11-8-76

Budgets

Budgets

AN ANALYTICAL
AND PROCEDURAL HANDBOOK
FOR GOVERNMENT AND
NONPROFIT
ORGANIZATIONS

Michael Babunakis

GREENWOOD PRESS
WESTPORT, CONNECTICUT • LONDON, ENGLAND

Library of Congress Cataloging in Publication Data

Babunakis, Michael.
    Budgets: an analytical and procedural handbook for government and nonprofit organizations.

    Bibliography: p.
    Includes index.
    1. Program budgeting. 2. Program budgeting—
California—San Diego. I. Title.
HJ2031.B3   658.1'54   76-5323
ISBN 0-8371-8900-4

Library of Congress Catalog Card Number: 76-5323
ISBN: 0-8371-8900-4
First published in 1976.
Greenwood Press, a division of Williamhouse-Regency Inc.
51 Riverside Avenue, Westport, Connecticut 06880

Printed in the United States of America

1937562

To My Father and Mother

CONTENTS

PREFACE

This study was undertaken to reexamine program budgeting and the independent Budget Analysis as well as their relationship to fiscal and land-use models. Hopefully, it will provide concrete evidence that such a comprehensive system is not only practical but also the best economic methodology available to government and to nonprofit corporations. The concept of program budgeting was first developed and implemented by the federal government in the early 1960s; since then, many state and local governments have also experimented with it.

The program budgeting examples in this work are from the city of San Diego and the state of California. San Diego has attempted to avoid some of the shortcomings of program budgeting experienced by other governments. The city has also instituted a Budget Analysis as an integral and independent process. To date, the city has been extremely satisfied with this new system of budgeting and analysis and will shortly be developing fiscal and land-use models.

This text describes the history of budgeting and the evolution of the program budgeting concept: that rationality in budgetary practices can result in more efficient and effective governmental operations. The advantages of program budgeting relative to previous budgetary systems, especially, the traditional line-item budget, are described, and numerous criticisms of program budgeting are presented with a response given for each critique. This work also strives to maintain a practical approach to the implementation of program budgeting and fiscal and land-use models. Hence, wherever possible, the practical applications of these concepts are provided.

By portraying the substantial and numerous advantages accruing, this text should give state and local governments a strong impetus to adopt a program budget and a Budget Analysis as well as fiscal and land-use models. Nonprofit organizations will find these concepts equally applicable to their goals and plans. A long-range fiscal model would be completely suitable to the corporation's long-range plans. However, the iand-use model should be replaced with a generalized economic model or overall organizational master plan following the logic of the corporation's ultimate goals. The Planning and Programming Budget (PPB) would interlock into this model or plan and provide the means of attaining those goals.

The author wishes to express his appreciation to the Mayor and the City Council of San Diego for implementing this new program budgeting and analysis system; to Ronald B. Frankum, director of the San Diego Urban Observatory, for his support of this project; to the city employees who fully cooperated with the author and provided him with such helpful assistance; and to Nancy C. Wheeler and Catherine P. Cleary who provided the dedication required for the completion of the text.

FOREWORD

Governmental expenditures, whether at the federal, state, or local level, are becoming exceedingly difficult to optimize or even describe satisfactorily to legislators and to the public they serve. The public is beginning to pressure governments to solve existing and future problems in the most economical and efficient way possible. The electorate has become more sensitive to the problem of where and how its tax dollars are applied and how much is spent. Because some programs appear to squander these funds, a disturbing lack of public confidence has resulted. A systematic budgetary method which defines objectives and quantifies data is necessary if governmental units are to manage their fiscal responsibilities well. For example, a generalized paragraph or two does not sufficiently describe the reality of a major and costly program. The reasons for such a program must be stated and justified, and its effectiveness must be measured by outputs of the program relative to objective criteria. Finally, the program must be evaluated to determine its efficiency, effectiveness, and priority ranking.

The Budget Analysis should identify diseconomies, while the program budget can provide a backbone upon which to build an organized and systematic means of implementing stated objectives. The budgetary process should be involved with far more elements than merely the historical allocation of the revenue pie from year to year.

This text details how a relatively new budgetary system (program budget and Budget Analysis), coordinated with fiscal and land-use models, can be vital to increasing the cost-efficiency, cost-effectiveness, and planning capability of state and local governments. The author has been as specific as possible and has utilized the experiences of the city of San Diego and the state of California in order to provide a practical guide to the implementation of this budgetary system.

I am quite pleased with the new budget process which has transformed the budget system of San Diego. This system, ably described in this work, allows the fullest possible legislative review. I have dealt with this system at the state level, and my fellow legislators in Sacramento are completely satisfied with the concept of a program budget and Budget Analysis as performed by the State Legislative Analyst Office. This success appears to have been duplicated at the local level of government in San Diego.

As a result of this process, I believe the city has saved multimillions of dollars annually and has found a mechanism which allows in-depth priority setting. The citizens of San Diego now have a budget they can fully understand, one that allows them to question governmental expenditures. We who represent the electorate greatly encourage such citizen participation and interest.

Let me express my thanks to all who participated in bringing about this budgetary process, which now permits the type of review that is a requisite at all governmental levels.

Pete Wilson,
Mayor of San Diego

Budgets

1

THE HISTORY OF BUDGETING

The concept of systematic budgeting in government is a relatively recent one. Although organized governments have existed for thousands of years, a budgetary system apparently was not needed until the nineteenth century, when state and local governments began to establish budgetary practices. The federal government had no formal executive budget until 1921. However, considerable progress has been made since that time.

Gradually, expenditure controls have improved, accountability has increased, and long-range planning has entered into budgetary practice. The end result ideally would be program budgeting and a Budget Analysis—the subject of this text.

BUDGETING: HISTORY AND PROBLEMS

In its early years, the United States government had a strong central executive budget under Alexander Hamilton. The men in Congress, however, with the excessive power of monarchial governments still fresh in their minds, felt this approach gave the President too much authority. Thomas Jefferson agreed, and so it was that Congress was given direct control over appropriations.[1] Congress maintained this control until the early twentieth century when the first major fiscal reform movement began. There was actually no formal budgetary procedure until the Budget and Accounting Act of 1921 which established the Bureau of the Budget and the concept of the executive budget.[2] Prior to this time,

budget requests were submitted to the Congress directly by the individual federal agencies. The President had no authority to amend those requests before they were submitted and no institutional mechanisms to influence the department in drawing up the requests . . . The great detail in which appropriations were made, the inability of department heads to transfer funds, and the lack of any central control mechanisms led to the widespread growth of deficiency appropriations . . . The Congress was principally concerned with limiting the power and discretion of the executive by specifying appropriations in detail and by controlling the tendency of executive departments to sidestep these restrictions through deficiency appropriations.[3]

Before 1921, lawmaking bodies were responsible for decisions concerning appropriations, as ordained in the U.S. Constitution: "No money shall be drawn from the Treasury but in consequence of appropriations made by law." Independently, each department would submit its request for funds to the legislative body, often at different times during the year. A standard method of accounting did not exist. Estimates of funds required were usually very general and unsupported. Requests were not related to projected revenues or to the general plan of government. Because of the fragmented nature of the process, a central authority could not effectively supervise or control departmental spending.[4]

Early in this century, a wave of reform swept over nearly all aspects of government in response to public objections to rising expenditures. Journalists exposed the corruption and incompetence of officials and administrators. The new discipline of public administration provided fresh ideas on both the functions of budgeting and methods to increase budgetary effectiveness.

Significant new techniques were adopted between 1911 and 1926. The system that evolved was termed *fiscal control budgeting*. In this system, the budget was viewed as the central instrument for administrative control over spending. Central budgeting authorities (budget bureaus) were established whose main duty was to prepare a government-wide budget for legislative action. Uniform accounting procedures were established; purchasing and personnel controls were centralized; and auditing methods were initiated to monitor administrative behavior. Fiscal control and responsibility were the primary needs at this time.

Although planning and policy determination were important, concern centered on regulating governmental activities, partly because of the political belief that government should be limited in scope. The electorate was fearful of government interference in areas of private concern.

Refinements in the fiscal control budgetary process were made during the 1920s and 1930s. The line-item budget, characterized by expenditures listed in broad categories (e.g., clerical help, number of pieces of equipment purchased), became firmly entrenched. Budget bureaus were more concerned with the spending process than with the preparation of budget proposals. Still, the budgetary process was not rationalized in terms of planning or program development.

Control over spending became even more important during the Depression as revenues declined and drastic curtailment of expenditures became a grim reality. With the advent of the New Deal, governments became concerned with meeting public needs, and budgets began to stress goals and activities other than fiscal control. The old system was simply not adequate to handle the administrative demands created by government entrance into new, wide areas of social action. The "limited government" philosophy was gradually replaced by the desire for alleviating the Depression problems of massive unemployment and lack of confidence in the democratic process.

The gradual change in orientation from fiscal control budgeting to management control budgeting occurred between the late 1930s and the early 1950s. World War II allowed the federal Budget Bureau to increase its managerial authority. The occurring change was clearly evident by the end of the war. Then Budget Bureau Director Harold D. Smith stated: "The main function of the Bureau is to serve as an agent of the President in coordinating operations and in improving the management of the Government."[5]

In 1949, the Hoover Commission recommended that "the whole budgetary concept of the federal government should be refashioned by the adoption of a budget based upon functions, activities, and projects: This we designate a 'performance budget'." This recommendation became law in the National Security Act Amendments of 1949 and the Budgeting and Accounting Procedures Act of 1950.[6] Performance budgeting focused on activities rather than objectives and emphasized the after-the-fact auditing of programs rather than prior revenue allocation.

According to Stephen Grossbard, a performance budget is an expression, in financial terms, of the major activities or functions of a unit. Program descriptions in a performance budget are based on the activities being performed rather than on the expenditures required. This change in emphasis marked a budgetary revolution in which management gained control from fiscal officials in development of the budget.[7] This new concept meant that changes in programs and activities governed the allotment of funds to the department.[8]

Performance budgeting was used with little success during the 1950s, the reason being that it was a purely mechanical innovation which made the budget neither more understandable nor more useful in planning and decision-making. Moreover, performance statistics tended to confuse the budget rather than to clarify it. According to Allen Schick, the absence of a mood of change in the nation may also have contributed to its failure.[9]

The earlier movement toward fiscal control was a by-product of reorganization efforts undertaken by all levels of government at this time. The Hoover Commission, however, gave it more importance than it actually merited. Schick states: "When there is overwhelming discontent with the current course, the prospects for reform are enhanced by portraying it as a complete break with the past. But when there is no strong groundswell for change, emphasis on the difference between the old and the new may diminish the attractiveness of the reform." [10] Once minor changes were made, administrators lost interest in performance budgeting.

The first state governments to implement performance budgeting were Maryland, New York, and Ohio, in that order. All three encountered problems. Maryland adopted performance budgeting in fiscal year (FY) 1954, but the changeover was not fully instituted or developed. Line-item detail still was required by the legislature, and the Budget Bureau, fearful of any loss of control, did not provide the leadership necessary to develop and sustain a new budgetary system. New York State experimented with performance budgeting between 1955 and 1960 in the operation of its tuberculosis sanitariums. Though a technical success, the system was discarded primarily because it was not in the best interests of those in power. New York's high government officials did not consider performance budgeting a priority item. Consequently, it was not implemented on a statewide level and was discontinued in the sanitarium budget. Ohio implemented performance budgeting during the early 1960s, but became overinvolved with detail. Those examining Ohio's budget felt that complexity had replaced clarity. Ohio discontinued the effort in 1965 when a new administration took over, having won the election on a platform that promised fiscal reform. [11]

From the perspective of the 1970s, performance budgeting cannot be termed a success. The performance budget dealt with how efficiently an activity was being accomplished, and ignored the question of the need for the activity altogether. [12] Its primary goal was to maintain efficiency and economy in government, not to see that government effectively responded to public needs. [13] In most cases, performance budgeting confused the real issues. It did not receive the enthusiastic support of officials and administrators necessary for its success, and it remained the brainchild of management and efficiency experts. Most governments that adopted performance budgeting soon returned to the line-item format until the advent of planning-programming-budgeting (PPB) in the mid-1960s.

THE HISTORY OF PROGRAM BUDGETING

The first efforts to include planning and program development with budgeting in state government were made at the turn of the century. The leading spokesmen were Frederick A. Cleveland, Frank J. Goodnow, and William F. Willoughby who realized the potential for planning in the budgetary process. [14] They felt that the chief executive should be the principal maker of the budgetary policy. The executive would be responsible for planning programs for governmental activities, and then these programs would be presented to the legislature for approval. The legislature would modify or delete items, but would not be responsible for suggesting or creating programs.

These theorists envisioned the budgetary process as a means of coordinating governmental activities previously initiated by the legislature in piecemeal fashion. Unfortunately, their ideas were not utilized because there were more urgent demands for fiscal control at this time and because resistance to a strong executive was still widespread.

There were several early efforts to use a program budgeting system. In 1907, the New York Bureau of Municipal Research published a sample "program memorandum" that contained 125 pages of functional accounts and data for the New York City Health Department. [15] During the 1920s, private businesses such as Bell Laboratories and General Motors began using systems analysis and program budgeting. The General Motors budget of 1924 "included a basic feature of the PPBS method, which is to identify major objectives, to define programs essential to these goals, to identify resources with specific types of objectives, and to systematically analyze the alternative available." [16]

Interestingly, the city of San Diego experimented with an embryonic program budget during the Depression. Its 1933-1934 budget contained detailed descriptions of its services or programs. This budget could have marked the beginning of a new era in budgeting, but it was used for only one fiscal year, for the sole purpose of alleviating the city's problems during the worst year of the Depression. The following year, San Diego returned to a line-item budget. [17]

Another effort to include planning in the budgetary process began during World War II. At the federal level, the Production Requirements Plan of 1941 and Controlled Materials Plan of 1942 attempted to give an overall picture of the needs and resources of the war effort as well as to provide a means of evaluating alternatives and priorities—the essence of PPBS. [18]

After the war, the RAND Corporation began to study new budgeting systems, realizing that existing forms were inadequate for long-range planning. RAND specifically concentrated on the field of weapons systems analysis. In 1954, it published *Efficiency and Economy in Government through New Budgeting and Accounting Procedures* for the Air Force. [19] Although the Air Force did not adopt the plan, RAND continued its research. In 1960, RAND published *The Economics of Defense in the Nuclear Age.* [20] This document came to the attention of the Kennedy Administration, and as a result the PPB system was adopted by the Department of Defense in 1961 under Robert McNamara. [21]

PPB worked so well for the Defense Department that it was adopted by all federal departments under President Lyndon Johnson in 1965. What proved to be optimal for the Defense Department, however, was not workable for the entire federal government. Discontent with PPB was soon widespread, for reasons to be discussed later in this text, and the system was finally abandoned in 1971. It was considered a failure primarily because it did not provide instant solutions for all federal ailments.

The country is now in a new era of program budgeting and Budget Analysis implementation. San Diego instituted this budgetary system in 1972 following its success at the state level and established a Legislative Analyst Office responsible for program analysis and evaluation. It produced a partial program budget in 1973 and a complete program budget for FY 1974-1975. As a result, San Diego's budget preparation has become more sophisticated and the budget itself more understandable to both the analyst and layman.

THE LINE-ITEM VS. THE PROGRAM BUDGET

Before examining program budgeting in more detail, it is important to understand its predecessor, the line-item budget, also known as an object budget. The line-item budget is a financial plan of estimated expenditures expressed in terms of the kinds and quantities of objects to be purchased and the estimated revenues needed to finance them during a specified period, usually one year. This budget generally includes the number of personnel employed by type of position.[22] Most governments still use this format.

The line-item budget has several key features. Budgetary divisions are listed by organization units (departments or agencies), and types of expenditures are listed by category. Its primary functions are expenditure control, the safeguarding of funds for their assigned uses, and the protection of fiscal resources. The line-item budget focuses on the attainment of a "balanced budget."[23] It forces a regular review of activities and policies because the process is repeated every year. [24]

The disadvantages of the line-item budget appear to outnumber its advantages. First, its fiscal orientation asks "how shall we increase or decrease what we are doing" rather than "what should we be doing?" Unless a new program is proposed, there is little examination of basic program structure.[25] Second, it is not conducive to long-range planning; line-item budgeting is a year-to-year process, and it thereby tends to postpone necessary action. Third, it is impossible to relate this budget to governmental objectives and to relate its expenditures to accomplishments or outputs. It makes no provision for examining alternative methods of accomplishing objectives.[26]

The line-item budget provides justification for decisions that have been made historically and does not yield systems data which can be used to evaluate alternative courses of action.[27] Also, it makes it easier for departments to conceal their activities, with the result that it becomes impossible to perform interdepartmental comparisons or reorganization by function or activity. Any duplication of effort remains undetected in the line-item budget, and program management control rather than planning and evaluation is emphasized.

The preceding year's line-item budget is accepted as the standard for the next year's budget, with little or no analysis of the effectiveness of the revenues spent.[28] Because the budget is revised annually, insufficient consideration is given to new program planning. The tendency is to meet only the most pressing demands and to avoid programs whose effects cannot be seen in the immediate future.

The line-item budget also encourages competition among departments for available funds. Naturally, each department wants as large an appropriation as possible, regardless of its relative importance to overall governmental objectives. Each department is responsible for preparing its own budget request, making comprehensive planning difficult. Because of this internal competition, there is little enthusiasm for interdepartmental collaboration on programs whose objectives are similar. [29]

The program budgeting system alleviates deficiencies of the line-item system. Each department states its goals and describes its programs designed to actualize those objectives. Output statistics are stressed along with inputs or personnel costs, thus permitting cost-benefit analyses.

With PPB, governments are committed to long-range planning. It permits the evaluation of (1) the efficiency and economy of programs, (2) alternative programs or alternative ways of implementing the same program, and (3) giving priority to various programs to determine their overall effectiveness. These evaluations *must* be generated in a separate document from the program budget itself in order to allow an independent appraisal. This other document, referred to as a Budget Analysis, originates from an office independent of the executive office responsible for preparing the program budget. The program budget provides the systems data required for this budgetary analysis.

In summary, program budgeting and the Budget Analysis offer a more rational approach to the budgetary process.

NOTES

1. Charles L. Schultze, *The Politics and Economics of Public Spending* (Washington, D.C.: The Brookings Institution, 1968), pp. 7-8.

2. S. Kenneth Howard, *Changing State Budgeting* (Lexington, Ky.: Council of State Governments, 1973), p. 3.

3. Schultze, op. cit., p. 8.

4. Allen Schick, *Budget Innovation in the States*, (Washington, D.C.: The Brookings Institution, 1971), pp. 14-25.

5. Harold D. Smith, *The Management of Your Government*, (New York: McGraw-Hill Book Co., 1945), p. 69, cited by Allen Schick, op. cit., p. 29.

6. Arthur Smithies, "Conceptual Framework for the Program Budget," *Program Budgeting, Program Analysis, and the Federal Budget*, ed. David Novick (Cambridge, Mass.: Harvard University Press, 1965), p. 31.

7. Stephen I. Grossbard, *PPBS for State and Local Officials*, Bureau of Government Research, Research Series No. 15 (Kingston, R.I.: University of Rhode Island, 1971), p. 7.

8. Schick, op. cit., p. 44.

9. Ibid., p. 64.

10. Ibid.

11. Ibid., pp. 69-85.

12. Howard, op. cit., pp. 22-23.

13. Stephen J. Knezevich, *Program Budgeting (PPBS)* (Berkeley, Calif.: McCutchan Publishing Corp., 1973), pp. 136-138.

14. Schick, op. cit., pp. 15-16.

15. New York Bureau of Municipal Research, *Making a Municipal Budget* (New York: New York Bureau of Municipal Research, 1907), pp. 9-10.

16. David Novick, "The Origins and History of Program Budgeting," *California Management Review* 11 (Fall 1968): 11.

17. Daniel E. Stone, "The Evolution of Municipal Budgeting in the City of San Diego, California," Master's diss., San Diego State College, 1966, pp. 84-86.

18. Knezevich, op. cit., pp. 25-26.

19. David Novick, *Efficiency and Economy in Government Through New Budgeting and Accounting Procedures*, R-254 (Santa Monica, Calif.: RAND Corp., 1954), cited by David Novick, "The Department of Defense," *Program Budgeting, Program Analysis and the Federal Budget*, ed. David Novick (Cambridge, Mass.: Harvard University Press, 1965), p. 86.

20. Charles J. Hitch and Roland McKean, *The Economics of Defense in the Nuclear Age* (Cambridge, Mass.: Harvard University Press, 1960).

21. Knezevich, loc. cit.

22. Stone, op. cit., p. 110.

23. Knezevich, op. cit., pp. 136-138.

24. Grossbard, op. cit., p. 6.

25. Howard, op. cit., pp. 102-107.

26. Grossbard, loc. cit.

27. Howard, loc. cit.

28. Schick, op. cit., p. 90.

29. Monty C. Lish, "Organizing for a New Approach to Budgeting," *Municipal Finance* 41 (May 1969): 157.

2

THE CONCEPT OF PROGRAM BUDGETING

There is a definite need for a more rational fiscal approach to budgeting. The public and their representatives are entitled to more accountability and evaluation in governmental expenditures. Increased demand for governmental services makes it imperative that a better method of evaluating existing and future expenditures be instituted. (For line-item budget examples, see pp. 12-14.)

Because of the many defects in line-item budgeting, program budgeting and a Budget Analysis are a *sine qua non*. This budget system is a systematic method of linking long-range planning with yearly budgeting and evaluation. It involves definition of public needs; preparation of programs with objectives to respond to those needs; and program implementation by the most efficient means possible. The program budget document makes possible the Budget Analysis. Both the program budget and the Budget Analysis optimize the process by allowing the interplay of ideas to determine allocations. The Budget Analysis tests program budget allocations via its programmatic evaluations which are made independently of the executive and departmental controls and requests.

INCREASED SYSTEMS INFORMATION

The most obvious advantage of program budgeting is that it increases the systems information available for making decisions. Without sufficient and organized data, rational decisions are not possible. For example, in studying a public library, one needs to determine how many books are circulated each year, how many requests for information are received, how many books are lost or stolen, what books are in demand which the library does not possess, how much effort is expended in shelving, and so forth. The operating effectiveness

ORGANIZATION REPORT
FY 1976

DEPARTMENT 18   BISHOP AIRPORT

CODE	DESCRIPTION	FY 1974 ACTUAL	FY 1975 BUDGET	FY 1975 REVISED BUDGET	FY 1976 BUDGET	FY 1975-76 DIFFERENCE AMOUNT	PERCENT
	OBJECTS:						
702.0	WAGES & SALR	280,664	283,935	323,832	371,302	47,470	14.7
709.0	OVERTIME	34,126	27,869	21,919	25,973	4,054	18.5
714.0	FRINGE BNFTS	0	62,538	81,471	104,498	23,027	28.3
718.0	SICK LV PAY	0	0	320	640	320	100.0
727.0	OFFICE SUPPL	1,346	600	1,000	1,000	0	0.0
727.9	OFFICE SUPPL	1,542	1,200	800	800	0	0.0
740.0	OPRATNG SUPP	7,106	6,800	6,000	6,800	800	13.3
740.9	OPRATNG SUPP	427	1,500	1,500	1,500	0	0.0
744.0	CLOTH RENT&C	0	0	0	4,000	4,000	NEW
751.0	GAS,OIL,FUEL	0			8,000	8,000	NEW
768.0	UNIFORMS PJR	4,372	3,000	4,000	1,000	3,000-	75.0-
775.0	REPR&MNT SUP	8,558	10,000	10,000	10,000	0	0.0
782.9	ASPHALT	63	0	46	1,000	954	>1000
801.0	PROF SVCS	53,390	45,000	45,000	10,000	35,000-	77.8-
850.0	COMUNICATIO	4,311	3,000	4,200	4,800	600	14.3
860.0	TRANSPORTATI	4,334	5,000	5,000	7,000	2,000	40.0
863.9	MTR VHC&EQUI	31,666	23,650	23,650	17,000	6,650-	28.1-
863.9	MTR VHC&EQUI	146	350	350	350	0	0.0
864.0	CONFRNC TRAV	3,053	3,000	5,000	5,000	0	0.0
880.0	COMUNTY PRO	1,740	2,300	2,300	2,000	300-	13.0-
885.0	ADVERTISING	360	6,000	6,019	15,000	8,981	149.2
900.0	PRINTG&PUBLS	411	750	500	500	0	0.0
900.9	PRINTG&PUBLS	164	250	500	500	0	0.0

11	321	Fire-Administration	EXPENDED 1970-71	EXPENDED 1971-72	ESTIMATED 1972-73	APPROVED 1973-74
	111	Salaries & Wages Regular	48,004	56,924	63,110	67,590
			48,004	56,924	63,110	67,590
	221	Transportation & Travel	777	802	1,050	1,155
	251	Other Agency Services	180	194	250	300
			957	996	1,300	1,455
	311	Office Supplies	1,526	1,582	1,700	1,850
	331	Uniforms, Badges & Tools	221	134	100	100
			1,747	1,716	1,800	1,950
	531	Retirement Plan	5,111	6,174	6,785	7,180
	541	Employees Insurance	388	515	780	1,080
	551	Compensation Insurance	1,682	1,984	2,100	2,200
	571	Building Rental			2,850	4,255
			7,181	8,673	12,515	14,715
TOTAL FIRE-Administration			57,889	68,309	78,725	85,710

11	322	Fire-Suppression				
	111	Salaries & Wages Regular	2,161,461	2,288,494	2,606,075	2,990,760
	141	Salaries & Wages Overtime	17,071	111,775	104,000	72,000
			2,178,532	2,400,269	2,710,075	3,062,760
	221	Transportation & Travel	387	362	3,350	3,350
	241	Janitorial & Housekeeping	1,810	1,969	2,350	2,720
	251	Other Agency Services			280	280
			2,197	2,331	5,980	6,350
	311	Office Supplies	1,732	2,015	2,000	2,050
	331	Uniforms, Badges & Tools	6,814	9,732	11,950	12,250
	361	Operating M & S Buildings & Grounds	770	1,705	3,500	3,850
	381	Operating M & S Equipment	1,407	400	750	750
			10,723	13,852	18,200	18,900
	531	Retirement Plan	240,592	263,820	291,730	317,640
	541	Employees Insurance	31,305	33,320	52,440	66,960
	551	Compensation Insurance	93,537	110,721	114,295	121,910
			365,434	407,861	458,465	506,510
TOTAL FIRE-Suppression			2,556,886	2,824,313	3,192,720	3,594,520

11	323	Fire-Prevention				
	111	Salaries & Wages Regular	95,892	132,199	139,565	151,060
	141	Salaries & Wages Overtime	500	763	2,260	2,000
			96,392	132,962	141,825	153,060
	221	Transportation & Travel	741	855	260	885
	251	Other Agency Services	179	526	1,000	1,100
			920	1,381	1,260	1,985
	311	Office Supplies	1,327	1,324	4,200	1,650
	331	Uniforms, Badges & Tools	1,172	711	1,100	850
			2,499	2,035	5,300	2,500

11 511 Public Works-Admin. & Engineering	EXPENDED 1970-71	EXPENDED 1971-72	ESTIMATED 1972-73	APPROVED 1973-74
111 Salaries & Wages Regular	392,167	448,855	471,270	505,140
131 Salaries & Wages Temporary	7,360	3,768	6,000	6,000
141 Salaries & Wages Overtime	1,477	2,590	1,000	1,000
191 Other Personal Services	3,232	3,839	4,000	4,000
	404,236	459,052	482,270	516,140
211 Communications	7,046	6,710	7,150	7,500
221 Transportation & Travel	746	1,425	1,500	1,800
251 Other Agency Services	613	868	1,500	2,000
281 M & R Machinery & Equipment	8,598	9,469	10,000	10,000
291 Other Contractual Services			500	500
	17,003	18,472	20,650	21,800
311 Office Supplies	14,756	15,942	16,300	15,000
331 Uniforms, Badges & Tools	191	139	300	300
361 Operating M & S Buildings & Grounds	101	107	300	300
371 Operating M & S Improvements	454	1,186	1,000	1,000
391 Other Materials & Supplies			50	50
	15,502	17,374	17,950	16,650
511 Rental City Equipment	8,429	11,416	9,285	11,500
531 Retirement Plan	33,184	39,038	37,015	49,075
534 Data Processing Services	8,000			
541 Employees Insurance	7,198	7,823	10,260	18,000
551 Compensation Insurance	915	1,424	1,060	1,480
571 Building Rental	14,925	14,925	34,540	34,540
	72,651	74,626	92,160	114,595
TOTAL PUBLIC WORKS-Admin. & Engineering	509,392	569,524	613,030	669,185
11 512 Public Works-Bus Transportation				
291 Other Contractual Services		108,650	10,400	
		108,650	10,400	
TOTAL PUBLIC WORKS-Bus Transportation		108,650	10,400	
11 521 Public Works-Refuse Collection				
111 Salaries & Wages Regular	7,236	8,224	10,920	10,430
141 Salaries & Wages Overtime	2,574	2,042	500	200
	9,810	10,266	11,420	10,630
251 Other Agency Services	450,397	544,087	591,245	624,000
	450,937	544,087	591,245	624,000
311 Office Supplies	804	908	1,000	1,000
331 Uniforms, Badges & Tools		8	20	20
	804	916	1,020	1,020
511 Rental City Equipment	434	648	600	960
531 Retirement Plan	444	495	690	975
551 Compensation Insurance	38	47	40	60
	916	1,190	1,330	1,995
TOTAL PUBLIC WORKS-Refuse Collection	462,467	556,459	605,015	637,645

of a library and its branches cannot be evaluated unless this kind of systematic information is gathered and available. With program budgeting, effectiveness is displayed in the output statements, and its evaluation in the Budget Analysis is not based on historicity. Hard systems information is provided to support any associative program costs. (Appendix A illustrates a three-year progression from a limited performance-type budget to a well-developed program budget. It is suggested that the reader note the improvements between the 1973 and 1975 fiscal year budgets. The 1975 fiscal year library budget incorporates the necessary components of a PPB.)

Lack of adequate systems information was one of the major problems the federal government encountered when it implemented PPBS in 1965. In her article concerning PPBS and HEW, Elizabeth R. Drew places the failure of PPBS on the fact that there was insufficient information available to conduct the kind of study that PPBS demanded. As an example, she uses a study on higher education. Those who did the study, she reports, were unable to determine what had happened to those who had received federal scholarships in the past or whether they had completed college. Drew concludes that the study was impeded by this lack of basic information.[1]

The first requirement of program budgeting should be to identify the need for hard data. When gaps in data are discovered, they should be closed, even though increasing the data base requires time and effort. In the case of HEW, PPBS *did* point out the gaps in knowledge. The system itself should not be faulted because it requires more data for analyses. Drew was not able to make the distinction between a data gap and the potential of a PPBS.

An increase in usable systems information is an obvious advantage to concerned administrators. "An agency head's ability to control the direction his department takes depends in part on his being able to face his operating subordinates with information and analysis about their own programs."[2] A department head needs facts not only to justify requests for funds, but to justify his program's existence as well. A program which is not serving a public need should be so identified and discontinued. Facts may reveal deficiencies in a program which would also provide the means to improve performance. In the library example, discovery that large numbers of books are not returned may lead to a solution and thus reduce costs.

Program budgeting requires heavy usage of computer data processing. The sheer volume of data requires that the most relevant information be organized and stored in an easily retrievable manner. Only a computer is able to sort and arrange such large volumes of data economically. An example of computer application is the ARMS (Accounting and Resources Management System) program now in operation in San Diego County.[3] ARMS integrates financial data, personnel and equipment utilization, workload statistics, and other data into one system for improved financial management. Every input is sorted, classified, and stored in the appropriate memory location. Concurrently, the impact of each transaction is updated. This system provides meaningful output data while decreasing the man-hours required to operate it.

MODERN BUDGETARY TECHNIQUES

Program budgeting achieves more efficient and economical government by utilizing numerous techniques:

1. Reorganization
2. Priority setting
3. Management improvement programs

4. Better coordination and cooperation
5. Capital improvements.

Reorganization

One of the main objectives of program budgeting is to increase government efficiency. Over the years, many departments have never had to justify or detail their activities. With program budgeting every program or program element undertaken by a government must have specific objectives relating to public needs. The most economical methods should be used to accomplish these objectives; diseconomies in organization will be identified under program budgeting. Thus, program budgeting reveals which departments or programs exist only for historical reasons; whether the departments are accomplishing the activities for which they are responsible; and whether interdepartmental communication is minimal or nonexistent.

A prime benefit of program budgeting is the opportunity it affords for reorganizing departments along functional lines. By emphasizing programs and objectives, it tends to reorganize departments along lines of similar activities, thereby resulting in savings and/or more efficient operations. A major restructuring of departments may be necessitated, but the end result will be a more economic and optimal means of meeting governmental responsibilities.

Reorganization will identify and resolve duplications between and within departments. In city government, for example, both the Park and Recreation Department and the Planning Department may be responsible for acquiring open space for creating new public parks. Ideally, only one department should be responsible, or a committee of personnel from each department might be assigned the responsibility. Without a program budget, it would be difficult to determine if duplication of effort existed. Examination of the budget document can also indicate whether a program which is currently the responsibility of one department should be transferred to another department. This is especially true of planning functions. A planning department should be responsible for all long-range planning activities, such as capital outlay expenditures, which would in essence reflect the general land-use plan for the city.

Examination of the program budget may also indicate the need to combine several small departments into one larger department to cut administration costs, or to merge small departments with other existing departments with similar activities. On the other hand, it may be more effective to transfer related programs from separate departments and to combine them into one new department. For example, several departments may be in charge of problems related to environmental quality; the Water Utilities Department may be concerned with waste from a de-salination plant, the Public Works Department with the environmental impact of its solid waste disposal programs, and the Transportation Department with air pollution from bus emissions. It might be more efficient and effective to combine these various departmental programs into one environmental quality agency. While this new department would need to maintain close ties with other concerned agencies, it would have the overall responsibility for environmental programs.

The program budget format can reveal two other diseconomies in a department's activities: (1) Departments may be ineffective in accomplishing the proper objectives. Programs may be designed to achieve the correct objectives but may be inefficient. The Fire Department, for example, may be seeking to increase its coverage capability. A relocation of fire stations could increase that coverage without requiring more personnel. (2) Programs may be efficient but not effectively meeting public needs. Program budgeting would disclose areas where new programs are necessary. It might reveal public needs that are not being satisfied by any existing programs. Existing departmental goals can be restructured to meet these needs.

As stated earlier, program budgeting requires that all departmental programs be justified. A program whose need cannot be proved should be eliminated. For example, once a city has developed and implemented a mass transit plan, there is no further reason to continue a program to plan a mass transit system.

Priority Setting

Detailed program information in the budget document can also provide decision-makers with the hard data to assist in setting priorities.[4] Funding for government programs is always limited; consequently, priorities must be set among programs to optimize benefits.

Once the departments are reorganized along activity lines, data in the program budget will allow the legislative body, analytical staff, and administrators to establish priorities. Within departments, the director is primarily responsible for establishing which programs have the highest priorities. For this task he relies on the budget document, and uses marginal analysis as his principal tool. For example, the director of the Fire Department has available the systems information necessary to judge whether shifting personnel from one fire station to another will increase departmental productivity. If a fire station is not receiving a sufficient number of calls to justify its current staffing, under-utilized personnel can be transferred to an understaffed fire station.

Management Improvement Programs

Program budgeting can provide the data necessary for management improvement programs. Such workload-oriented programs are important when costs continue to rise because of annual salary increases and an inflationary economy. The programs may be conducted by inhouse staff or outside consultants. These programs can (1) improve the level of service, (2) reduce expenditures per unit of service provided, (3) improve management capability, and (4) stimulate the desire to provide better service. They are not designed to eliminate management responsibility, but rather to provide management with improved tools. For example, the California Department of Motor Vehicles uses a MARC (Management Reporting and Control) program. The state program budget provides analysts with the workload data necessary to evaluate the department's operations. The program has resulted in (1) annual savings of $6 million because of increased productivity, (2) reduction in staff through attrition and increased workloads, (3) increased service levels, and (4) acceptance of the department's budget by the Legislature when other departmental budgets were reduced. Without program budgeting, it would have been difficult for the MARC study to have been accomplished.

Better Coordination and Cooperation

Program budgeting can increase interdepartmental and intergovernmental cooperation. Each department has specific, well-defined responsibilities, and as all activities are organized along program lines, there is less opportunity for departments to overstep or shirk these duties. Interdepartmental programs are designed so that each participant is fully aware of its role. Such coordination occurred in the city of San Diego after the PPB was introduced in 1972, when a new park was developed. The Park and Recreation Department was responsible for the overall development of the park program, and the Engineering Department oversaw the park design and construction. This awareness of specific role resulted in better coordination and cooperation between departments.

Program budgeting should also promote better coordination among different levels of government participating in joint programs. San Diego's involvement in the Model Cities and the Urban Observatory are examples of such intergovernmental programs. A government using program budgeting is better able to provide the sponsoring federal agency with data on the program and its achievements. The result should be better organization and implementation of such programs.

Better coordination of interrelated activities is possible when two jurisdictions (e.g., city and county) use the same or similar program budget formats. Program detail can identify duplication of efforts, and intergovernmental tradeoffs can then be considered. San Diego is currently involved in making such tradeoffs with federal revenue-sharing monies. For example, San Diego could use its allocation for joint Human Care Service programs, while San Diego County could assist the city with land acquisition purchases for regional parks. In this way, duplication of effort can be reduced, overlapping activities minimized, and unique areas of expertise shared.

Capital Improvements

With the line-item budgetary format, the operating budget is traditionally separated from the capital outlay budget both in format and in concept. The operating budget includes all the actual costs of running governmental programs. The capital budget includes all expenditures for capital improvements such as new buildings, acquisition of open space, and park development. The funding sources of the two budgets are generally not the same. Operating expenditures are usually financed by the general fund via tax revenues, collection of fees, licenses, and so forth. Capital improvements are frequently financed by bonds or special funds earmarked for capital improvements.

Both capital improvements and operational expenditures are incorporated in a program budget. S. Kenneth Howard believes that, in time, the distinction between the two will disappear:

> As rationalistic budgeting systems mature, and planning becomes more inclusive, the distinction between operating and capital budgets will probably fade. . . . Thorough analysis requires that *all* costs, both operating and capital, be evaluated. Under this emphasis, distinctions between operating and capital outlays may become less critical, since both are relevant in evaluating *total* program costs and results.[5]

This combining approach has many advantages for budgeting capital improvements. Program budget analysis can provide data for identifying the facilities to be constructed, the priorities among projects, and the level of funding necessary.[6] For example, analysis can inform the decision-maker whether it will be better to construct a new fire station or to assign more firemen to existing stations. The first alternative is a capital expenditure, and the other, operational. The most efficient alternative should be selected, regardless of the fund source. Thus, the union of these two budgets in a PPB format permits such alternative analysis.

Another advantage of PPB is that it allows easier review of capital projects. The operating budget points out which projects are of a high priority and can be justified. For example, the Park and Recreation Department may request funds for construction of additional tennis courts. Program budget data will indicate the current tennis court usage and reveal if there is a greater demand than existing courts can fulfill. On the other hand, if the program budget reveals uneven usage of the courts, it may be more effective to use the revenue to direct tennis players to lesser used courts.

The operational budget also provides data concerning future needs for capital improvements. For example, there may be an urgent need for a future police station in a certain precinct. At the same time, a study may already be under way on citywide relocations of police stations. It would make little sense to build a new police station before the results of the relocation study are released. The need for the new station might be eliminated by redistricting areas covered by existing stations. The multiyear approach to planning and budgeting that PPB entails makes future projections of needed capital improvements easier to estimate.

PPB emphasizes programs that accomplish a government's stated objectives. Capital improvements needed to implement these programs in the most effective way will be clearly delineated. The program budget can provide systems information on programs necessary to maximize the benefits of capital expenditures. For example, the program budget may reveal that a certain public facility (e.g., a museum) is not being sufficiently utilized. As a means of improving attendance, the facility might be renovated to make it more attractive to the public, or publicity might be increased. In other words, operational costs and capital costs are completely interrelated with program budgeting. The emphasis is on the achievement of the objective, regardless of the type of the expenditure.

The program budget allows more objective analysis of capital project priorities. Sources of revenue as well as expenditures are included in the budget document. Analysis of program alternatives allows priorities to be set among these alternatives. If requests are simultaneously made for, say, a new police station, a new library, and the acquisition of open space, cost-benefit and cost-effectiveness analysis assists in establishing priorities among them.

PROGRAM BUDGETING, ANALYSIS, AND DECISION-MAKING

Program budgeting and Budget Analysis improve decision-making in government by providing more data and illuminating issues and problems. (For examples of Budget Analyses, see Appendix B.) This system focuses the decision-making process by:

1. Sharpening issues
2. Instituting annual review of programs and long-range planning
3. Providing more systems information
4. Allowing more objective decisions
5. Making evaluation easier
6. Providing understandable data

The program budget contains data on allocation of money, manpower, and capital expenditures. These statistics assist decision-makers by clarifying programs. The annual review of the budget, the second half of the budgetary process, provides program evaluation and reveals the necessity for long-range planning.

The increased data allow special interest groups, lobbyists, and other involved parties to present their case more intelligently to the public. Consequently, the entire decision-making process is improved and policy decisions can be made more objectively. The program budget provides data to determine if the existing programs are satisfying the intent of the legislative body. Finally, the breakdown of the budget into program categories allows the citizenry to become better informed as to governmental expenditures.

Sharpening Issues

According to Marvin Hoffenberg, program budgeting not only sharpens the judgment of decision-makers, but the issues themselves as well, and focuses on areas of conflict.[7] Inspection of the program budget can clarify what may have been initially a very general question.

The mass transit issue is a good example. Legislators may believe that their city needs a mass transit system or improvement of the existing bus system. The program budget provides data with which to initiate a new inquiry into the mass transportation question. An analysis of alternatives may raise the question of additional need or may make clearer the specific needs of the city. Does the city require a new mass transit system, or are its current methods of transportation sufficient? The inclusion of capital improvements projects in the budget is vital, as mass transit entails major capital outlays extending far into the future. The capital improvements data would indicate the fiscal impact of implementing a mass transit program. Analysis would answer the question of whether the city should establish a new mass transit system, or whether it should upgrade its existing bus system. Conflict surrounding the issue may increase, but the debate should be based on hard calculations, not speculation.

Analysis of the budget may reveal an entirely new problem. Elizabeth R. Drew states that the mere existence of defined alternatives may result in new demands for action.[8] Review of the program budget may raise questions regarding the efficiency of a city's fire department because of slow fire response times. In order to answer these questions, an analysis of relocating fire stations to decrease response times on a citywide basis may reveal possible new uses of fire department equipment and personnel in emergency situations.

The question may be raised as to which department can best perform a service and whether there is a public need for it. Thus, a whole new arena of budgetary action has opened. If the policy-makers envision that a service is a proper responsibility of city government, the question still will remain as to what department should provide the service, and still further analysis will be necessary. As the program budget document contains program descriptions for all departments, it would assist in answering this question. For example, should a new program or activity be established to provide emergency medical service? Will this involve the establishment of a new agency, or can it be incorporated into an existing one? These questions were not even considered when the initial study on fire station relocation was undertaken. Subsequent analysis led to the examination of the city's role in providing auxiliary medical emergency services to the public. As Drew points out, program budgeting and analysis can lead to involvement in totally new areas of public concern and create new conceptions of the scope of public service.

Annual Review and Long-range Planning

The program budget format includes operating expenditures for the past year, the current year, and the coming fiscal year. It provides systems information useful for an annual review of programs and for long-range planning. In the annual Budget Analysis of the proposed budget, programs are continuously evaluated as to how well they are meeting public needs. This cycle of evaluation is institutionalized, thus becoming an integral part of the budgetary process.[9]

The multiyear aspect of the program budget is especially useful in long-range planning, allowing measure of the effects of past expenditures and the future impact of current expenditures as well. Inclusion of each program's capital improvements expenditures for a longer time period (usually five to six years) is particularly helpful in long-range planning. The budget provides systems information on the amount of capital expenditures required in the future and their effect on operating costs.

The program budget can also assist in the implementation of new programs. Knezevich states: "Program budgeting helps to minimize the danger of deceptively low expenditures during the first fiscal year of a new program." In other words, it illuminates the long-range cost implications of proposals.[10]

Used together, the fiscal and land-use models and PPB/Budget Analysis can assist in predicting the long-range trends in population growth, expected revenue, and future demands for services. Any fiscal difficulty of the city of San Diego could be predicted if the city had fiscal and land-use models in addition to its budgetary system. On March 13, 1974, the city manager announced that San Diego would not have sufficient funds for the current fiscal year because of unforeseen increases in the cost of utilities, fuel, paper, and construction. Each department was asked to make a 10 percent across-the-board decrease in expenditures to counter the effects of rising costs. The city had predicted a 5 percent rise in costs due to inflation, but the actual increase was between 9 and 17 percent.[11] This rise in costs, partly the result of the energy crisis, might have been predicted with greater accuracy if a fiscal model for San Diego had existed. The city would have had contingency plans ready for such a crisis and would not have been forced to consider cutbacks on a quasi-emergency basis.

More Systems Information

In addition to providing decision-makers with hard data, program budgeting and Budget Analysis increase the rationality of debates on budgets.[12] The Budget Analysis provides recommendations concerning program alternatives based on the hard data in the program budget, thus reducing subjectivity in debates, though not eliminating it altogether.

This separate analysis of the program budget is needed to identify alternatives and to allow comparative analyses. It must be stressed that the Budget Analysis is separate from the budgetary process and not an integral part of the program budget preparation. The program budget advocates a previously selected alternative without documenting its comparative desirability. The separate and independently prepared Budget Analysis would either confirm the selected alternative or identify other preferred alternatives. After examining all pertinent data, a rational partisan should be able to justify his position and also be more knowledgeable about opposing positions. He may even alter his original position.

The mass transit question is again offered as an example. It is becoming more apparent every day that cities need more mass public transportation. The Budget Analysis would identify programs dealing with this service. Certain factions may desire a monorail system, others may favor an underground subway system, while still others may feel that the bus system is sufficient. There may be those who desire a combination of these transportation systems. Analysts would study these alternatives, and the Budget Analysis would provide systems analyses as to which system would be optimal for the city, depending on its size, topography, and other related inputs. Such an analysis allows partisans to defend their position against opposing viewpoints from a common basis of understanding. The program budget provides the beginning data inputs for such an analysis.

In theory, the most efficient and effective means of mass public transportation would be selected from the existing alternatives. Political constraints on decision-making sometimes interfere with objectivity, however. The decision made should be the best possible one if the partisans involved are well informed. Intuitive reasoning is a fiscal luxury which can no longer be afforded. Partisans with the soundest and most objective argument are most likely to get the attention of legislators.

More Objective Decisions

The primary role of program budgeting is to improve the decision-making process. As stated in UCLA's 1972 study, "The purpose of PPB is to improve the likelihood that there will be a rational allocation of tax dollars that will have maximum impact on attaining stated purposes. This reflects the continuing concern of public executives that public funds should not be allocated merely on the basis of intuition and conventional procedures."[13] Schick describes PPB as "an effort to extend the bounds of collective rationality."[14]

Program budgeting improves the quality of the decision-making process since it provides systems information for better analysis, which in turn results in better economies and efficiencies. California's PABS manual observes: "The system is operating in a political world. No one is going to change the fact that political decisions are made, nor are decision-makers going to stop using subjective judgments. . . . What this system does is marshall the best facts that there are, state their limitations, analyze the facts with the best tools that are available, and provide the decision-maker with recommendations."[15] PPB's data-gathering and data-processing techniques and the associative Budget Analysis, utilizing such methods as cost-benefit, cost-effectiveness, and marginal analysis, advance the cause of good governmental management. As Howard states: "most men are rational and will make better decisions if they are given better information. Decisions will be better if the decision-maker knows what he is trying to do, if the objectives are stated, and if the resources devoted to their accomplishment are grouped together."[16]

San Diego's recent review of its water utility rates is an example of how program budgeting and Budget Analysis aid the decision-making process. The city's demand for construction of new water conduction facilities had increased because of population growth and new housing developments. The program budget revealed that these facilities would cause a deficit since the cost of providing new service could not be offset by existing water rates. The Budget Analysis of the water utilities program recommended that the cost of providing water service to new areas be charged to those developments receiving the new service rather than to the existing population. The Council decided to charge the additional cost of new services to the new users, thus following a user-fee philosophy espoused in the Budget Analysis.

Easier Evaluation

The program budget document can provide a legislative body with the data to determine if its legislative intent is being implemented as envisioned. Legally, a government can perform only those functions specifically named in its constitution or charter, or other activities mandated by the legislative body.

One of the outstanding features of the program budget is that every program format must include its legal authority or citation. For example, the authority for the central library program in the Library Department of San Diego is given as Municipal Code, Chapter II, Article 2, Decision 2, Section 22.0201; Article 2, Division 18, Section 22.1801 (see Appendix). These provisions establish the Library Department as a legal department of the city of San Diego which cannot be eliminated without amending the Municipal Code. Such data can be helpful in determining the goals, objectives, outputs, and general description of each program. When programs do not correspond with what the legislation has specified, changes in the program are necessary. This is an obvious advantage over the line-item form of budget.

Only the program budget can reveal areas of legislative discrepancy. It can indicate whether legislative policies are being ignored. The executive branch (or the agent responsible for administering legislative policy) is made more accountable for its actions through the program budget. The program budget can also indicate misinterpretations of legislative intent and suggest new legislation.

Understandable to Laypersons

Officials and administrators sometimes look on the increase in systems information provided by the program budget as a mixed blessing. Governmental actions and policies will be made more visible to the public and press via the PPB document. Citizens are able to see exactly the kind of services their government is providing, the level of funding for each program, and the effectiveness of programs. Furthermore, the program budget will indicate public concerns that are being neglected or ignored. Those elected to office will become more accountable to their constituencies, especially if there is an active and interested press. To cite an example, a certain public dissatisfaction may exist regarding the adequacy of recreational facilities. Officials could indicate in the budget document that the city is deeply involved, or they could be faulted in the budget document if significant steps were not taken to respond to an area of responsibility. On the other hand, the fact that data are readily available to the public and press can sometimes ease the pressure on government officials. If the public has understandable data, it is more likely to be convinced that government is seriously attempting to carry out its responsibilities.

The program budget can also be useful to the press and, therefore, to the public by providing systems information necessary for writing news stories and editorials. Not only does PPB make hard data available, but it also yields information that is understandable even to those without a background in finance, budgeting, or economics. The program budget can also make data available to public-concern groups, such as the League of Women Voters and taxpayers' associations.

NOTES

1. Elizabeth R. Drew, "HEW Grapples with PPBS," *Politics, Programs and Budgets*, ed. James W. Davis (Englewood Cliffs, N.J.: Prentice-Hall, Inc., 1969), pp. 163-165.

2. Charles L. Schultze, *The Politics and Economics of Public Spending* (Washington, D.C.: The Brookings Institution, 1968), pp. 92-94.

3. Hal Schwartz, "Accounting, Resources Management System," *Business Association Review* 11 (Fall 1973): 20-21.

4. *Program Budgeting in State and Local Governments: The Practitioner's View* (UCLA: Institute of Government and Public Affairs, 1972), p. 19.

5. Kenneth Howard, *Changing State Budgeting* (Lexington, Ky.: Council of State Governments, 1973), p. 258.

6. Larry N. Blick, "A New Look at Capital Improvements Programming," *Municipal Finance* 42 (November 1969): 110.

7. Marvin Hoffenberg, "Program Budgeting in Education: Some Organization Implications," *Strategies of Educational Planning*, ed. Richard H. P. Kraft (Tallahassee: Educational Systems Development Center, Florida State University, 1969), pp. 193-199.

8. Drew, op. cit., p. 177.

9. State of California, Department of Finance, *Programming and Budgeting System: The Overall,* (Sacramento, 1968), p. 2.

10. Stephen J. Knezevich, *Program Budgeting (PPBS)* (Berkeley, Calif.: McCutchan Publishing Corp., 1973), p. 131.

11. *San Diego Union*, March 14, 1974.

12. Allen Schick, *Budget Innovation in the States* (Washington, D.C.: The Brookings Institution, 1971), pp. 201-202.

13. *Program Budgeting in State and Local Governments: The Practitioner's View*, op. cit., p. 2.

14. Schick, op. cit., p. 201.

15. State of California, Department of Finance, *Programming and Budgeting System (PABS)* (Sacramento, 1968), p. 11.

16. Howard, op. cit., p. 112.

3

THE IMPLEMENTATION OF PROGRAM BUDGETING

The city of San Diego has recently undertaken program budgeting and Budget Analysis on a full-scale basis. In 1972, as a result of recommendations by the Legislative Analyst Office (the agency responsible for the Budget Analysis), the first steps were taken to change from an essentially performance budget to a program budget. Fiscal 1973-1974 became a transition year to the program budget. Although there were still refinements to be made, San Diego had a complete program budget format in all city departments for the fiscal year 1974-1975.

THEORIES AND PLANS FOR IMPLEMENTATION

Many different plans are useful for the implementation of program budgeting and the Budget Analysis. This section describes plans for policy, especially for decision-makers, and general considerations about adopting program budgeting and the Budget Analysis.

Policy and Implementation Guides for Creation of a PPB System

Before a program budget and Budget Analysis can be instituted, the legislative body must be convinced of their desirability. In the case of San Diego the role of persuading the legislature was undertaken by the Legislative Analyst Office. Next, those responsible for program budgeting and the Budget Analysis must set up guidelines for a successful implementation program. If these guidelines are ignored, disillusionment may arise during the transition period, leading to the abandonment of the budget system before it has been given a fair opportunity.

Standard policy guides for those instituting a program budget and the Budget Analysis are as follows:

1. A strong high-level commitment must exist.
2. The legislative body must be involved in implementation.
3. Political realities cannot be ignored.
4. The implementation effort must be strong and determined.
5. There must be a complete overall plan for implementation.
6. The initial efforts should be centralized as much as possible.
7. Expectations of what the system can do must be realistic.
8. The person in charge of the implementation must have well-defined authority and must be an expert in the field.
9. The support of department or agency personnel is necessary.
10. Implementation should be carried out from within the government, avoiding the use of outside consultants whenever possible.
11. Those involved must feel they will benefit.
12. Good communication at all levels is imperative.
13. Enthusiasm for and confidence in the system is necessary.

1. *Strong high-level commitment:* A requisite input for successful implementation is strong support from the top levels of government, especially the chief executive and his staff. They must believe in the system and transfer this confidence to their subordinates. Next in importance is top administrative support. Opposition to change at lower governmental levels can be minimized if high-level support for program budgeting is well publicized.[1] S. Kenneth Howard describes the experience of the state of California:

> We have learned the advantage of having top-level support and the difficulties of getting the job done in its absence. Without this support, the job can be done, but it is tough. With it, the program and fiscal people fall in and do a job because they know their boss means business. Something as important is that they feel the effort will be worthwhile and will be used. Top support makes a big difference.[2]

Unless those engaged in the implementation program feel that they are strongly supported by high-level officials, enthusiasm for program budgeting will be difficult to maintain. The need for high-level support was well demonstrated in the early 1960s when the federal government implemented PPB in the Department of Defense. Secretary Robert McNamara was the system's strongest enthusiast, and he is given major credit for PPB's success there. McNamara's support led the entire department to welcome the innovation.

2. *Involvement of the legislative body:* In addition to the active support of the chief executive and other high-level officials and administrators, legislative involvement is necessary.[3] The legislative body is responsible for enacting into law any modifications in government and for appropriating funds to implement new programs. Thus, its role in PPB must not be unintentionally minimized. The legislature should be well informed of the advantages of program

budgeting and the Budget Analysis and the progress made toward its successful implementation.

The degree of legislative involvement sometimes influences the form that the budgetary system takes. In Hawaii and Florida the impetus for PPB implementation was provided by the legislature. In Pennsylvania, however, the legislature was not enthusiastic. Consequently, PPB was used by Pennsylvania's executive branch as an aid to fiscal planning; there was little legislative involvement.[4] If the legislative body is not provided with status reports regarding the new budgetary system, it will not have developed the necessary background, and the budget committees will be less likely to understand or to support the new system with adequate appropriations. In cities with a city manager form of government, such as San Diego, legislative support is important as it provides direction to management. In San Diego, before approving PPB, the City Council had to be convinced that the new system would lead to more effective government. The legislative body should also be included in the planning stages of implementation so that it can keep informed about the system in progress.

3. *Political realities:* A program budget and Budget Analysis system operates in a political environment.[5] Political constraints influence decision-making at all times.[6] Even the decision to adopt the system is political as it has implications for the executive and legislative branches of government, operating departments, and vested interests.[7] Departmental administrators therefore must not fear that the program budget and Budget Analysis will lessen their power and control.

4. *Strong and determined effort:* The success of a program budget and Budget Analysis largely depends upon how strongly it is supported. Those in charge of its implementation must be determined to make the system work. Aaron Wildavsky, in a discussion concerning ways to implement change, states that efforts at persuasion must be strong and persistent because of the resistance and inertia of those who are not directly involved with the plans for change.[8] McKinney and Kiely also mention the importance of inertia.[9] Supporters of program budgeting must convince lower level employees that the system is advantageous for them. Fear of the unknown increases resistance to change; this fear must be allayed to gain support for the implementation program.

5. *Complete overall plan for implementation:* Major difficulties in the implementation of a program budget format can be expected by "starting without an overall plan for the entire period of development from design through implementation, evaluation and revision."[10] Every stage must be planned before the actual changeover begins so that all participants can have an orderly sequence of events. Activities can be gauged to adhere to the overall plan. The plan should be flexible enough to accommodate unexpected obstacles, but comprehensive enough to anticipate some of these difficulties. For example, the San Diego PPB Task Force issued instructions to all departments, includ-

ing a timetable, for program budget preparation. After departments had made an initial attempt to design a program budget, their efforts were reviewed, revised, and improved as needed. The plan was completely charted before the transition began.

6. *Centralized efforts:* Wildavsky believes that the more that change can be limited to central management, the greater the probability for success. He states: "The program budget group that McNamara established had to fight with generals in Washington but not with master sergeants in supply. Anyone who knows the Army knows what battle they would rather be engaged in fighting."[11] In other words, efforts at persuasion should be directed toward the higher administrative levels. These persons are more likely to accept program budgeting if they understand that it will improve their administrative effectiveness.

Persons lower in the hierarchy may consider program budgeting an unnecessary increase in their workload, requiring alteration of their daily routines. While their support is also important, lower level bureaucrats will be more cooperative if their superiors are committed to the budgetary system. Consequently, efforts at persuasion should be directed toward those with the power to implement the change in their departments: the department directors. Without such support, resistance will be greater and the implementation of program budgeting more difficult.

7. *Realistic expectations:* Those in charge of implementation must set realistic goals for the system. It is a major fallacy "to assume that major deficiencies in existing systems (planning, finance, personnel, operating and capital budgeting, accounting, and management control) will be overcome easily through PPBS."[12] Program budgeting can lead to more efficient government, but difficulties will always be present primarily because of political constraints. The program budget can provide the information necessary for rational decision-making, but it cannot guarantee that all decisions will be made objectively.

Program budgeting must also be given a reasonable chance for success. As Sidney Sonenblum warns: "Do not expect too much too soon. Do not set excessive goals in the early stages."[13] As stated earlier, unrealistic expectations were a major flaw of the federal implementation program during the 1960s. President Lyndon B. Johnson's announcement of PPB implementation illustrates the unrealistic advantages attributed to the system. In his August 26, 1965, press conference, he announced the start of "a new and very revolutionary system of planning and programming and budgeting throughout the vast federal government *so that through the tools of modern management the full promise of a finer life can be brought to every American at the lowest possible cost.*"[14] PPB was expected to revolutionize all federal operations, and, of course it was unable to solve all problems for all individuals.

The primary objective of the system is *not* to produce program budgets.[15] Rather, it is a tool to obtain better program descriptions, better performance data and standards, and better program evaluation. The production of systems data does not lead to better government in and of itself. The data must be absorbed, understood, and responded to for program budgeting and Budget Analysis to succeed.

8. *Well-defined authority:* The individual who is put in charge of implementation should have both theoretical and practical experience with the system. He should be given sufficient authority to accomplish its implementation[16] and adequate resources to act upon departmental budgets.[17]

When San Diego was considering its program budget implementation, the city manager formed the Committee of Program Budgeting consisting of one staff member each from the Financial Management, Auditor and Comptroller's, and Data Processing Departments, with two members of the Comprehensive Management Planning staff. This committee was chaired by the city's legislative analyst who had previous experience with program budgeting and Budget Analysis at the state level and the necessary expertise on both practical and theoretical levels. He was familiar with many of the concepts used by the state of California and was able to apply them to San Diego. His experience at the state level also alerted him to the problems to be expected during the implementation period. The legislative analyst was granted the authority to carry out the PPB implementation by the mayor and City Council. He had the full cooperation of the departmental directors and their budgetary staffs, as well as the city's Mayor and Council.

9. *Support of department personnel:* In addition to the support of elected officials, it is also necessary to have the backing of departmental and agency administrators. They should be well informed and involved in the implementation program.[18] The San Diego Committee on Program Budgeting relied heavily on departmental budgetary personnel for support. Participating individuals must be convinced that program budgeting is a realistic approach to better government and to better administration of their individual departments. The system should not be regarded as a means to budget-cutting or as a political strategy to reduce a director's control.

10. *Implementation initiation from within:* The implementation of program budgeting will be more successful if the system is developed by the in-house governmental bureaucracy rather than by outside consultants.[19] In reference to state budgeting, Howard remarks that "professional outside consultants are probably more easily resented than existing state personnel and more readily charged with not appreciating the needs of current employees and with showing too little concern for them."[20] In other words, program budgeting will encounter more resistance if it is thought to be forced on governmental employees by persons with no real inside knowledge of the government's particular needs. Consultants should be utilized only when absolutely necessary.

In San Diego, the Committee of Program Budgeting consisted solely of city employees with a working knowledge of the city's operations. Consequently, there was less internal resistance.

11. *Benefits identified:* Officials and administrators must believe that a program budget will improve governmental operations. Government officials should also feel that *they* will benefit personally. [21] Thus, those in charge of the program should convince all officials and employees that the program budget is to their advantage. [22]

12. *Good communication:* Since implementation requires a significant amount of change, open channels of communication must be maintained among all levels of government. [23] Not only must there be direct communication between the implementation staff and administrative and elected officials, but also among and within departments. Most important, the implementation staff must communicate with all officials affected by the change. [24] The staff should also receive adequate feedback.

13. *Enthusiasm and confidence in the system:* The implementation staff must strive to generate enthusiasm for and confidence in program budgeting at all levels of government. First, they need to be enthusiastic themselves. One way of transferring this enthusiasm to others is to demonstrate that the system is "of proved quality, [and] its effects demonstrable." [25] Participants must feel certain that program budgeting will work.

Program Budgeting Implementation
Several strategies must be considered before implementation can begin; otherwise, less than satisfactory progress can be expected. Major considerations are:

1. Sufficient time for implementation
2. A step-by-step approach
3. Adequate personnel and fiscal resources committed to the implementation program
4. Minimizing differences between the program budget and the line-item budget
5. Program structure related to public needs

1. *Time period for implementation:* Government should expect to implement program budgeting, at the minimum, over a three-year period. PPB requires an increased amount of data collection in addition to many format and procedural changes which cannot be resolved immediately. Therefore, PPB should be given sufficient time to be phased in.

The state of California's PABS Manual suggests five years as a proper period for transition to a full PPB system. [26] While efforts must be made to move as quickly as possible, unreasonable demands must be avoided. The Data Processing and Auditor and Comproller's Departments in San Diego stated more time would have been helpful when they changed over to a PPB system. The data requirements were so massive that existing personnel had to work over-time.

2. *Step-by-step approach:* A government should not try to implement a complete program budget immediately, but should plan to adopt and improve the system gradually over five years. [27] Implementation should begin in a few key departments and proceed step by step until all departments are included. It is doubtful that a full PPB system could be successfully implemented in even one department in one year.

A time-phased approach (as used in San Diego) would seem to be more effective. The advantages of this approach are that all departments would face the same problem at the same time and the central PPB staff could anticipate and assist in alleviating problems more efficiently. For example, San Diego concentrated on the development of program structures, objectives, and output measurements in fiscal 1973-1974 (the second implementation year). Results were highly variable from department to department. In fiscal 1974-1975, efforts were made to make improvements in these three areas. At the same time, the capital improvements budget and all sources of revenue were included in the program budget.

While the city now has a complete program budget document, implementation is far from complete. There is need for improvement in the area of quantifying and relating program objectives and outputs. The transition process in San Diego has been fairly smooth, however, because program implementation was phased.

3. *Adequate personnel and fiscal resources:* The individual in charge of PPB implementation must be given adequate staff to plan the program and fiscal resources to keep it going. [28] A central PPB staff such as the Comprehensive Management Planning Task Force in San Diego is continuing the work of implementation and improvement on an on-going basis. This is a necessary follow-up procedure. It is also vital to include Department of Finance personnel in the implementation. The Auditor and Comptroller's and Data Processing Departments will participate as key implementation inputs. In San Diego, these two departments were required to create and design new systems in order to accommodate the larger volume of programmatic data. Consequently, high-level personnel from these departments were included in the PPB Task Force.

4. *Minimizing the distinction between the program budget and the line-item budget:* Some PPB advocates have suggested that both a program budget and a traditional line-item budget should be prepared during the initial implementation stages. But those in charge in San Diego felt that this would entail an enormous duplication of effort, with the result that the staff would be reluctant to substitute the program budget for the line-item budget. Sonenblum suggests that as little distinction as possible be made between the program budget and the "real" or line-item budget. [29] Not only was his advice followed

in San Diego, but it was carried one step further. Line-item budget preparation was discontinued once the program budget format was adopted.

5. *Relating program structure to public needs:* Werner Hirsch and others maintain that, to be effective, the program structure of a program budget must relate to public needs.[30] Program structure is of little value unless it deals with areas of public concern. It must not be viewed as an end unto itself. Legislative review and the Budget Analysis of the PPB document will greatly assist policy-making decisions as PPB provides the necessary input for objective analysis.

PERSONNEL CONSIDERATIONS

Those in charge of implementing a program budget should consider the human element, since the full participation of staff at all levels is needed for success. Thus, successful implementation requires that:

1. Agency heads be kept well informed in order to promote cooperation between the PPB staff and the agencies.
2. Agencies be involved in issue identification.
3. Provisions be made for adequate training of personnel.
4. Cooperation be promoted between fiscal and capital improvement planners.
5. The work schedule to meet time requirements be given consideration.

Consideration of these five points before implementation begins will facilitate the changeover to a program budget.

1. *Well-informed governmental agencies or departments to ensure their cooperation.*[31] According to Wildavsky, experienced personnel can be a barrier to change because they are aware of numerous alternatives and may rationalize that the change will not work.[32] Administrative personnel may fear that program budgeting will limit their flexibility. Administrators, on the other hand, may fear that they will lose their discretionary power of allocation if they are forced to itemize all expenditures in a programmatic format.[33] In order to counter these apprehensions, the PPB staff should make every effort to include agency personnel in the developmental and implemental stages of program budgeting.[34]

The PPB staff must design a plan which can be implemented by the agencies. Therefore, agency involvement in the planning stages is necessary to avoid future difficulties. If the PPB staff has the cooperation and confidence of agency heads and other executive personnel, the departmental staff will be more willing to accept program budgeting.[35]

2. *Agency involvement in issue identification:* Agencies should define and offer solutions for any problems anticipated during PPB implementation. They should also be encouraged to identify how program budgeting can be of

assistance in areas of concern.[36] Increased agency involvement will decrease apprehensions and promote confidence in PPB.

3. *Adequate training of personnel:* Program budgeting requires that governmental personnel learn new skills and techniques and develop a new attitude toward the budgetary process. Consequently, large-scale training programs must be provided for all involved personnel.[37] Resistance to PPB will be greater if people are not properly trained.[38]

First, the central PPB staff itself must be trained in the economic theory, statistics, and analytical techniques of the system. They must understand the concepts of program budgeting and its methodologies. A "PPB expert" can be utilized for a few years to train the staff.[39] This is a reasonable solution if the staff does not have these capabilities. Hostility may arise, however, should PPB be viewed as a system designed by "outsiders." It is preferable to create in-house training programs if possible.

Once the central staff is trained in PPB methodologies and concepts, these capabilities must be transferred to the individual agencies. Agency involvement in the implementation program will thereby become more meaningful. In San Diego, for example, group workshops were held on program budgeting for department heads and their budgetary staff. Individual meetings between departmental staff and members of the PPB task force also assisted in the educational process.

Training should be an on-going process. Inevitably, the departments' first efforts to prepare a program budget will be less than perfect,[40] and additional assistance will be necessary. Examples of both good and bad program budgets can be provided. San Diego used this technique. After each department had prepared its first program budget, the PPB task force reviewed and evaluated this first attempt. A list was made of exceptional efforts, adequate efforts, and unsatisfactory efforts, by category. Those departments with unacceptable program budgets were requested to use the better ones as models for their next attempt. Training of agency personnel in the methodologies of program budgeting was made an on-going process. The training effort continues in San Diego since improvements in the departmental program budget formats are made each year.

4. *Close cooperation between fiscal and capital outlay planners:* Traditionally, planning departments have been concerned with capital planning, and budget departments with fiscal or operational expenditures. A PPB system requires every department to prepare long-range projections for its operating and capital expenditures. This process can best be done with cooperation between capital and fiscal planners. Examples of questions which must be answered are: (1) Where should new utilities be located in regard to population patterns? (2) What capital construction projects fit into a priority structure? (3) How will population growth affect revenue projections and capital requirements?

If the staff responsible for long-range fiscal planning is not aware of long-range capital plans, its tasks will be impossible. Conversely, capital planners must be aware of future population and revenue projections to adjust their capital planning accordingly. In this way, major projects will not be designed on an inadequate funding and/or demographic base. Neither fiscal nor capital planners can operate independently in program budgeting. Revenues and expenditures over a five-year period should be coordinated in a successful PPB system.

5. *Work schedule to meet time requirements:* Initial attempts by departments to produce program budgets will very likely be deficient. Moreover, not all departments and personnel work at the same pace. Some departments will be more than eager to undertake the development of a program budget, while others will need constant encouragement. The PPB implementation staff should be aware of these differences and schedule a workload geared to varying capabilities, so that all departments will complete their budgets at the same time. In order to provide such assistance, the PPB staff must know which departments will require encouragement and support.

IMPLEMENTATION ACTIVITY CONSIDERATIONS

Because more time will be spent gathering hard data by program detail, PPB staff should allow for these circumstances in their implementation plan. Thus, PPB staff should organize the following activities:

1. Increased workloads
2. Progress reports of the implementation program
3. Procedures for appraising program structure

Increased Workloads

In the initial stages of implementation, workloads increase for all governmental units. The departments especially affected are the Auditor and Comptroller's and the Data Processing.

The PPB staff has a sizable task in supervising the changeover. Before implementation can begin, an appropriate budgetary format and instructions for its use by the various departments must be developed. The PPB staff must design and approve the format of the budget document. It should prepare detailed instructions and examples of acceptable objectives, goals, and outputs to lessen initial confusion. In San Diego, all departments received a program budgeting instruction packet which gave definitions of the various program budget components, along with individual examples. Two articles on program budgeting supplemented the definitions. The instructions were both an introduction to program budgeting for those not familiar with the concepts and practical guide to budget preparation. The format was simple, straightforward, and easily understandable by a layperson.

The Data Processing Department will experience a greater workload because it must develop new systems for the data. [41] (The Data Processing Department in San Diego, for example, has experienced increased workloads in programming its computer for additional data necessitated by the program budget. [42]) In fact, if these new data-gathering systems were not generated, effective program evaluation would be impossible. [43] These systems provide input and output data necessary to create program and program element structures. Output quantifications permit evaluation of a program's efficiency and effectiveness. Therefore, the Data Processing Department staff must be included in the initial and on-going planning of a program budget implementation effort.

Data Processing Department personnel should be required to collect only meaningful and useful data. Here they must strike a careful balance between collecting too little and too much data. With too little data, a program budget is not meaningful; with too much raw data, those examining the budget document become confused and those collecting the data, frustrated. [44]

Governments that insist on excessive data collection often end up producing budgets that are of mammoth size and unreadable. For example, the state of Hawaii's first efforts at program planning produced a document containing 600 program elements, 10,000 pages in length and three feet in width. Printing costs for 250 budgets would have exceeded $150,000. [45] The Data Processing Department has enough responsibility without having to assume the additional burden of unnecessary data collection.

Program budgeting requires that the accounting system be structured by program and program element activity. As a result, PPB implementation usually necessitates changes in the accounting system. [46] The following questions should be asked about accounting systems when evaluating their suitability for PPB: "How accurate and flexible is the expenditure accounting system? Does it allow recording and reporting by both program (or activity) and by organizational unit? Does the revenue accounting system link income to its source (such as federal matching funds)?" [47]

Alan Steiss has identified the four most important requirements which an accounting system needs to be useful for program budgeting: (1) comprehensive procedures for expense distribution; (2) unit cost accounting procedures; (3) general ledger accounts for work in progress; and (4) suspense accounts for distribution of such expenditures as compensation and retirement insurance. [48]

Before any changeover takes place, the current accounting system should be evaluated. Insofar as the Auditor and Comptroller's Department in San Diego had to alter its systems to accommodate PPB, a supervising member from the department was included in the PPB task force. This individual, aware of what was to be required of his department, was in a position to inform the task force of the necessary changes and timing requirements the department faced.

When the Auditor and Comptroller's Department in San Diego developed a new accounting system to meet the city's requirements for program budgeting, the department's personnel expended a considerable number of man-hours on the task. William G. Sage, director of the department, has stated that the new system allows for future expansion and will maintain such flexibility.[49]

San Diego now itemizes expenditures within programs rather than aggregating them. Some of the items now charged to individual programs are utilities (power, water and heating), social security, retirement, and unused sick leave. Prior to PPB implementation, these items were budgeted on a citywide, aggregated basis; they are now included in the individual program's budget summaries as cost items associated with the individual program or program element. Consequently, budget organization is more meaningful since a program's total cost is available. This format change necessitated additional modification of San Diego's accounting procedures, but the benefits are notable. Reimbursable programs could now finance their full cost for the first time.

Progress Reviews

The central PPB staff should review and evaluate the progress of implementation at regular intervals.[50] An implementation program will not be flawless, regardless of how complete the planning phase has been. Difficulties can be detected early and corrected by scheduling progress reports. Ideally, these reviews should be made biweekly at the beginning of PPB implementation and yearly once the full changeover has been accomplished. The progress of program budgeting must be evaluated and analyzed regularly to permit improvements on an on-going basis.

Program Structure Evaluation

Definite procedures must be established for program structure appraisal once implementation has begun. Departments are initially requested to create their own program structures, including goals, objectives, and output measures. As previously stated, first efforts are usually mediocre. The PPB staff should assist departments by reviewing their program structures and suggesting methods for improvement. In San Diego, the staff in charge of budget preparation for each department met with members of the PPB task force as well as the assigned department.

The review of program structures should continue and become a regular part of the budgetary process. The budget preparation period is the best time to examine the effects of operational changes on program structure.

THE PROGRAM BUDGET FORMAT

The fiscal year 1974-1975 Library Department Budget in the Appendix is an example of San Diego's program budget format. A general description of the budget document is given first, followed by more detailed definitions and explanations of the various components of the format.

The entire city budget document is divided into the budgets of the various individual departments. The first part of a departmental budget, the *Budget Summary*, lists expenditures for the operating program and capital improvements program of the department. The operating program is broken down into staffing (position- or man-years), personnel expenses, and nonpersonnel expenses for the coming fiscal year and the two previous fiscal years. This format (the inclusion of the two previous years' expenditures in the current budget) is followed throughout the entire operating program budget. It facilitates multiyear comparisons, indicating whether expenditures and position- or man-years are increasing or decreasing. The change from one year to the next is provided in percentage form for total operating program expenditures. Personnel expenses include salaries and wages, employee pensions, and injury and health insurance. Nonpersonnel expenses include supplies, services, and equipment outlay.

The next component is the *Fund Source Analysis* which itemizes revenue sources for the operating and capital improvements programs. Examples of revenue sources for operating programs are general funds, federal revenue-sharing monies, and employee pension tax funds. Sources of revenue for the capital improvements program are general funds, motor vehicle fees, bonds, and noncity funds such as federal, state, and private sources.

The next format categories are *Department Goals* (Objectives) and the *Operating Program Summary*. The latter is broken down into position-years and expenditures for each operating program within the department.

Following overall departmental budget information, budget detail is provided for each program. The first component of the individual program's budget is again a *Budget Summary*, the same format used for the overall departmental budget description. Program information is next provided under the headings of *Need, Objectives, Authority*, and *General Description*. A large program is divided into program elements. If program elements are included, the next section of the program detail is the *Summary of Program Elements*, in which a breakdown of position-years and expenditures is provided for all the program elements. This section is followed by a description of *Operating Program Revenues/Reimbursements*. The format is identical to the departmental *Fund Source Analysis* except that revenues and reimbursements are itemized in the individual program elements.

Following the overall program information, *Program Detail* is given, providing more comprehensive information on the individual program elements. A *General Description*, a summary of objectives, input, and output, is given for each program element. *Input* has the same format as the departmental *Budget Summary* (i.e., position-years, personnel expenses, and nonpersonnel expenses). *Input Detail* shows where these inputs are located within the various program element activities.

Outputs are quantifiable and reflect numerous categories; therefore, they are covered in more detail. Output data are important because they make program evaluation possible; consequently, output statistics should be as meaningful as possible.

After each program and program element has been described, an overall *Position and Salary Schedule* is given for the entire department. This schedule is broken down into the various programs and program elements, but only the previous year's and the present year's information are included. Each position is listed by its classification title with the number of man-years and the expenditures required to fund each position. In addition, personnel expenditures, such as vacation pay, unused sick leave, injury leave, and education incentive, are listed under the program or program element to which they have been charged. In a line-item budget, these expenditures are usually hidden, that is, they are not charged to individual programs.

The *Position and Salary Schedule* is the last item in the operating budget for each department in the San Diego budget.

Following this schedule is the *Capital Improvements Detail*, which provides a description for each capital project undertaken. Every project has a title and a brief description. Also itemized are the type of project and the revenue sources. The previous year's expenditures for each project are given with the present year's expenditures and planned expenditures for the next five years. In this way, long-range planning capability is built into the operational and capital program budget. Capital improvements are an integral component of the program to which they are associated. In the PPB format, the effects of the operating program on capital improvements (and vice versa) can be analyzed more readily.

Program Budget Components

Certain components of San Diego's program budget mentioned above should be elaborated on for a complete understanding of the budget document. This section explains the aforementioned elements of the program budget:

1. Program
2. Program element
3. Goals
4. Need
5. Objectives
6. Authority
7. General description
8. Input
9. Output

1. *Program:* "A program should be a group of interdependent, closely related services or activities, contributing to a common objective. A program should be clearly delineated, have a minimum of overlapping with other programs, be end-product oriented, and lend itself to quantification."[51] Examples of programs within the Library Department are administration, central

library, extension division, and technical services. All activities within individual programs are functionally related and are designed to satisfy common objectives which are part of the overall departmental objectives.

2. *Program element*: "If a program has distinct subobjectives then it should be divided into *program elements*, each with its own subobjectives."[52] A program element is a subdivision of a program, with specific objectives within the program.

An example of a program with program elements is the extension division program of the Library Department. Program elements are the extension division headquarters and the extension division agencies. The elements divide the extension program along organizational lines. Each program element helps satisfy the overall objectives of the extension program.

3. *Goals*: "A goal should be a *broad statement of intended accomplishment of an entire department or major division*. A goal should be viewed as an end state of ideal condition to be attained at some time in the distant future. However, whenever possible, goals should not be stated so broadly that their accomplishment cannot be measured . . . The most essential characteristic of a goal is that it be community-oriented. That is, it ought to describe *intended effects on citizens and the community*."[53] Goals, in other words, are more general than objectives but not so broad as to be meaningless. In San Diego, each department lists its overall goals. Objectives are stated by the individual programs of the department. For example, the goals of the Library Department are as follows:

> To provide a major source of high quality research material and recreational reading for the entire City community; to serve as the public's cultural and intellectual center for individual development, and the continuation of education; to assist the community in social growth, business endeavor, and governmental progress.[54]

These goals are broad and idealistic but progress toward their attainment can be measured. It is possible to quantify the library's use of reference materials and recreational reading material and the number of persons using the facilities.

4. *Need*: "First of all, no objectives can be formulated, no plans for action made without the identification of the need. It may be expressed in terms of market demand or in terms of a target group, but in any event, it should be so stated that it can be quantified."[55] A need is a statement of the problem which the program is designed to alleviate, phrased so that it is possible to measure its effectiveness. A need does not have to be elaborate.

The Library Department's needs are fairly simple and straightforward. For example, the need of the central library program is stated as: "A comprehensive collection of research and information resources . . . needed by the community to facilitate the pursuit of information. The effectiveness and efficiency of such a program is maximized by a centralized facility."[56] The need of the extension division program is simpler yet: "Easy access to library service is needed by the entire community."[57] A need must be real, however, for a program to justify its own existence. If no such need can be identified, the program should not be continued.

5. *Objectives*: "Objectives should be elements of a goal, and accomplishment of an objective should constitute partial fulfillment of a goal. Further, an objective should be a *specific* and *quantitative* statement describing *what* is to be achieved, by *how much*, and within what time frame."[58] Objectives are the ends toward which a program is directed. They must be realistic and attainable and must contribute to the achievement of overall governmental goals.

Definition of objectives is a critical aspect of the program budget because they influence a program's activities and success. Some departments may be tempted to formulate objectives which merely justify an existing program. Objectives in this case support existing activities rather than guide the direction of activities. Objectives should be stated in terms of satisfaction of public needs, and programs should be designed to accomplish these objectives.

In the San Diego program budget, programs, and sometimes program elements, are required to have objectives. The objectives of the program elements will be subordinate to those of the overall program. The objectives of the central library program of the Library Department are:

> To achieve a higher per capita attendance figure; to initiate the recording of patron unfilled needs and complaints per capita; to maintain the amount of library materials available per capita; to increase the circulation of library materials per capita; to initiate the recording of materials used in the library besides those circulated in order to gauge collection use; and to increase the answering of information, reference and research questions.[59]

These objectives satisfy the criteria of being quantifiable, specific, and realistic. Fulfillment of these objectives is measured by output.

6. *Authority*: Authority is that section of the legal code which allows or requires the existence of a program or program element. It may be local, state, or federal.

7. *General description*: The general description of a program or program element is a brief explanation of the program or program element activities. It provides a nonprofessional with a basic understanding of the program. For example, the general description of the central library program is as follows:

> The Central Library includes five adult-oriented sections, a children's section, a young adults' collection, a rare books collection (Wangenheim Room), and supportive services, supplemented by a full depository of United States and State of California documents. The staff selects mate-

rials in anticipation of public use, and assists the public in obtaining the most benefit from these resources. The proposed budget includes the addition of 4.17 position years to continue the Director and Information Service, and to handle the increased workload for the Art, Music, and Recreation Section. The increase in Non-Personnel Expense for FY 1975 reflects price increases for books, periodicals, and binding. 60

The purpose of the general description is to provide anyone examining the budget document with an understanding of a program, its activities, and any changes from the previous fiscal year.

8. *Input*: Input is a description of manpower and resources used by a program. It is a further breakdown of the expenditures listed in the Budget Summary. Personnel expenses are subdivided into the program's various activities. For example, input for the central library program includes the number of man-years required, including temporary positions such as PEP and YEP (respectively, Public Employment Program and Youth Employment Program). It also lists total personnel and nonpersonnel expenses. The input represents the actual cost of the program or program element.

9. *Output*: "Outputs should be *measurements of the degree of achievement of objectives*. Thus, outputs must necessarily relate to objectives and may generally be separated into three different types:

> *Effectiveness*—a valid indicator of the success of a program in terms of effects on citizens and the community. Measures of effectiveness focus how well an objective is accomplished, without particular regard to the costs.
> *Efficiency*—measures how economically input (costs, position-years) is converted to output . . . usually expressed as a ratio of input to output.
> *Basic Work Load*—measures level of activity, amount of processing, or magnitude of basic work load. This type of measure will usually not be a good indicator of achievement of objectives since it is process-oriented rather than results-oriented. 61

Output measures are probably the most troublesome elements of the program budget. They must relate to the objectives to measure the program's effectiveness or efficiency. They must be quantified but simplified so that all can use and understand them. Finally, collection of output data must not be so time-consuming that it becomes an end unto itself or that the time lag is too great for the information to be used. The San Diego PPB Committee believed that quantifying outputs and relating them to objectives was the most difficult aspect of San Diego's implementation program.

The Library Department has performed an exemplary job of developing output measurements which are related to objectives. One objective of the central library program is to increase per capita attendance, one of the outputs listed. Another objective is to maintain the amount of library materials available per capita; this statistic is also provided in the output section of the program's budget. An objective must be measurable by an appropriate output statistic. The Library Department has attempted to connect the two wherever possible.

THE TRANSITION PROCESS

San Diego began to implement program budgeting in 1972, with the first real attempt at a program budget in fiscal year 1973-1974. A completed program budget format is being used for fiscal 1974-1975. This section will describe the budgets for the last three fiscal years and explain the changes that have been made. Once again, the budget of the Library Department is used for illustration. Copies of its budgets for fiscal 1973, 1974, and 1975 can be found in the Appendix.

San Diego's budget for fiscal 1972-1973 (the year before program budgeting was initiated) can best be described as a performance budget. A great deal of emphasis was placed upon unrelated workload statistics (performance measurements of departmental personnel and operations). The divisions of this budget are as follows:

1. *Budget summary*: Only the operating program of the Library Department is included in this summary. In fiscal 1973 the capital improvements budget was a separate document from the operating budget issued and approved by the City Council two months before the operating budget. The summary lists the number of man-years in the entire department, along with expenditures for personal and non-personal expenses and equipment outlay for fiscal 1971, 1972, and 1973.

2. *Description of purpose and functions*: This section describes the purpose and activities of the Library Department. It is analogous to the goals section of the program budget but does not mention goals per se.

3. *Significant workload statistics*: This section is unique to the 1973 budget and is not found in the program budget format. It lists general workload statistics for the entire department, which are not specifically identified with various programs or activities. Examples of workload statistics for the Library Department are: number of books on the shelves, number of books per capita, and number of books purchased. Listed also is a percentage value of the amount of change in these statistics from the previous year—a good indicator of performance.

4. *Activity analysis*: This section includes a breakdown of input in the same format as the budget summary; a program description providing information about the activity; and amount of change in input from the previous year. For some activities, significant workload statistics are sometimes given.

5. *Position and salary schedule*: This section lists the number of personnel

in each classification and the total amount of revenue allocated to it. The format is the same as that of the program budget.

San Diego's budget for fiscal year 1973-1974 was not a complete program budget because major elements were missing. Thus, fiscal 1973-1974 was a transition year.

The following are the divisions of the 1974-1975 budget:

1. *Budget summary*: This is basically the same as for the fiscal 1973-1974 budget, but for the first time capital improvements are included with the operating program detail.

2. *Revenue source analysis*: This section is new in this fiscal year. For the first time, sources of revenue for the Library Department are listed for both operating and capital improvements programs. Examples of revenue sources are the general fund, county grants, service charges, and bonds. In this way, accountability is identified by source relative to the Library's revenues to operate and to fund capital improvements.

3. *Department goals*: This section replaces the description of purpose and functions section of fiscal 1972-1973. More information is provided than was formerly included.

4. *Program requirements analysis*: Also new in this year's budget is a breakdown of expenditures for the operation of each departmental program. The format is the same as for the budget summary.

5. *Program detail*: The Library Department has been organized by program instead of by activity. Each program has a statement of need, goals, authority, general description, input, and output. Program goals are eventually termed objectives in the 1974-1975 budget. Workload statistics have been replaced by outputs.

6. *Position and salary schedule*: There is no change from the previous year.

7. *Capital improvement project detail*: This is the first attempt to include capital improvements data in San Diego's budget. San Diego also prepared a separate capital improvements budget in fiscal 1973-1974. This section lists only the project's title and number and total expenditures for fiscal 1972, 1973, and 1974.

The new items in the 1974-1975 budget are worth repeating because more data were included in this program budget than in the budgets of the previous two years.

1. *Budget summary*: Both operating and capital improvements summaries are given. For the first time, however, temporary federal manpower (PEP and YEP) and items such as unused sick leave and health insurance payments are included within the department summary. In previous years, these had not been broken down by department. Consequently, a more complete picture of resources used by each department is provided.

2. *Fund source analysis*: This is basically unchanged from the previous year.

3. *Goals*: This section is also the same as for the previous year.

4. *Operating program summary*: This too contains the same data as the 1973-1974 budget.

5. *Operating program revenue*: For the first time, sources of revenue are broken down into the separate departmental programs. This is especially applicable to the Library Department which obtains a certain portion of its revenue from fines and charges for lost and damaged books. In this way, the percentage of each program paid for by its own revenue sources can be estimated.

6. *Program detail*: This section is basically the same as the previous year's except that program goals are now stated as program objectives. The extension program contains program elements; consequently, the Library Department has provided output measures for both the program and its elements.

7. *Position and salary schedule*: This section is unchanged from the previous year.

8. *Travel budget*: This section is new in the fiscal 1974-1975 program budget. It includes a description of each trip made, the number of persons attending, the time period involved, and the appropriation necessary to cover expenses.

9. *Capital improvements program detail*: In 1974, San Diego had no separate capital improvements document; capital improvements were included within the departmental budgets. More data are provided than in the 1973-1974 budget. In addition to its title and number, a detailed description of the project is given. Expenditures are broken down into various categories such as land, engineering, construction, and furnishings. Sources of revenue are also identified by categories such as capital outlay, gas tax, bonds, and federal grants. A six-year projection of expenditures for each project is made, beginning with expenditures incurred in fiscal 1973-1974 and running through 1980. In this way, the future expenditure implications of each capital improvement project can easily be determined.

The 1974-1975 budget document is the first one that San Diego can properly call a program budget. This budget provides more data than either the performance budget of 1972-1973 or the transition budget of 1973-1974. There is much greater accountability concerning city operations and what San Diego can expect in the future. In this way, the efficiency and effectiveness of governmental operations in the city of San Diego can be increased.

Extracts from San Diego's *Budget Preparation Manual* prepared as a guide for department heads are given in Appendix C.

ACCOUNTING PROCEDURES MANUAL

Appendix B includes a *Program Accounting Procedures Manual*, which details the data requirements of a PPB. A summary of this manual follows:

When San Diego decided to change from a line-item to a program budget, it was faced with the problems of (1) gathering quanitifiable input, output, revenue, and expenditure data necessary for budgetary purposes on a programmatic rather than a line-item basis, and (2) how best to provide reports reflecting actual versus budgeted data to management.

The major source documents for the input category were labor cards reporting position-hours spent on a particular job; equipment cards reporting usage of equipment; photocopy usage reporting usage of xerox machines; and other expenditure reports, such as purchase orders. The output category called for work unit reports which recorded the total work units completed for each work unit category.

It was determined that the data should be provided at the fund, department, division, program, program element, and activity levels. In order to implement this system, each program element was assigned a four-digit number, the first two digits designating the department or division, the third the program, and the fourth the program element. In addition, each activity within the program element was assigned a job order number. The other number set up for reference, the operation account was established to reflect specific output measurements expressed as work units. (An operation account can serve more than one job order if the output measurements on the job orders are the same.) The operation account was also used to accumulate position-hours.

The labor card was used to report position-hours by job order and operation account. Thus, if a person spent time on one job order but the output was of two distinct types, there would be two entries on the labor card. Similarly, the work unit report can use the same operation account in conjunction with two or more job orders (or vice versa). All other source documents used only the appropriate job order number, not the operation account number.

There are several ways to accumulate and report the available data. San Diego uses these source documents (input requirements) for end-of-period reports to provide (1) the position-hours and total work units by work unit category, and (2) the expenditures by type and by activity. In each case, the data are provided as a total for each program element, program, division, department, and fund. The end-of-period reports also compare the actual data to the amounts budgeted for the current fiscal year. (The actual data are also expressed as a percentage of the budgeted amounts.) Thus, management has an effective tool for monitoring the rate and objects of expenditures and for monitoring and controlling the output efficiency of each department and its component units. After this accounting system was established, it was possible to make accurate estimates regarding input requirements and the related output for the city departments. This improvement allowed more accurate cost-benefit analysis for use during the budget process. Thus, the city was able to allocate its resources to the most effective and efficient programs.

In order to provide both timely and useful data, it was deemed necessary to computerize the accounting system. By keypunching the data from the source documents onto cards, which were then read into the computer, the reports to management could be produced within a reasonable time. This process made it possible to correct actual problems, such as a potential deficit situation, before they became serious. In order to increase their usefulness, the end-of-period and end-of-month reports were prepared using the same basic format as the budget, thereby facilitating the comparison of budgeted versus actual data.

One major change has been made since the development of the system: the city has switched to a thirteen-period year, with the end of the period coinciding with the end of every other biweekly pay period (with a final period from the date of the last report to June 30, the end of the fiscal year). This change facilitates comparison between periods since each period (except the first and the fourteenth) covers the same time span. This change has proved most useful.

NOTES

1. Sidney Sonenblum, *The Environment Facing Local Government Program Budgeting* (UCLA: Institute of Government and Public Affairs, 1973), p. 69; S. Kenneth Howard, *Changing State Budgeting* (Lexington, Ky: Council of State Governments, 1973), p. 167; Stephen J. Knezevich, *Program Budgeting* (*PPBS*) (Berkeley, Calif.: McCutchan Publishing Corp., 1973), p. 255.

2. State of California, Department of Finance, *Programming and Budgeting* (Sacramento: 1967), p. 43, cited by Howard, loc. cit.

3. Sonenblum, loc. cit.; Haldi Associates, Inc., *A Survey of Budgetary Reform in Five States* (Lexington, Ky: Council of State Governments, 1973), pp. 36-37; Allen Schick, "A Death in the Bureaucracy: The Demise of Federal PPB," *Public Administration Review* 33 (March-April 1973): 154.

4. Haldi Associates, Inc., loc. cit.

5. Howard, op. cit., p. 347.

6. Knezevich, op. cit., p. 278.

7. Jack Rabin, *Planning, Programming, and Budgeting for State and Local Governments*, Bureau of Public Administration, University of Alabama, Citizen Information Report No. 9 (Birmingham, Ala.: Commercial Printing Co., 1973), p. 38.

8. Aaron Wildavsky, "Rescuing Policy Analysis from PPBS," *Public Administration Review* 29 (March-April 1969): 191.

9. Jerome B. McKinney and Edward S. Kiely, "Has Success Spoiled PPB?" *The Federal Accountant* 22 (September 1973): 62.

10. "Introduction to Planning Programming and Budgeting Systems," *Management Information Service* 1 (September 1969): 12.

11. Wildavsky, op. cit., p. 192.

12. "Introduction to Planning, Programming and Budgeting Systems," loc. cit.

13. Sonenblum, loc. cit.

14. *New York Times*, August 26, 1965.

15. State of California, Department of Finance, *Programming and Budgeting System* (*PABS*) (Sacramento 1968), p. 54.

16. Ibid., p. 52.

17. "Introduction to Planning, Programming and Budgeting Systems," op. cit., p. 11.

18. Sonenblum, loc. cit.

19. Werner Z. Hirsch, Sidney Sonenblum, and Ronald Teeples, *Local Government Program Budgeting: Theory and Practice* (UCLA: Institute of Government and Public Affairs, 1973), p. 150.

20. Howard, op. cit., p. 168.

21. Richard L. Hays, "Analysis of the Feasibility of Instituting a PPBS in a Line Agency," Master's diss., San Diego State College, 1968, pp. 88-90.

22. Howard, op. cit., p. 165.

23. Ibid., p. 345.

24. *Implementing PPB in State, City and County* (Washington, D.C.: State-Local Finances Project of The George Washington University, 1969), p. 48.

25. Howard, loc. cit.

26. State of California, *Programming and Budgeting System (PABS)*, op. cit., p. 53.

27. Sonenblum, loc. cit.; State of California, *Programming and Budgeting System (PABS)*, loc. cit.; Knezevich, op. cit., pp. 258-260.

28. Sonenblum, loc. cit.; "Introduction to Planning, Programming and Budgeting Systems," loc. cit.; Knezevich, op. cit., p. 256.

29. Sonenblum, ibid.

30. Hirsch, Sonenblum and Teeples, op. cit., p. 138.

31. "Introduction to Planning, Programming and Budgeting Systems," op. cit., p. 12.

32. Wildavsky, loc. cit.

33. State of California, *Programming and Budgeting System (PABS)*, op. cit., p. 26.

34. Sonenblum, loc. cit.

35. Howard, op. cit., p. 345.

36. Sonenblum, loc. cit.

37. Ibid.; Hirsch, Sonenblum, and Teeples, op. cit., pp. 188-189; "Introduction to Planning, Programming and Budgeting Systems," op. cit., p. 11; Knezevich, op. cit., pp. 256-257; Hays, op. cit., p. 88; Statement by David Knapp and Ken Fabricatore, personal interview, March 20, 1974.

38. Howard, op. cit., p. 165.

39. *Implementing PPB in State, City and County*, op. cit., p. 107.

40. State of California, *Programming and Budgeting System (PABS)*, op. cit., p. 53.

41. Sonenblum, loc. cit.

42. Statement by Robert A. Mitchell, personal interview, March 26, 1974.

43. Hirsch, Sonenblum, and Teeples, op. cit., p. 185.

44. Knezevich, op. cit., p. 278.

45. *Program Budgeting in State and Local Governments: The Practitioner's View* (UCLA: Institute of Government and Public Affairs, 1972), p. 10.

46. Haldi Associates, Inc., op. cit., p. 31; State of California, *Programming and Budgeting Systems (PABS)*, op. cit., p. 54.

47. "Introduction to Planning, Programming and Budgeting Systems," loc. cit.

48. Alan Walter Steiss, *Public Budgeting and Management* (Lexington, Mass.: Lexington Books, 1972), p. 175.

49. Statement by William G. Sage, personal interview, March 20, 1974.

50. "Introduction to Planning, Programming and Budgeting Systems," loc. cit.

51. *Program Budgeting-The PPBS Task Force* (San Diego: Comprehensive Management Planning Program, 1973), p. 4.

52. Ibid.

53. Ibid.

54. *City of San Diego, California, Annual Budget, A Program of Municipal Services, Fiscal 1975*, Volume 1, (San Diego, Calif.: City of San Diego Print Shop, 1974), p. 339.

55. State of California, Department of Finance, *Programming and Budgeting System-The Overall* (Sacramento 1968), p. 2.

56. *City of San Diego, California, Annual Budget, A Program of Municipal Services, Fiscal 1975*, op. cit., p. 342.

57. Ibid., p. 343.

58. *Program Budgeting-The PPBS Task Force*, op. cit. p. 5.

59. *City of San Diego, California, Annual Budget, A Program of Municipal Services, Fiscal 1975,* op. cit. p. 342.

60. Ibid.

61. *Program Budgeting-The PPBS Task Force,* op. cit., p. 5.

4

THE IMPORTANCE OF
AN INDEPENDENT BUDGET
ANALYSIS

A program budget created the environment for comprehensive program analysis and evaluation as programmatic and systems data are available. Together, the program budget and the Budget Analysis comprise the most responsive system possible (assuming that fiscal and land-use models are integrated in this process) for positive, rational legislative action. This chapter examines the need for an independent Budget Analysis and discusses both the general concepts of a Budget Analysis; and evaluation and analysis methodologies.

The concept in this chapter is that the Budget Analysis must be separate from the program budget, thus allowing the analysis staff independent status. The integration of the two has been partly responsible for the failure of program budgeting in the past. Evaluative analysis and the program budget document are two separate and independent responsibilities which cannot be combined without creating confusion and conflicts of interest. Departments cannot analyze their own programs while involved in and justifying the very same on-going programs (i.e., self-evaluation).

CONCEPTS OF BUDGET ANALYSIS

Separating the Analysis from the Program Budget
An important feature of San Diego's budgetary system is the separation of PPB responsibilities and the city's independent Budget Analysis, as performed by the Legislative Analyst Office. In San Diego and the state of California, the Budget Analysis is the responsibility of an independent analytical staff employed by the legislative body. The unit at both levels of governments is the Legislative Analyst Office. This office has no responsibility for program administration, budgetary policy, or preparing the budget document. These are the

responsibilities of the Governor's Office (Department of Finance) at the executive level, and the city manager, at the city level. Consequently, the Legislative Analyst Office does not have any conflicting duties as, in both cases, it represents the legislative rather than the executive branch. The executive branch is in charge of budgetary programs.

The Legislative Analyst Office conducts both long- and short-term fiscal studies. Because it is independent of the executive or administrative branch as well as departmental control, it can examine programs objectively and make recommendations as to program performance. Departmental personnel cannot be required to present program alternatives or evaluations while administering the department. The budget that the director presents is his choice of action. Aaron Wildavsky makes this point clearly in his paper, "Rescuing Policy Analysis from PPBS":

> The shotgun marriage between policy analysis and budgeting should be annulled . . . It is hard enough to do a good job of policy analysis, as most agency people now realize, without having to meet arbitrary and fixed deadlines imposed by the budget process. There is no way of telling whether an analysis will be successful. There is, therefore, no point in insisting that half-baked analyses be submitted every year because of a misguided desire to cover the entire agency program.[1]

This does not mean that budgeting and analysis are not related. To be of practical value, recommendations made by the analysis need to be incorporated within the program in order to reflect actual changes. The Budget Analysis for San Diego bears the title *Report of the Legislative Analyst*. This document is presented to the City Council during the budget review conferences of the coming fiscal year. This office is accountable only to the City Council; consequently, the analysts are free of many constraints commonly found in governmental administration. The program budget provides quantitative data in a comprehensive and understandable format necessary for analysis and research. Without a program budget, it would be difficult, if not impossible, to conduct a meaningful Budget Analysis.

What Is Analysis?

Analysis can be defined in simplistic terms as being the process of systematically posing incisive and relevant questions about program alternatives, specifically the full costs of each and the magnitude of benefits that can reasonably be anticipated from each option seeking to satisfy one or more objectives. At its heart is the quantitative evaluation of alternatives.[2]

Analysis can be thought of as "quantitative common sense." It is "the application of methods of quantitative economic analysis and scientific method."[3] It is not merely the application of computer technology to problem-solving, although it may frequently rely on such data bases and expertise. Analysis is more than that; it is a systematic method of examining specific problems and seeking alternative solutions while identifying the cost/benefits of each solution.

The purpose of analysis is to provide meaningful alternatives and priorities in the decision-making process. Analysis can (1) narrow the scope of debate by focusing attention on important issues,[4] (2) enlighten decision-makers about *realistic* choices,[5] and (3) provide more data.[6] Wildavsky summarizes the purpose of analysis:

> Policy analysis aims at providing information that contributes to making an agency politically and socially relevant ... Analysis evaluates and sifts alternative means and ends in the elusive pursuit of policy recommendations. By getting out of the fire-house environment of day-to-day administration, policy analysis seeks knowledge and opportunities for coping with an uncertain future.[7]

How does analysis assist the decision-making process? Analysis attempts to determine whether resources are allocated in the best way to be effective in achieving objectives.[8] At the same time, it measures progress toward achievement of these goals.[9] Analysis also questions whether current and future programs are designed to meet present and future demands[10] and examines the consequences of alternatives, weighing costs and benefits.[11] Creativity in the search for alternatives is emphasized, with attention given to innovative, in-depth analysis.[12] As Wildavsky states:

> Policy analysis is expensive in terms of time, talent and money. It requires a high degree of creativity in order to imagine new policies and to test them out without requiring actual experience. Policy analysis calls for the creation of systems in which elements are linked to one another and to operational indicators so that costs and effectiveness of alternatives may be systematically compared.[13]

The Need for Analysis

In short, analysis helps make decisions to modify, expand, curtail, continue, or terminate programs. Government has a direct responsibility to the taxpayer to ensure that tax revenues are being optimally spent, and the best way to fulfill this duty is to test whether programs are accomplishing their objectives. Constant review is needed to weed out obsolete or lingering programs as public demands change. Analysis of program objectives and the means of attaining these objectives will optimize governmental expenditures.

Analysis can also lessen administrative inertia. Because of bureaucratic resistance to change, it is frequently difficult to replace existing programs with new ones. The Budget Analysis, acting as a catalytic agent, provides the stimulation for change. Finally, the Budget Analysis can help administrators demonstrate to the legislative body and the public that existing programs and planned future programs accomplish their stated objectives. [14]

Benefits of Analysis

Analysis results in increased economies, efficiencies, and effectiveness in governmental operations. It also provides:

1. An early warning system to avert fiscal or program crises. [15]
2. Justification for elimination of uneconomical projects and programs. [16]
3. Information to set priorities among programs competing for limited resources. [17]
4. Evaluation of programs to ensure accomplishment of objectives. New objectives may be discovered during the course of analysis.
5. "New organizational alignments and assignments of responsibilities" (i.e., reorganization). [18]
6. Recognition of unperceived problems in need of solution.
7. Strengthening of executive and legislative ability to deal with administrators. It increases their ability to coordinate the administrative organization. [19]
8. Tradeoff identification. [20]
9. Establishment of an analytic staff within a government, providing an alternative to the use of crash task forces and outside consultants. [21] Studies can be undertaken without outside help.

The most important benefit, however, is the introduction of increased rationality into the decision-making process. Wildavsky makes this point clear:

> The very idea that there should be some identifiable objectives and that attention should be paid to whether these are achieved seems a great step forward. Devising alternative ways of handling problems and considering the future costs of each solution appear creative in comparison to more haphazard approaches . . . The policy analyst seeks to reduce obscurantism by being explicit about problems and solutions, resources and results. The purpose of policy analysis is not to eliminate advocacy but to raise the level of argument among contending interests. [22]

Limitations of Analysis

As has been demonstrated, analysis has many advantages and benefits. But even the best technical capability cannot solve all the problems of modern government. Analysis can help greatly in the optimal allocation of scarce resources, but it should not be expected to be a substitute for legislative determination on broad policy issues. Expectations should be realistic, and analysis should not be promoted as the means of instantly reducing untold millions or billions of dollars:

> Let me hasten to point out that we have not attempted any grandiose cost-benefit analyses designed to reveal whether the total benefits from an additional million dollars spent on health programs could be higher or lower than that from an additional million spent on education or welfare. If I was ever naive enough to think this sort of analysis possible, I no longer am. The benefits of health, education, and welfare programs are diverse and often intangible. They affect different age groups and different regions of the population over different periods of time. No amount of analysis is going to tell us whether the Nation benefits more from sending a slum child to pre-school, providing medical care to an old man, or enabling a disabled housewife to resume her normal activities. The grand decisions—how much health, how much education, how much welfare, and which groups in the population shall benefit—are questions of value judgments and politics. The analyst cannot make such contribution to the resolution. [23]

METHODOLOGIES OF ANALYSIS

Qualifications of Analysts

Many authorities stress the shortage of qualified analysts. They do not clearly specify, however, what characteristics or training are necessary for these unique professionals. The most important characteristic appears to be the ability to think creatively. Analysts should be able to conceptualize and determine solutions for difficult problems. They should be "persons who can perceive and articulate a problem, choose appropriate objectives for its solution, define relevant and important environments or situations in which to test alternatives, judge the reliability of cost and other data, and invent new systems of alternatives to evaluate." [24]

Organization of the Analytic Staff

The organization of the analytic unit and its placement in the governmental hierarchy can be done in many ways:

(1) Program analysis can be performed by *departments* on their own programs. Besides the obvious disadvantage of letting managerial personnel evaluate their own programs, this method has other shortcomings. Analysis will be less comprehensive, and persons capable of performing high-quality analysis on an on-going basis are required. [25]

(2) Program analysis can be performed by the *budget department*. The inadequacy of this plan is obvious. Program analysis *must* be separated from

budget preparation for either to be successful. The budget department (i.e., Department of Finance) is too busy with day-to-day problems to be capable of annual and long-range analyses; neither are budget personnel trained in analytical skills.

(3) Program analysis can be performed by *"team approaches"* comprised of members of various mixes from departments. Some of the mixes that have been suggested are: members from agencies, the budget office, and planning; agencies and budget office only; and budget office and planning only. All of these plans involve the budget office, which should not be included in the analytic unit for reasons cited above. Planning departments usually do not have the personnel or time for year-round analysis, and agency involvement tends to bias analytical objectivity. Some authors recommend a team approach for local governments because it avoids extremes of overcentralization or decentralization. 26

(4) A similar approach is to have *two analytic units*—one under the jurisdiction of a central authority, and the other comprised of staff from the various agencies. This is the so-called two-track approach. This method will not work, unless the analytical responsibilities given to each unit are clearly defined. If they are not, the two units may work against each other rather than in coordination. 27

(5) A *separate analytical staff* under legislative control can be established. San Diego and the state of California use this form of Budget Analysis organization. This analytical unit can conduct objective and probing analyses because it is independent of both agency and administrative control. Merewitz and Sosnick suggest this organizational structure as it avoids conflict of interest. 28 Agencies tend to analyze only those projects which do not overly criticize their own operations. Outside consultants may make minor or noncontroversial recommendations so that they will receive future contracts. Consequently, the best placement of an analytical unit appears to be under legislative authority independent of executive control. San Diego's Office of the Legislative Analyst was established in this manner. This office is accountable to the Mayor and City Council (the legislature), and it prepares an annual Budget Analysis as well as independent reviews of fiscal allocations and programs of the executive or administrative branch (i.e., city manager). At the state level, the governor is responsible for the state budget, and the legislature approves the allocations with advice and input from the state Legislative Analyst Office (which is responsible only to the legislature).

Analysts in the Legislative Analyst Office working independently of the various departments perform budget analyses and undertake special studies such as a study for metropolitan water rates. The Legislative Analyst Office makes recommendations to the Mayor and City Council to increase government effectiveness and efficiency and provides them with unbiased and objective data concerning all city activities. The most important advantage of the separate staff is that it offers freedom from organizational constraints.

Methods and Techniques of Analysis

There are many types of analyses, but they all tend to share the following elements, as described by E. S. Quade:

a. *The objective* (or objectives). Systems analysis is undertaken primarily to help choose a policy or course of action.

b. *The alternatives* are the means by which it is hoped the objectives can be attained.

c. *The costs.* The choice of a particular alternative for accomplishing the objectives implies that certain specific resources can no longer be used for other purposes.

d. *A model* is a simplified, stylized representation of the real world that abstracts the cause and effect relationship essential to the question studied.

e. *A criterion* is a rule or standard by which to rank the alternatives in order of desirability. [29]

An orderly sequence of events is needed to ensure that the Budget Analysis will improve the efficiency and effectiveness of governmental operations. Wildavsky suggests the following procedure:

a. Secretary of agency and top policy analysts review major issues and legislation and set up a study menu for several years. Additions and deletions are made periodically.

b. Policy analysts set up studies which take anywhere from 6 to 24 months.

c. As a study is completed for a major issue area, it is submitted to the secretary of the agency for review and approval.

d. If approved, the implications of the study's recommendations are translated into budgetary terms for submission as a program memorandum in support of the agency's fiscal year budget. [30]

This is a rational approach to the problem of study selection, although it may have to be modified to suit specific requirements. In any case, the analytical staff should have an orderly sequence to follow. The following order is more generalized than Wildavsky's and is therefore offered as a possibility:

1. *Select what is to be analyzed:* Selecting the programs to be analyzed is an art in itself. [31] The program potential for recommendations must be sufficient to justify the time and expense of any analysis. The program must be studied in the time available so that the recommendations made can have maximum ef-

fect. Analyses should not be performed if a policy decision has already been made and a new alternative has no chance of implementation.[32]

It is very important to select the right "problem" program. As Quade states: "An accurate answer to the wrong question is likely to be far less helpful than an incomplete answer to the right question."[33] Schultze believes that for the best results new, rather than older, established programs should be selected.[34] Whereas the available data of older programs are generally greater, there is also more resistance to change. Most new programs suffer from a lack of data, but present more opportunity for innovative recommendations.

2. *Identify the problem that the program is trying to solve:* Once a program had been selected, the next step is to define clearly the problem area requiring a solution. "Develop a clear statement of the need that the program is designed to meet or the problem it is intended to solve."[35] A program budget is a great assistance in this step as each program is required to state its objectives in the budget document.

3. *Select performance criteria:* The next step is to determine the criteria which will measure a program's effectiveness. These criteria are the quantitative outputs in the program budget. Output is generally expressed in monetary terms. Cost/benefit analysis based on nonmonetary criteria would determine the "payoff."[36] For example, a measurement of the effectiveness of the Police Department's crime prevention program would be the actual reduction in crimes during a given year. A verbal description of effectiveness would not provide a quantifiable output to allow measurement of performance.

4. *Collect data:* There will never be enough data for an analysis. The problem must be approached with the awareness that data are a scarce resource along with tax revenues.[37] Consequently, the Budget Analysis must be so designed that maximum insight into a problem can be gained from existing or readily obtainable data.[38] A program budget can provide much of the data necessary for analysis. In fact, analysis would be impossible without the systematic organization of data found in the detailed program budget.

One source of data sometimes overlooked is census tract data. Statistics concerning unemployment, per capita income, suicide rate, crime rate, and the like can be developed from census data. No potential sources of information should be overlooked, for the analysis will be more comprehensive if every source of data is included.

5. *Identify areas of uncertainty:* "Data gaps" must be identified, and, if possible, attempts must be made to quantify them by indirect methods (i.e., identify compatibles). The limitations imposed by these data gaps should be made explicit in the analysis.[39] Uncertainty will always exist and should be identified as such.

6. *Identify alternatives:* After the data have been collected and the uncertainties defined, the next step is to formulate alternative programs, alternative levels of activity within a program, or alternative combinations of programs.

Alternative objectives may even be considered.[40] Analysts should formulate alternatives as well as improvements to existing programs.[41]

Creativity is important to alternative selection. An analyst must be able to formulate new and innovative courses of action and to adapt methodologies used by other jurisdictions to the program under review. The success of an analysis depends upon this ability. The purpose of analysis is not merely to criticize and reveal inadequacies, but also to recommend how improvements can be made.

7. *Estimate the effects of each alternative:* As alternatives are being formulated, the social costs and cost-benefit effects need to be identified.[42] Future demands should be anticipated and included in the analysis. For example, a proposed alternative may result in immediate cost-savings; the long-term effect, however, may be such that programmatic social objectives are not met. Analysis should attempt to predetermine these effects when comparing alternatives.

8. *Estimate the cost of each alternative:* Every program and every alternative involve an outlay of revenue and expenditure of man-hours. Analysts should specify all costs (operating and capital) of each alternative under consideration.[43] An alternative that results in immediate cost savings may be more expensive in the long run if it requires large expenditures at a later date. For example, a decision to postpone a capital project may not necessarily be cost-wise. Growth studies may reveal that the need will definitely increase in the future and that the cost of present construction may make it more economical to begin the project in the next fiscal year.

9. *Specify where tradeoffs can be made:* Cost and benefit data facilitate "tradeoff" analysis. Available resources are a finite factor in program adoption; therefore, tradeoffs are necessary. Analysis should reveal where economizing tradeoffs are possible without impairing the effectiveness of governmental operations.[44]

10. *Present analysis recommendations:* The completed Budget Analysis must be presented to legislators for their approval. The analysis should include a summary in a format understandable to both specialists and laypersons.[45] This step requires special attention, since the clarity of the document will influence the impact of the recommendations. The analysis should also identify the major assumptions as well as indicate how "sensitive" the results of the analysis are.[46] The presentation should be as technical as possible without jargon.[47]

The analytic staff may view itself as an educational unit which informs, criticizes, and recommends.[48] The conclusions and recommendations of the analysis should be clearly presented to the legislative body both verbally and in a written report, with an opportunity for response from the executive branch. The logic of the recommendations is the essence of the study.

Major Techniques of Analysis for Budget Review

The following techniques of analysis can be performed, utilizing the general categories previously outlined:

1. *Cost-benefit and cost-effectiveness analyses:* Cost-benefit and cost-effectiveness analyses have led to a more scientific means of choosing among alternative courses of action. Cost-benefit analysis is not a new technique. It was used in 1844 by the French engineer Jules Dupuit for a study of public works [49] and more recently, in the 1930s, by the Tennessee Valley Authority for developing water resource use plans. [50] In cost-benefit analysis, costs and benefits of proposed alternatives are expressed in monetary terms. The ratio of benefit to costs is calculated for each alternative and is used as the basis for comparison among the alternatives.

For example, a desired objective in police protection might be to reduce the cash value of goods stolen per year by a certain percentage identified as a crime index statistic. Several alternative methods of accomplishing this objective could be proposed. One method would be to increase police surveillance; costs would include equipment (maintenance and operation of squad cars) and personnel (salaries of policemen). Another alternative would be to conduct public education programs on burglary; costs would include salaries of personnel conducting educational door-to-door surveys, group meetings, and the like. By stating these costs in dollar terms, it is possible to learn which alternative would cost less for the same amount of benefit. A program that costs twice as much as another and produces the same result would not be recommended. Subsequently, the choice is less likely to be made on the basis that one program is more easily implemented or readily available than another.[51] Nor do program budgeting and the Budget Analysis accept the intuitive feeling that one alternative appears better than another. Emphasis on quantification requires that costs and benefits be identified. Cost-benefit analysis can also assist in making tradeoffs between unrelated programs (beneficial in testing overall priorities and benefits).

Cost-effectiveness analysis is closely related to cost-benefit analysis. Whereas cost-benefit analysis is concerned with dollars, cost-effectiveness analysis permits more alternative criteria. Cost-effectiveness analysis may be defined as the "systematic examination of an alternative in terms of its advantages as measured by a fixed level and quality of an outcome, and disadvantages, as measured by the economic cost. The measure of desirability (effectiveness) is *not* the same as the measure of costs. The index or ratio shows the costs of various alternatives that produce the same degree of effectiveness."[52]

Cost-effectiveness analysis is preferred to cost-benefit analysis when it is difficult to place a dollar value on objectives. For example, the costs of alternative ways of reducing the crime rate can be stated by a fixed percentage. (*Note:* This objective is *not* expressed in dollar terms.) Or one can calculate the crime rate reduction by spending equal amounts on each alternative. In *Changing State Budgeting*, Howard states that cost-effectiveness analysis is a more realistic way of examining differences among alternatives, since some objectives are impossible to quantify in financial terms.[53]

2. *Marginal analysis:* Another technique used to compare alternatives, marginal analysis, examines the new benefits that accrue from additional dollar and/or personnel inputs. The amount of new benefits derived from varying levels of input can be compared to test for diminishing or increasing returns (benefits) per unit of additional input. For example, personnel costs are a major source of increased governmental costs. Additional benefits or output should result from additional manpower. Marginal analysis benefits can indicate whether additional salaries could produce more benefits if used in other programs. For example, an increase in police personnel may not result in a sufficient decrease in the crime rate to warrant the cost. Therefore, it might be more effective to allocate these funds to a more sophisticated management, or even communication, system. Thus, through marginal analysis the effectiveness of alternative new inputs can be compared. The best alternative is that which produces the greatest increase in benefit per unit cost of input.

Marginal analysis of additional benefits as compared to additional costs is most useful when applied to existing, on-going program evaluation. A cost-benefit or cost-effectiveness study can be very helpful when alternative ways of implementing a totally new program are reviewed. Marginal analysis is used to test alternative ways of improving existing programs. Past expenditure levels can be of little value as they may have no future impact relative to increasing or decreasing additional benefits. The marginal effects of new inputs are the important considerations.

3. *Opportunity cost analysis:* In *Changing State Budgeting*, Howard describes opportunity costs as follows:

> The cost of doing one thing is the benefit that would have been derived if the same resources had been applied to their next-best use. Every allocation of scarce or limited resources means that some other allocation or opportunity must be foregone. In this sense, the real cost of doing one thing is *not* being able to do another—that is, foregoing the benefits that the other opportunity would have provided.[54]

Opportunity cost analysis can show the alternative that provides the most benefit while minimizing the benefits lost by not implementing other alternatives. A department director can use opportunity cost analysis to justify the rejection of a new program. Analysis may reveal that the opportunity cost of the new program outweighs the benefits received. Resources, therefore, would be better allocated to existing or other new programs.

For example, the director of a parks and recreation department may be studying open space acquisition for future park development. Opportunity cost analysis may reveal that implementation of a program will not allow necessary improvement of existing parks and recreation areas. The cost of purchasing new land may be so prohibitive that any opportunity to improve existing parks must be foregone. On the other hand, once available land is developed, it is irretrievably lost for open space usage. If such land is not purchased now, it may be sold to another agent, or the purchase price may increase beyond the reach of public revenues. Existing parks can always be improved in the future, but available lands for additional parks may be lost forever. Thus, opportunity cost analysis can provide a department director with systems information concerning not only direct costs of implementing a new program but the potential value of lost benefits as well.

4. *Comparative analysis:* This technique is undertaken to examine the effectiveness and efficiency of specific governmental programs. Studies are made of the programs of other jurisdictions for comparative purposes. The results of these studies are then applied to the specific operation of the governmental activity. For example, when conducting a comparative analysis of waste disposal operations in a city, the analyst will compare waste disposal activities of one city with those of other cities. In this way, better methods used by other governments could be applied.

5. *Systems analysis:* The systems approach is an attempt to study a program in its entirety, including all outside influences and all internal interactions within the system. Kraemer summarizes the concept as follows:

> Systems are made up of all sets of components that work together for the overall objective of the whole. The systems approach is a way of thinking about these total systems and their components. It is an effort to consider a system in its entire context, with all of its ramifications, with all of its interior interactions, with all of its exterior connections, and with full cognizance of its place in its context.

According to Kraemer, the systems approach to problem-solving is contrary to the natural inclinations of most decision-makers. Legislators will usually attempt to cut down a problem to understandable size and study it out of context.[55] The systems approach, on the other hand, is concerned with the workings of the total system. It can be a useful technique for analysis as it permits the entire problem to be studied in its natural environment. Systems analysis is especially applicable to the study of major governmental operations such as fire, police, and public utilities.

REQUIREMENTS OF A BUDGET ANALYSIS

The following policy and operational commitments would be necessary to establish or improve analytical capabilities within governmental responsibilities.

Use a Program Budget

A program budget is mandatory for successful analysis. California's Finance Department indicates that it is necessary to "recast the budget document in program terms, since one of the first essentials in conducting program evaluation is program identification."[56] Program budgeting provides the systems data necessary to perform analysis that is readily incorporated and understandable in terms of existing programs. Without PPB, the analyst will be required to spend excessive time trying to collect raw data which in some cases may be found to be unattainable.

Obtain Support from High-level Officials

The success of any analysis depends upon support from the executive branch, the legislative body, and top administrators. It should not be difficult to get the legislators' backing as Budget Analysis increases their resource allocation potential, allows new priority mixes, and provides an independent data source.[57] Concerning the legislative body, Wildavsky states: "Policy analysis must be relevant to what congressmen want . . . The purpose of analysis would be, in its simplest form, to enable Congressmen to ask good questions and to evaluate answers."[58]

Administrative support (the formulators of the budget and department heads) is not as easily obtained. Administrators might oppose the Budget Analysis on the basis that if it uncovered inefficiency or ineffectiveness in their programs they might be embarrassed. The analytic staff must attempt to assuage these concerns. With administrative support, the Budget Analysis will proceed more smoothly. "The first requirement of effective policy analysis is that top management want it. . . . The inevitable difficulties of shaking loose information and breaking up old habits will prove to be insuperable obstacles without steady support from high agency officials.[59]

Obtain an Adequate Analytical Staff

As suggested earlier, qualified analysts are in short supply, considering the extent of the creative analysis required.[60] The analytical unit must be provided with sufficient and qualified personnel. An inadequate staff will be overworked and the quantity and quality of analysis will suffer.

Protect the Analytic Unit from Political Harassment

The recommendations of the analytical unit can be controversial. Analytical staff should be protected from political harassment should staff recommendations not follow the politician's desires for specific changes. "Political officeholders bring with them campaign promises and their own perceptions of what needs to be done. The advice of an analyst who tells them they are wrong is not always welcome."[61] A political officeholder may resent, or even fire, an analyst whose analysis, albeit competent, conflicts with the officeholder's perceptions and/or campaign promises. As Schultze has pointed out, analysis "is in tension with political dialogue because it emphasizes resource efficiency and stresses economic opportunity costs while political dialogue has its own set of efficiency criteria and emphasizes political opportunity costs."[62] Consequently, the analytic unit must be protected from potential attacks: "In other words, an analysis unit must have some protection or a power base of its own if it is to survive the slings and arrows that its work necessarily draws."[63] The analysis is not intended to further the political interests of the executive, legislative body, or administrators. The analytical unit must operate independently and free of politics if their recommendations are to be objective.

Maintain a Balance Between Long- and Short-Term Studies

If an analytical unit has proven successful, demands will be made on the staff to undertake both long- and short-term analyses. Pressure will be applied to assist in "fire-fighting"—that is, to solve current day-to-day problems that need immediate remedy. The analytical staff must also have sufficient time and personnel to do long-term studies which have far-reaching consequences (e.g., land-use, growth, and governmental reorganization studies). While such studies are not as urgent as "fire-fighting," they are just as necessary for better government:

> Immediate usefulness to top management may be secured by working on problems with short lead times while attempting to retain perhaps half of the available time for genuine policy analysis. To the degree that serious policy analysis enters into the life of the organization and proves its worth, it will be easier to justify its requirements in terms of release from everyday concerns.[64]

Contract Large Studies

Because of limited time and personnel, "a ... tactic would be to contract out for studies that are expected to take the longest period of time."[65] This approach is often utilized by San Diego. For example, the analytical study for relocating fire stations was performed by an outside firm because the city did not have sufficiently trained personnel.

Establish Training Programs

Training programs will increase in-house analytical expertise. Qualified analysts are always in demand, and in-house training programs can increase interest and promote technical skills.[66] Training programs will educate departmental personnel in the use of such techniques.

OBSTACLES TO ANALYSIS

Sufficient Time Is Not Always Available

Analysis should provide refined recommendations, but often time constraints preclude even a rudimentary analysis.[67] These are the "crisis" situations, such as when it is suddenly discovered that more revenue is needed to balance the budget. Long-term fiscal analysis can identify, predict, and provide alternatives before any crisis has a chance to develop, or it can at least provide a prepared study for such contingencies.

Some Programs and Their Objectives Are Unclear

Often, departmental programs are not stated specifically, and objectives are unduly generalized. Analysis cannot be performed successfully on program objectives which are ill defined or provide insufficient data. The solution lies in the correct implementation of program budgeting. A program budget requires that every program be clearly defined and that its objectives be identified and rationalized by department heads.

Some Programs Are Difficult to Analyze

Certain programs are difficult to analyze due to their outputs. For example, programs whose main activities involve research, analysis, or creative thinking are hard to evaluate, but output measures are available even in these particular cases. The analysis can test the outputs or recommend different ones.

Social Costs Are Hard to Determine

Merewitz and Sosnick believe that social costs are the real concern of government but that they are very elusive. [68] Only some social costs can be quantified; thus, a complete analysis will be difficult. While this constraint may exist, analysis can utilize whatever systems data are available and appropriate, thus reducing areas of uncertainty.

PROBLEMS AND SHORTCOMINGS OF ANALYSIS

Shortcomings Can Be the Fault of Analysts

Even though analysts, ideally, are objective and utilize quantitative techniques, they are also subject to human frailties. Such failings might show up in their work and should be identified as soon as possible. For example, analysts may promote the recommendations of a report to justify their research. Or else an on-going study may be used as justification for continuing research, regardless of the benefits or costs. Analysts may also attempt to promote major programmatic changes as a result of personal biases or to justify or exalt their positions.

On the other hand, analysts may feel constrained and compromised because of their employers: "The study must cater to the information wants of decision makers and, at the same time, investigate program alternatives that would, if adopted, alter the distribution of power among government employees." [69] Needless to say, this may place an analyst in an untenable situation.

Results May Be Manipulated

The results of an analysis can be used to further a position or to support a decision. An analysis may be designed to further a conclusion rather than to reveal the most efficient and effective alternatives. [70] Ida Hoos is the most outspoken critic of this shortcoming: "Just so long as assessment of economic feasibility remains in the hands of agencies with vested interest in the outcome of such studies, cost-benefit analyses will be a useful vehicle for substantiating a particular position." [71]

San Diego has minimized this difficulty by establishing an independent analytical staff under the direction of the City Council. Program analysis is performed by the Legislative Analyst Office, not by the concerned departments. In this way, analyses can be more objective.

Analysis Deals Only with Quantifiable Facts

Many critics have complained that analysis ignores intangible and nonquantifiable factors which can sometimes be more important than quantifiable statistics. [72]

> Many factors fundamental to public policy are not subject to any sort of quantitative analysis. Even though systematic procedures exist . . . for handling factors that cannot be quantified unless an effort is made to overcome the analysts' bias toward quantitative and mathematical models, we may find the more elusive political social aspects neglected, improperly weighted, or even deliberately set aside. [73]

Ida Hoos is even more critical of the quantification emphasized by analytical techniques.

> In our review of this technique in the management of public affairs, we find a need for greater attention to the intangible costs for which this method provides little accommodation . . . Critical review suggests that the approach has generated numerous problems, perhaps more than it has settled. Identifying, quantifying, and relating service objectives with the costs and benefits of various courses of action have forced concentration on the measurable elements rather than the whole . . . It is often likely that these portions are relatively less important than those which could not be objectively weighed or meaningfully weighted . . . Through the show of formulas and calculations, there has been conveyed to the unenlightened not only an impression of accuracy that does not exist, but also the notion that solely that which is quantifiable is significant. [74]

It is true that analytical techniques rely heavily on factual and quantifiable data, but serious analysis does not purposely ignore nonquantifiable factors.

What other method of fact-finding can better deal with intangible factors? No critic has provided a solution that is better than the attempt to quantify existing data. Certainly, intangible factors cannot be ignored, but it is the responsibility of decision-makers to understand these variables. Analysis provides the decision-makers with alternatives and their associative costs and benefits. Recommendations are made on the basis of available data, not on the assumption that one alternative *seems* better than another. The social costs will inevitably be weighed by the political realities to which the legislature will always be responsive.

Some Types of Alternatives Are Neglected

If certain alternatives are controversial, they may be neglected. For example, alternatives that threaten existing monopolies owned or regulated by the government (e.g., water, power, and waste treatment) are often discounted because of their political nature. Alternatives that modify existing organizational structures (i.e., reorganization) are avoided. As long as the analytical unit is independent of political constraints, it should be able to study controversial issues which others might wish to avoid.

Examples of Bad Analysis

Some critics of analysis have pointed to specific studies that arrived at fanciful conclusions. One study, mentioned by Hoos, concerns the feasibility study of the SST (supersonic transport). An analyst decided that an executive making at least $20,000 per year would be willing to pay an additional $10 for every hour of flight time saved. Nowhere in the study was the problem of congested airports, including the time lost circling the airport or waiting for baggage, considered. The study also overlooked the cost considerations of sonic booms, noise pollution, and possible degradation of environmental quality. Analysis of the sonic boom was conducted without the help of physicians, psychiatrists, or psychologists. [75]

Another study mentioned by Hoos concerned health care for the poor. She cited this study as an example of how analysts who have no expertise in a specific field can reach biased conclusions. The analyst concluded that the poor should be provided with the kind of health care they desired rather than the type of care medical experts stated they required (i.e., face-lifts rather than preventive health and dental care). [76]

These two examples illustrate how an analysis could be distorted. Clearly, those conducting these studies did not concern themselves with all relevant systems information. A thorough systems analysis should utilize all available data. But the studies cited above merely illustrate analytical deficiencies and do not compromise the need for such analyses.

EXAMPLES OF GOOD ANALYSIS

Two examples (see Appendix, pages 210-229) have been chosen to illustrate analyses made possible by data provided within a program budget. The first example is the San Diego Fire Department's operating and capital improvement Budget Analysis for fiscal year 1973-1974. The recommendations in the Budget Analysis led to a study on fire station relocation, which resulted in a decrease in citywide response time, better fire protection coverage, and annual cost-savings in both the operating and capital budgets. The second example is the analysis of the budget of California's Department of Motor Vehicles. This last analysis recommended savings of an estimated $9 million for this department. These analyses are further described in this section and are illustrated in the Appendix.

City of San Diego—Fire Station Location Analysis
The impetus for a study on relocating San Diego's fire stations resulted from the capital improvements Budget Analysis for fiscal 1973-1974. The Budget Analysis revealed many discrepancies between the department's operating and capital improvements budgets. For example, the operating budget included equipment appropriations for fire stations which were scheduled to be abandoned in the capital improvements budget. The Fire Department had scheduled for elimination stations that had been constructed as recently as 1963, without giving any clear indication of any cost-effectiveness. The department justified relocation on the basis of decreasing response time, but it failed to give actual hard data on current response times or the expected times decreases. The Legislative Analyst Office concluded that the department was unsure of its short- and long-term objectives for locating these stations. Therefore, it recommended that the Fire Department undertake a master plan for capital improvements and study actual response times by clocked trial runs, so that hard cost/benefit data could be evaluated.

Shortly after the Budget Analysis of the capital improvements program was completed, the Legislative Analyst Office evaluated the Fire Department's operating budget. Once again, it recommended that no further capital or related operating expenditures be approved until a computerized study of fire station location was made available. Both the city manager and the Fire Department concurred with this recommendation. Subsequently, the department and an outside consultant, Public Technology, Inc. of Washington, D.C., jointly began such a study.

The memorandum dated November 29, 1973, in the Appendix details the study approach. It involved three phases:

Phase I (describing the geographic area) pinpointed areas of need and identified target hazards, geographic centers of groups of like occupancies, and fire demand zones. Fire potential and risk were considered, and a response time for each fire demand zone was determined. Existing locations of fire stations were identified.

In Phase II (path program), the data collected in Phase I were fed into the computer. The output report displayed the actual path and response time required from each proposed site to every focal point in the system.

Phase III (location program) involved computer simulation and was an effort to decrease response times by relocation of fire stations.

The results of the relocation study were significant: (1) an estimated one-time savings of $800,000, as well as annual operational savings of approximately $1 million were made, (2) citywide resonse times were decreased by an average of approximately 30 seconds, and (3) total city coverage by the Fire Department was increased by 12 percent.

State of California—Department of Motor Vehicles Analysis, FY 1971

The Legislative Analyst Office of the state of California is responsible for budget analyses for all state departments. If all of the DMV recommendations in the Budget Analysis had been implemented, a first-year savings of approximately $9 million would have resulted. Briefly, the analysis recommended that the DMV adopt a new fee schedule for driver and vehicle information. In addition, the State Legislative Analyst Office recommended that the price for vehicle registration information be increased from $7 to $25 per 1,000 names. This recommendation was adopted and, as a result, increased DMV revenues by approximately $850,000 the first year.

The Legislative Analyst Office also recommended that the price for individual items of vehicle registration information be raised to $1, which would have increased revenues by $86,000. A compromise measure of a 25c to 75c charge depending on the type of information requested, was adopted. Additional charges are now levied for the history of a vehicle ($1) and various other searches. The price per item for driver's license information was raised to 75c rather than $1 as recommended by the Legislative Analyst Office; this measure resulted in a revenue increase of $2,874,000 instead of $3,832,000, a total that still represents a substantial annual savings. The recommendation that the driver improvement program be discontinued at a savings of $4 million was not implemented, but a study was initiated to make the program more effective. The results of this study have not yet been released.

Although all of the recommendations of the Legislative Analyst Office were not fully implemented, there was a major reduction in the DMV budget and, concomitantly, substantial savings for California taxpayers. The program budget of the state of California provided the necessary data for such an analysis. And without the independent Budget Analysis, the recommendations would, in all likelihood, not have been made or implemented.

NOTES

1. Aaron Wildavsky, "Rescuing Policy Analysis from PPBS," *Public Administration Review* 29 (March-April 1969): 196.

2. Stephen J. Knezevich, *Program Budgeting (PPBS)* (Berkeley, Calif.: McCutchan Publishing Corp., 1973), p. 183.

3. A. S. Enthoven, "Systems Analysis and the Navy," *Planning-Programming-Budgeting*, eds. F. J. Lyden and E. G. Miller (Chicago: Markham Publishing Co., 1971), pp. 265-280, cited by Knezevich, ibid., p. 175.

4. Stephen I. Grossbard, *PPBS for State and Local Officials*, Bureau of Government Research, Research Series No. 15 (Kingston, R.I.: University of Rhode Island, 1971), p. 22.

5. Werner Z. Hirsch, Sidney Sonenblum, and Ronald Teeples, *Local Government Program Budgeting: Theory and Practice* (UCLA: Institute of Government and Public Affairs, 1973), pp. 178-179.

6. Robert D. Lee, Jr., and Ronald W. Johnson, *Public Budgeting Systems* (Baltimore: University Park Press, 1973), pp. 178-179.

7. Wildavsky, op. cit., p. 190.

8. State of California, Department of Finance, *Program Evaluation—From Concept to Action* (Sacramento: 1968), p. 1.

9. Grossbard, loc. cit.

10. State of California, *Program Evaluation—From Concept to Action*, loc. cit.

11. Grossbard, loc. cit.

12. Yehezkel Dror, "Policy Analysts: A New Professional Role in Government Service," *Public Administration Review* 27 (September 1967), pp. 200-201.

13. Wildavsky, op. cit., p. 191.

14. State of California, *Program Evaluation—From Concept to Action*, op. cit., pp. 1-2.

15. *Program Budgeting in State and Local Governments: The Practitioner's View* (UCLA: Institute of Government and Public Affairs, 1972), p. 23.

16. Murray L. Weidenbaum, "Program Budgeting—Applying Economic Analysis to Government Expenditure Decisions," *Policy Analysis in Political Science*, ed. Ira Sharkansky (Chicago: Markham Publishing Co.), p. 386.

17. Ibid.

18. *Program Budgeting in State and Local Governments: The Practitioner's View*, loc. cit.

19. Grossbard, op. cit., p. 29.

20. Kenneth Howard, *Changing State Budgeting* (Lexington, Ky.: Council of State Governments, 1973), p. 127.

21. *Program Budgeting in State and Local Governments: The Practitioner's View*, loc. cit.

22. Wildavsky, op. cit., pp. 189-190.

23. William Gorham, Statement before the Joint Economic Committee, Congress of the United States, *Hearings, The Planning, Programming-Budgeting System: Progress and Potentials*, 90th Congress, 1st Session, September 1967, p. 5. cited by Wildavsky, ibid., p. 195.

24. Howard, op. cit., p. 176.

25. Hirsch, Sonenblum, and Teeples, op. cit., p. 180.

26. Ibid., p. 181.

27. Ibid., p. 180.

28. Leonard Merewitz and Stephen Sosnick, *The Budget's New Clothes: A Critique of Planning-Programming and Budgeting-Cost Analysis* (Chicago: Markham Publishing Co., 1971), p. 276.

29. E. S. Quade, *The Systems Approach and Public Policy*, RAND Corp. Paper P-4053 (Santa Monica: 1969), p. 28.

30. Wildavsky, op. cit., pp. 196-197.

31. Charles Schultze, *The Politics and Economics of Public Spending* (Washington, D.C.: The Brookings Institution, 1968), p. 82.

32. Howard, op. cit., p. 173.

33. Quade, loc. cit.

34. Schultze, op. cit., p. 88.

35. State of California, *Program Evaluation—From Concept to Action*, op. cit., p. 5.

36. Howard, op. cit., p. 127.

37. Ibid., p. 175.

38. Haldi Associates, Inc., *A Survey of Budgetary Reform in Five States* (Lexington, Ky.: Council of State Governments, 1973), p. 12.

39. Howard, loc. cit.

40. Ibid.; Knezevich, op. cit., p. 185.

41. Quade, loc. cit.

42. Howard, loc. cit.

43. State of California, *Program Evaluation—From Concept to Action*, loc. cit.; Howard, loc. cit.; Knezevich, loc. cit.

44. Howard, loc. cit.

45. State of California, *Program Evaluation—From Concept to Action*, op. cit., p. 6.

46. Howard, op. cit., p. 128.

47. Quade, loc. cit.

48. Wildavsky, op. cit., p. 199.

49. Merewitz and Sosnick, op. cit., pp. 9-12.

50. Knezevich, op. cit., p. 15.

51. John Rehfuss, *Public Administration as Political Process* (New York: Charles Scribner's Sons, 1973), p. 167.

52. Knezevich, op. cit., p. 326.

53. Howard, op. cit., pp. 128-129.

54. Ibid., p. 110.

55. Kenneth L. Kraemer, *Policy Analysis in Local Government* (Washington, D.C.: International City Management Association, 1973), p. 22.

56. State of California, *Program Evaluation—From Concept to Action*, loc. cit.

57. Wildavsky, op. cit., p. 198.

58. Ibid.

59. Ibid., p. 197.

60. Howard, op. cit., p. 174.

61. *Program Budgeting in State and Local Governments: The Practitioner's View*, op. cit., p. 20.

62. Schultze, op. cit., p. 92.

63. Howard, op. cit., p. 176.

64. Wildavsky, op. cit., pp. 199-200.

65. Ibid., p. 199.

66. State of California, *Program Evaluation—From Concept to Action*, loc. cit.

67. *Program Budgeting in State and Local Governments: The Practitioner's View*, loc. cit.

68. Merewitz and Sosnick, op. cit., p. 278.

69. Schultze, loc. cit., cited by Hirsch, Sonenblum, and Teeples, op. cit., p. 18.

70. Lee and Johnson, op. cit., p. 196.

71. Ida Hoos, *Systems Analysis in Public Policy: A Critique* (Berkeley Calif.: University of California Press, 1972), p. 132.

72. Howard, op. cit., p. 180; Hoos, op. cit., p. 133.

73. Quade, loc. cit.

74. Hoos, op. cit., pp. 138-139.

75. Ibid., p. 143.

76. Ibid., p. 191.

5

CRITICISM OF PROGRAM BUDGETING AND THE BUDGET ANALYSIS

Numerous criticisms have been directed at program budgeting and the Budget Analysis. The demise of PPB at the federal level further exacerbated the PPB issue. Many critics still do not fully understand the reason for PPB's failure in federal government. This chapter examines and responds to criticisms directed toward PPB and the Budget Analysis. While the responses to such criticisms are brief, they demonstrate that shortcomings can be avoided by successfully implementing a *workable* program budget and Budget Analysis.

CRITICISM AND RESPONSE

1. *Criticism*: The time has not yet come for PPB.

But the decisive factor has been the prematurity of PPB. The conceptual side of PPB presents something of a paradox. The important ideas are few in number and easy to understand. But they happen to run counter to the way American budgeting has been practiced for more than half a century. The concepts which took root in economics and planning will have to undergo considerable mutation before they can be successfully transplanted on political soil. PPB is an idea whose time has not quite come. It was introduced government-wide before the requisite concepts, organizational capability, political conditions, informational resources, and techniques were adequately developed. A decade ago, PPB was beyond reach; a decade or two hence, it or some updated version, might be one of the conventions of budgeting. For the present, PPB must make do in a world it did not create and has not yet mastered.[1]

Response: PPB cannot be criticized on the grounds that governments are not ready for it. There will be no trouble-free day in the future when governments automatically will be ready for program budgeting or the Budget Analysis. Program budgeting and the Budget Analysis are tools that can assist governmental operations to become more effective. The demand for public services is increasing geometrically; therefore, program organization and analysis must be introduced to alleviate the constraint of scarce revenues. Program budgeting and the Budget Analysis permit rational decision-making and testing. The need is definitely now and not at some utopian future date.

2. *Criticism*: PPB is unrealistic because it is too ambitious.

> From one viewpoint, it is too ambitious in that it is attempting to apply economic and systems analysis to all of the vast gamut of civilian government operations simultaneously.[2]

Response: This critique is another misconception of PPB and is illustrative of why PPB failed at the federal level. PPB was expected to revolutionize governmental operations instantly. Most of PPB's current enthusiasts, however, make more realistic claims. They assert that program budgeting is a means of providing increased systems data for better decision-making and not an instant panacea for every governmental operation deficiency. However, a properly conceived PPB and analysis system is the closest approximation to instant problem-identification and solving which governments will ever have.

The expectations of San Diego's program budgeting system were realistic. Its PPB was not expected to solve all of the city's problems instantly. San Diego's PPB has contributed to a great extent in providing more in-depth programmatic systems data to all concerned. "Some of the more enthusiastic advocates of PPBS seem to suggest that it can work miracles in all corners of government. But it is not a magic wand. . . . It may be used as easily to rationalize a decision as to make a rational choice. It is not a substitute for experience and judgment, though men of experience and judgment may find it helpful."[3]

Finally, the test of a governmental operation should lie in the applicability of scientific methodological procedures, as there is no other method of evaluation. Otherwise, with no acceptable objective criteria in existence, anything and everything would be fiscally permissable.

3. *Criticism*: The expertise of PPB specialists has been criticized.

Ida Hoos, for one, is very critical of PPB experts in government. She states that government will be served better by employing political scientists for decision-making rather than economists. In other words, government is looking to the wrong experts for assistance:

> Expertness in the new managerial techniques is nebulous and elusive of definition, however. And the ranks of specialists are swelled with accountants, economists, econometricians, systems engineers, and business analysts who have seized the opportunity to offer themselves as consultants, presumably capable of introducing and implementing

PPBS at any level of government, from local to national. Notable here is the lack of specificity with respect to qualification; the major requisites appear to be self-imputed and honorific . . . for they come to their task with little understanding, less interest, and no experience in the political and policy implications of cost-benefit calculations and program-budgeted objectives in the public sector.

On the home front, his employment and steady advance have been virtually assured with the widespread adoption of PPBS. Ready to advise the uninitiated on program budgeting and the information system and cost-benefit studies that are an intrinsic part of it, the cadre of emergent experts often graduate to the ranks of "public planners," where they perpetuate the kind of management philosophy their techniques stand for.[4]

Hoos also believes that the use of consultants removes the responsibility of decision-making not only from officials and administrators but from the consultants as well. Consequently, no one can be called to account for a wrong decision:

> While use of outsiders to perform specialized tasks is not new, what is noteworthy here is the growing incidence of government-by-contract that removes from public officials responsibility of the decisions made. Because consultants are never held accountable for bad advice, the arrangement shields everyone from criticism . . . Moreover, because of the way in which systems analysis can be crafted to suit the occasion, the use of hired specialists may serve the politically useful purposes of masking bureaucratic ineptness and inadequacy, of providing support for a course of action already decided upon, or of working as a red-herring, diversionary tactic.[5]

Response: Economists and systems analysts have more of the requisite theoretical and technical knowledge to implement a program budget and a Budget Analysis than political scientists. After all, budgeting is an economic process which attempts to identify economic benefits and tradeoffs, using quantifiable techniques; it is not a political theory. Consultants may have failed in the past because they oversold their ability to streamline government. This fault should be laid upon the individual, then, and not the professional area of competence.

The economic specialist can provide a budgeting and analysis system, which in turn can provide decision-makers with more and better systems data. He neither makes the decisions nor assumes responsibility for them. Economists are most suited for PPB implementation. As for specialists in general, McKinney and Kiely state:

The predicted overshadowing of the generalist administrator by the expert with the rise of PPB appears at closer range to be unfounded. If properly utilized, the expert analyst can be an invaluable aid to the decision-maker. Fear that the expert analyst will usurp the role of the decision-maker cannot be supported. . . . Possibly the first thing that both the administrator and analyst should recognize is that each has only partial answers to problems.[6]

4. *Criticism*: PPB is not sensitive to the needs of the public. It is too mechanistic.

"Some fear that PPBS means decision-making by technicians and computers and will prove insensitive to the preferences of people as expressed through their elected representatives."[7] They fear that program budgeting implies that decisions will be left to "specialists" and "experts" who have neither the knowledge of the actual governmental operations nor any responsibility to an electorate. They fear that efficiency will become more important than fulfilling the public needs.

Response: This critique is somewhat similar to the previous one. Program budgeting and the Budget Analysis provide the means for a citizen-centered service outlook. Specialists are needed during the initial phases of PPB implementation to direct data-gathering activities and objectives, but they are by no means in control of governmental operations. The increased data in the budget document require that computers and advanced data-processing techniques be used as data banks to assist decision-makers. Sophisticated techniques and adequate data-gathering systems do not jeopardize legislative authority in decision-making or encourage computerized solutions. Furthermore, as McKinney and Kiely state:

Paradoxically, when they find it difficult or impossible to apply scientific criteria and techniques and come up with predictable results, the same people say that one of PPB's main weaknesses is its lack of universally acceptable techniques . . . To view PPB as a set of mechanistic techniques to be mastered in various and sundry ways without taking due recognition of the environment and/or contextual situations is a gross simplification.[8]

In brief, systems information enhances legislative decisions by applying a background of logic and data. PPB should be feared only when decision-making procedures exclude such input.

5. *Criticism*: PPB ignores intangible factors.

Numerous critics believe that program budgeting's insistence on greater quantification is a weakness rather than an asset. Immeasurable and intangible factors are thereby overlooked or ignored.[9] Ida Hoos summarizes:

In fact, because techniques of PPBS are quantitative, they can deal with only the measurable aspects of programs underway or under consideration . . . The result, in terms of what is learned and what is achieved, is much like the horse-and-rabbit stew described so ably by Anthony Downs. The variables that are selected because of their tractability (the rabbit) are treated meticulously, but there is almost total neglect of the incommensurable aspects which are enormous (the horse). [10]

Response: Intangible factors remain intangible with or without the quantification stressed by program budgeting. The program budget can itemize those outputs capable of being quantified. Without program detail, all data become "intangible." The program budget systems information decreases the number of variables not measured and indentifies nonquantifiable social costs or benefits. Therefore, PPB reduces the areas of vague understanding and increases the data base for decision-making. This last statement does not imply that PPB ignores intangibles; all factors should be indentified and incorporated within the PPB format. The General Description category in the PPB format allows for "intangible" inputs and considerations of a qualitative nature.

6. *Criticism*: Some PPB critics believe that the benefits derived from program budgeting do not outweigh its costs. [11] A program budget has more programmatic detail and, hence, is more costly to prepare than the line-item budget. The budget document itself is larger, so printing costs are also higher. In addition, more time is spent in budget preparation as each department must submit detailed program descriptions. Finally, accounting and data-processing departments have increased workloads and costs.

Response: This criticism can be refuted by numerous examples in the San Diego experience. As a result of the increased systems data in its budget, analyses and decisions made in specific program areas have produced annual savings far in excess of the modest costs of implementation.

The economic benefits that San Diego or the state of California has derived from program budgeting and Budget Analysis have greatly outweighed any cost of implementation. The benefits have been actual annual dollar savings, increased effectiveness of operations, and greater service to the public—not to mention increased accountability.

7. *Criticism*: Goal formulation and priority-setting required by PPB is difficult, if not impossible.

As was described in Chapter 3, the program budget format requires every department or agency to state its goals and its programmatic objectives. Quantifiable output measures are used to evaluate the achievement of these goals and objectives through the separate Budget Analyses. Program budgeting has been criticized because goal formulation is too difficult:

In theory, formulating goals should be easy; in practice it is not. Goals stated too broadly are little more than truisms and have little analytical value. In many, ultimate goals cannot be formulated except by achieving agreement on value judgments. A single program may promote the achievement of more than one goal; the goal which, due to political criteria, is dominant at any one time will color spending decisions. Programs pursuant to the same goals can cross agency lines; achievement of agency coordination on objectives adds more difficulties.[12]

Ida Hoos is more critical. She believes that the goals formulated by program budgeting are in error: "But, when government accepts business as its model and economics as its decision-making means and depends for guidelines on experts whose techniques have a strong bias, its goals are calculated with measuring devices of limited scope."[13] The goals are of little value because program budgeting is not suitable for government.

Once goals have been formulated, they must be assigned priorities so that limited resources can be allocated to the most important programs. Some critics insist that this cannot be reasonably done. They assert that it is nearly impossible to set priorities for goals and to maintain public consensus. Constraints on government, such as intergovernmental revenue requirements, city council approval, municipal union, and ethnic group considerations, prevent priority-setting by strict objectivity.

Response: The definition of goals and objectives is one of the more difficult aspects of the program budget. An attempt must be made, however, to identify and set priorities to goals. As governments obtain more experience with program budgeting, this process is more easily accomplished. Without goals, governmental participation or effectiveness cannot be measured or even known. No meaningful programs or activities can be designed and continued unless there is some direction and testing for those programs or activities.

Hoos' argument is simply not valid. Governments were created to provide public services in an organized manner. They can use organizational techniques from business and economics to maximize benefits and reduce costs in order to optimize effectiveness rather than profits. Governmental "profit" can be measured in dollar savings, more services, or reduced taxes.

Priorities are established by legislative review and program evaluations. The Budget Analysis evaluates key programs establishing cost-benefits, thus allowing a scale or schedule of "tradeoffs" between or among departmental programs. It would be difficult, if not impossible, to categorize priorities without program identification and specification (PPB) or program evaluation (the Budget Analysis). Consensus, "nontangibles," and so forth can be weighed as part of the priority-setting technique. If priority-setting is to be rational, it should be arrayed in the process formulated by this text.

8. *Criticism*: PPB's products have become endproducts.
Allen Schick makes the following criticism of program budgeting:

> Those who had hoped that PPB would not succumb to the tyranny of technique can find much disappointment in what has happened. PPB's products have become its endproducts. For so many practitioners, PPB is not some majestic scrutiny of objectives and opportunities, but going through the motions of doing a program structure, writing a program memorandum or filling in the columns of a program and financial plan.[14]

The activities required by program budgeting have become ends unto themselves. Filling out the proper form is more important than using the information in a meaningful way.

Response: Every time a new idea is introduced, certain individuals become unduly involved with techniques and methodologies. This temptation must be foreseen by those in charge of PPB implementation. The federal government's PPB emphasized the preparation of program structures, program memoranda, multiyear financial plans, and special analytical studies. Proper emphasis should be placed on data-collection methodologies; the implementation and followthrough system would be at fault if data collection simply became an end in and of itself.

San Diego and the state of California do not use program memoranda or other artificial constructs of the old PPB. The program budget document itself provides the vehicle for systems information requirements and serves as the data base for the separate Budget Analysis.

9. *Criticism*: Zero-based budgeting, if used by program budgeting, may be disadvantageous.

In zero-based budgeting, every expenditure must be justified from the start every year as if it were a new expenditure. Departments are required to justify not only increased levels of allocation, but the continuance of their current expenditure levels as well. Many critics believe that this is a disadvantage of program budgeting as past expenditures are not given their due weight when future expenditures are being considered.[15]

Response: Program budgeting and the Budget Analysis do not necessarily imply zero-based budgeting.[16] It would be impossible to analyze and justify each expenditure in this manner in one fiscal year. It is important, however, to analyze more than fiscal increases in program expenditures. Limitations of resources, time, and manpower necessitate compromise. Time and resource constraints permit a Budget Analysis to be conducted only on a selective basis anually. The selection of what programs are to be studied depends upon the level of expenditure in relation to the total budget, the percentage of change from one year to the next, program effectiveness and need, and so forth. PPB can provide the data necessary for a zero-based Budget Analysis, provided it is deemed desirable as a technique for a selcted program. However, it is not a generalized requisite to either a PPB or the Budget Analysis.

10. *Criticism*: The concept of PPB is political.

> At the local level, where power and its holders are open to closer and more immediate scrutiny and where the relation between money and results is often painfully clear, the power implicit in PPBS becomes even more vivid. Against the backdrop of urban administration, the concepts of PPBS are no longer (if they ever were) simply technical; now they are political as well.[17]

In other words, program budgeting has political ramifications. It is a powerful tool which can be manipulated by officials and administrators to their benefit.

Response: The essential argument within this criticism is invalid. Utilizing PPB, governments can achieve better operational effectiveness. Program budgeting and the Budget Analysis are analytical, not political, tools and, therefore, should not be criticized per se if abused on this basis. PPB and the Budget Analysis objectively permit the best program or alternative to surface, regardless of political bias. The political dialogue takes place *after* the PPB and the Analysis are presented.

11. *Criticism*: PPB is in conflict with the political decision-making process.
Many critics insist that program budgeting is in direct conflict with political bargaining and decision-making processes. They object to PPB for the following reasons: In the name of rationality, program budgeting has sought to eliminate politics from the decision-making process altogether.[18] "PPBS may represent the even more disastrous triumph of economic rationality over the political and social rationality which reasonably, logically, and necessarily belong in government decisions on resource allocation."[19] Levine also criticizes program budgeting on this point:

> On the one hand, every decision-maker . . . might be treated . . . as a rational, reachable individual, so that the planner is best advised to lay out his recommendations for the national good and to count on their rationality to convince all the necessary actors. The PPB system came close to this, assuming a community of interest not only among federal operating agencies, the Budget Bureau, and the administration, also of the states, localities, and quasi-public instrumentalities. In doing this, it denied for practical purposes the validity of the kind of competitive process that, it has been suggested, really pervades the bureaucracy. This was a major limitation of program budgeting as it was operated.[20]

McKinney and Kiely believe that PPB tries to eliminate political decision-making because its heavy reliance on mathematics makes it nonunderstandable to all but the PPB specialists. "The whole process of pricing programs could easily become a mystery to all but the analyst. This would raise immensely the stature and prestige of the analyst . . . The decline of the legislator and the generalist administrator would thus follow.[21]

As described by Schultze, Charles E. Lindblom believes that program budgeting is unrealistic because it is incompatible with political realities. Lindblom prefers his "muddling through" approach to decision-making. This alternative stresses consensus rather than rationality and efficiency. Some "muddling through" methodologies are:

1. Minimize the debate to alienate as few people as possible.

2. Proceed in small increments; do not plan ahead. Lindblom calls it the "Lewis and Clark" approach of "plan as you go" rather than PPB's "Cook's Tour" approach where everything is planned in advance.

3. Make pragmatic decisions rather than idealistic ones. "A good decision is one which gains consensus rather than one which meets outside criteria of efficiency or effectiveness.[22]

It would also appear that legislators may even prefer to operate without fiscal evaluation:

> Very often they have to vote for or approve programs, expenditures and taxes—regardless of their inefficiency—because their constituents want or demand them. Such decisions are made more difficult when quantitative program budgeting information becomes available. Local elected and appointed government officials may find PPBS embarrassing because they operate in a fish bowl in close proximity to their constituents.[23]

Response: Program budgeting *does not separate or eliminate* political bargaining and decision-making. PPB and the Budget Analysis provided legislators with a wider and more substantive systems data base, as well as alternatives, so that decisions can be more rational. PPB does not make the final decisions on budgetary appropriations. The so-called experts do not take over governmental operations. Program budgeting and the Budget Analysis neither attempt to eliminate nor to bypass politics. PPB should provide systems information to facilitate decision-making. Anderson describes the role of program budgeting and the Budget Analysis in the decision-making process:

> Even in the absence of political barriers to PPBS-type decision procedures, the role of human judgment looms large at several critically important crossroads:

> 1. The definition of basic objectives,

2. The translation of basic objectives into operational "intermediate type" goals,

3. The coordination of various agencies which jointly determine the degree of success in achieving a given intermediate objective,

4. The framing of alternatives to be considered,

5. The interpretation of results as they may apply to decisions at hand.

Reasonable men looking at the same set of facts can—and do—disagree at each of these crossroads. Yet the PPBS format makes a significant contribution in that it tends to pinpoint these areas of potential disagreement, so that differences can be readily exposed for rational discussion.[24]

The "muddling through" technique appears to encourage no planning, control, or evaluation, as though a program or budget were a chimera which should be dealt with by sacrificing rationality on its altar. The "fish bowl" technique, or total disclosure of tax expenditures, needs no defense; local expenditures and objectives should be tested as to results. The alternative approach suggested encourages "hidden" governmental decisions inimical to democratic principles.

It would appear that the critics of PPB maintain that political decisions should be made in a vacuum free from all objective inputs. It is difficult to believe that they would seriously suggest that political decision-making be divorced from objective data.

If anything, PPB and the Budget Analysis can provide the opposition with the support to criticize the final political decision and thus encourage political debate. Once again, this criticism indicates the lack of understanding of the political and budgetary processes which generally results from an *a priori* research methodology.

12. *Criticism*: Program budgeting will allow too much centralization of power within a government.

Critics complain that budgeting implies too much centralization of power.[25] They do not agree, however, on where power is centralized. Some state that PPB gives too much power to the executive and to department heads.[26] Some, on the other hand, believe that by enhancing executive power PPB will remove power from the agency heads.[27] Lee and Johnson maintain that PPB gives power to the executive at the expense of the legislative body.[28] Payad and Chouari believe that, with program budgeting, financial management officials will become more powerful because they have PPB expertise. They also fear that the more aggressive and articulate department heads stand a better chance of obtaining adequate fund allocations.[29] Other critics warn that, with increased centralization resulting from program budgeting, the possibility of making a major misallocation is greater than if a suboptimal decision had been made at a lower level of government.[30]

Response: "As to enhancing central control, no one knows how much centralization is desirable."[31] Furthermore, none of the PPB critics states *specifically* how much centralization results from program budgeting. Program budgeting and the Budget Analysis do not remove the responsibility of decision-making from those who have the same responsibility with a line-item budget. The system advocated in this text is a balanced process recommending competing alternatives between the executive and legislative branches. Executives, legislators, and department heads have the same responsibilities as before. What *is* different is that everyone is provided with more meaningful systems information with which to make decisions. Program budgeting and the Budget Analysis do not concentrate power among top officials. They have always had this power and, if anything, the process herein advocated will allow objective evaluation of program accomplishments and, therefore, will temper decisions made by "power" loci.

13. *Criticism*: PPB has not altered the bureaucracy.

PPB enthusiasts claim that program budgeting facilitates more effective government, but some critics point out that bureaucratic practices continue unchanged. Most of these criticisms are directed toward the federal government's PPB. As Ida Hoos states: "Far from providing guidelines for 'legislative and budgetary changes,' PPBS seems to have failed to achieve any improvements in the executive budgetary process or to respond to the needs of Congress."[32] Levine discusses the problem in more detail:

> During 1965, however, McNamara was riding high and program budgeting looked good. For this reason. President Johnson directed that the system be generalized throughout the federal government . . . In retrospect, it seems to have made very little difference . . . for the most part it made very little dent on the bureaucratic way of doing things. For one thing, most federal agencies never really implemented program budgeting as it had been intended. They imposed a new nominal structure on the old way of making decisions and they left it at that . . . And this is the point: Program budgeting at its best improved the system a bit; it changed nothing fundamentally.[33]

Response: PPB failed in the federal government because the bureaucracy was too established and resistant to substantive changes. PPB by itself cannot be expected to eliminate bureaucratic resistance. PPB's failure at the federal level did not stem from internal flaws in conception; bureaucratic inertia played the key role. This "failure" can be overcome by well-executed implementation procedures. As McKinney and Kiely state, "Too little credit is given to the idea that people's behavior can be modified if the right conditioning process and environment are created."[34] A comprehensive implementation plan, as herein identified, for program budgeting and the Budget Analysis will wear down bureaucratic resistance and result in meaningful legislative controls to replace bureaucratic "in-house" control.

14. *Criticism:* Defining objectives may make decision-making more difficult.

Every program in a program budget must specify its objectives. Some critics believe that this requirement may actually hamper the decision-making process. Individuals with interests different from those expressed by the objectives may become dissatisfied with governmental programs. They may create pressure to change or modify these programs. The more data available, the more room for controversy.

Response: Data in the program budget provide programmatic detail about governmental activities and objectives. These disclosures may increase debate surrounding programmatic objectives. Ideally, competition among the competing objective alternatives will encourage public input into the very programs which seek to provide public services. In addition, program detail can be used to justify and rationalize existing objectives or decisions. The adversarial process encourages competition; hopefully, the best alternative or objective will surface and be adopted.

15. *Criticism:* In the long run, politics will undermine PPB.

Some critics maintain that political factors will preclude program budgeting from succeeding in areas where controversy might arise. They fear that the political obstacles to its success will eventually undermine its effectiveness, even if it is well implemented.

Response: Program budgeting and the Budget Analysis may encounter difficulty in controversial political areas. Legislators, who are informed of the advantages of the system, must support it. A certain type of political bent could pervert this or any other system, and the only safeguard would be the protection guaranteed by the entire legislative process.

16. *Criticism:* PPB is too static to adapt to changing political conditions.

Response: Program budgeting and the Budget Analysis are not a static system. Program evaluation is an on-going, ever-changing, dynamic, creative struggle. Modifications in governmental programs required by a changing political environment are, in fact, made easier by this two-part budgetary system, as changes are easily assimilated into the PPB format and the analysis will identify marginal or new benefits.

17. *Criticism:* You do not need PPB to do Budget Analysis.

Snyder believes that program analysis can be done without a program budget format.[35] A Budget Analysis need not be a separate document or independent effort.

Response: Whereas Budget Analysis is possible without a program budget, it would result in a substantial qualitative and quantitative improvement if a PPB format were available. Governments conduct departmental operations programmatically; unfortunately, the line-item budget document does not reveal this structure. Consequently, analysts must seek additional sources for program information which is often not available. The program budget provides *more* useful programmatic systems information for analysis. Therefore, it is strongly recommended that the Budget Analysis be based upon a PPB as suggested throughout this text.

Departments preparing their own budgets cannot be made responsible for evaluating their own programs. Program budgeting has failed in the past partly because its supporters insisted that program analysis be incorporated into budgets. However, such analysis would be developed by the same individuals administrating these programs. This approach cannot avoid a conflict of responsibilities. Therefore, the Budget Analysis must be a separate and independent operation distinct from the administration of departmental responsibilities.

18. *Criticism:* Planning and budgeting cannot be linked.

Schick believes that the day-to-day routine of the budgetary process prevents it from being combined with long-range planning.[36] Long-range planning is necessary, but it does not require a PPB to be successful.

Response: The increased systems information in a PPB allows for better planning, especially since PPB data are collected and identified in three-year cycles.

Land-use and fiscal models (indicating five- to ten-year projections) should be undertaken and incorporated as separate studies complementing a PPB and the Budget Analysis to create optimal, long-run planning ability. With its systems data base, PPB will assist both models, but a PPB cannot be expected to include these separate special studies. Planning and budgeting can be and, indeed, should be linked. But as with the Budget Analysis, a separate effort is required as it would be unrealistic to expect five- to ten-year planning data to be incorporated in full detail in a PPB.

19. *Criticism:* There are disadvantages to committing yourself too far into the future.

One function of program budgeting is to provide systems information for multiyear projections. Opponents to PPB state many reasons for not making multiyear estimates of revenues and expenditures. Some of the reasons given are:

   a. Multiyear projections tie the hands of the executive and other officials dependent upon public support. Politicians do not want to commit themselves too far into the future because it could prove embarrassing if they made the wrong commitment, conceivably lessening their chances for reelection.[37]

   b. Governments are too busy taking care of present business to conduct effective future planning.

   c. Multiyear projections tend to be poorly done because they draw from an inadequate data base.[38]

   d. The recommendations of multiyear studies are not implemented. Therefore, such studies are a waste of time and effort.[39]

   e. Multiyear projections may fail because departments will not voluntarily eliminate their own programs, even after their usefulness has expired.[40]

f. "It may even be the case that multi-period exhibits will *reduce* feelings of commitment on the part of decision-makers because the end result of activities can be more accurately and completely described for periods that exceed their immediate period of political concern."[41]

g. Public knowledge of multiyear projections may mobilize opposition to controversial programs.

Response: Multiyear projections are just that—*projections*, not commitments. The concept of program budgeting and Budget Analysis does not require that these projections be followed to the last proposed expenditure. Flexibility for modifications from one year to the next is always present and more than possible. The program budget does provide data on current revenues and expenditures so that it is possible to make realistic projections. Legislators are not forced into rigid positions by PPB. They are still able to reallocate expenditures if a given situation changes.

Governments must plan for the future, regardless of the budgetary format. A program budget provides a better data base to conduct long-range planning (realistically, a five-year period). If long-range projections are accurate, better implementation, allocations, and priority-setting are inevitable. By encouraging better long-range revenue and expenditure projections, program budgeting disallows a crisis approach to emergencies as contingencies are programmed into the system. Therefore, rationality is programmed into the present and future.

The proposed budgetary process would indicate the life expectancy of temporary programs or program elements, and the termination date would be identified in the PPB format under the heading General Description. The program budget should indicate that such a program had reached its cutoff date. If no cutoff date were indicated, it would be the direct responsibility of the Budget Analysis to recommend the program be eliminated. To do less would mean that the Budget Analysis was not responding to its area of responsibility.

The assumption that politicians will not be concerned with long-range results is, of course, without foundation, for political or policy commitments tend to follow a politician throughout his career. Usually, a politician or legislator will point to a commitment that has benefited the community or, if that is not the case, the opposition will be more than happy to indicate where he failed. Therefore, long-range planning is a matter of political concern unless a political career is viewed as short term, involving one to three years.

Public reaction and input should be encouraged in a democratic government in both long- and short-term programs. Since program budgeting informs the public about current and future expenditures, more and better public input may serve to create better programs, as the final objective of the program is to serve the public.

20. *Criticism:* There is a lack of accountability and control with PPB.

Program budgeting has been criticized for its lack of accountability and control (i.e., the program budget does not allow department heads and executives to control expenditures adequately and to account for all revenues spent). The legislative body will resist plans for PPB implementation by the executive branch if it feels it already has adequate fiscal control without program budgeting. It does not want to lose whatever control it already has.

Response: PPB does not eliminate line-item accounting, which is the main ingredient of a "control-oriented" budget. On the contrary, PPB augments this accounting method with specific program costing data which aid officials in their efforts to control expenditures or to charge fees to cover full operational costs. The program budget provides for *more* accountability and control than a line-item budget because it is more comprehensive toward implementing full-cost accounting procedures. All PPB input is derived from line-item data; therefore, line-item data are still available and are not lost should they be required.

21. *Criticism:* The data obtained from PPB are of limited value.

A program budget provides increased data on the operation and expenditures of programs. Such data have been criticized, however, as not being necessary for decision-makers. Some of the specific critiques are:

a. Program accounting supposedly will produce better decisions by enabling decision-makers to see how much money is being spent for each purpose and by enabling high-level officials to exercise greater control in budget formulation. However, the information being generated has limited value: it reflects arbitrary cost allocations, and it tells little about how much money a partial, or even a total, cutback in a program would save. [42]

b. Data in the program budget are statistically oriented. This method for measuring program effectiveness is inadequate. [43]

c. The program budget does not provide data to assist in "fire-fighting" problems (decisions that must be made on the spot). PPB is of value only when there is ample time for planning and analysis. [44]

d. Program budget data suffer because the purpose is established before the data are collected:

Facts are accepted as relevant only if they fit into the preconceived scheme and relate to the pre-determined goal. And to be considered, they must be in quantitative form, either by nature or by arbitrary assignment of a price. If, as has been claimed by PPBS promoters, the technique forces the decision-maker to seek information on how resources are being used, then one wonders what kind of accounting system he used previously. [45]

e. "The case most frequently made for the structural budget process in PPBS is that, at the very minimum, it can provide a catalyst for initiating change... Even this claim, however, has been challenged. Program budgets have been criticized as being not very informative for policy formulating purposes, not displaying alternatives, and not indicating what is received for the money expended, let alone who gets what and who pays for it." [46]

f. PPB includes no data to assist in new program implementation. Program budgeting is a mechanical procedure rather than a process to establish policies. [47]

Response: No advocate of program budgeting believes that the program budget in and of itself is a panacea:

> Long discarded has been the suggestion that PPBS would permit a rational allocation of resources among precisely defined goals on the basis of the results of quantitative analysis. Most practitioners of the art now claim only that PPB techniques can provide information that will help public officials make *better* decisions. In this context, PPBS, adapted in terms of depth and sophistication to the unique needs and capabilities of each city, would seem to offer considerable potential as an aid to decision-makers of municipalities, both large and small. [48]

Payad and Chouari criticize PPB's statistical orientation, yet they offer no better method for measuring program effectiveness. Effectiveness is measured by comparing input, output, and objective achievement (i.e., cost/benefit analysis). This methodology can only succeed if great care is given to the definition of objectives and output measurements.

The criticism that a program budget does not facilitate on-the-spot decisions is misleading. Certainly, more sophisticated systems data can only assist "fire-fighting" decisions.

The use of the proper output statistics which also emphasize nonmonetary criteria, as exemplified in the Library Department budget in the Appendix, permits cost/effectiveness as well as cost/benefit analyses. Dollar values are not the only values assigned output statements.

The very heart of program budgeting is to state a program's objectives and to compare the input (personnel requirements and costs) and output (workload data)—indicators of the program's cost and effectiveness—to the objectives. The program budget format allows a technical review of all stated objectives, as well as measurement of the degree of the effectiveness of programs in terms of cost and efficiency. Should the goals or objectives be invalid, only the program budget format and the Budget Analysis will identify these shortcomings. The program budget and the Budget Analysis not only identify the objective, but test its effectiveness as well, by citing the objective in the PPB and evaluating alternatives in the Budget Analysis. Therefore, rather than reflecting data weaknesses, as suggested in this criticism, the very strength of the program budget and the Budget Analysis is their well-organized systems data base.

Perhaps the most convincing response to these criticisms is a statement by the deputy mayor of the District of Columbia on the city's first program budget:

It revealed gaps and contradictions in information of such proportions that the document became a highly visible stimulus for questioning by the City Council and Congress of program alternatives, program effectiveness, and basic city policies and objectives. [49]

There is no preconceived PPB requirement to create artificially a Procrustean bed to fit data. This particular criticism shows a peculiar lack of insight as to PPB requirements. A departmental director states his own objectives or goals and then tests their success by the output statements. The output can be measured quantitatively or qualitative outputs can be stated in the PPB document. This criticism can only be valid if the implementation of a PPB is at fault. A successfully implemented PPB would not require an artificial match of a goal and an output.

To state that a PPB does not display alternatives or cost analyses for policy formulation indicates that the criticism precludes the independent Budget Analysis control of the PPB. A PPB cannot be expected to include budgetary data over a three-year period while simultaneously displaying alternatives and presenting cost/benefit analyses. As stated, the administrators should not be put in a position of analyzing their own budgets by presenting alternatives and cost/benefit analyses between alternatives. This information and this type of analysis can only be performed by the separate and independent Budget Analysis staff, as described in the budgetary process advocated in this text.

PPB provides data of new program implementation in the three-year data comparisons. Thus, the value of a new program or of increased expenditures of existing programs is clearly indicated in the PPB format. If the additional expenditure does not result in sufficient output increases, the new program, because of its low cost/benefit ratio, may be recommended for deletion.

PPB is an organizational method of identifying programmatic activities. The result of such a methodology is to allow more informed policy decision-making. The program budget does not establish policy. Only a legislative body can make policy; a PPB and the Budget Analysis seek to provide a method of presenting budget data and an analysis of such data. This method subsequently permits the legislators to formulate the best policy, taking into consideration budgetary as well as policy requirements.

22. *Criticism:* PPB does not facilitate tradeoffs among broad objectives.

Some critics believe that program budgeting should provide enough information to allow tradeoffs among broad objectives. [50] When the system is unable to do so, they blame PPB. Objectives of different programs are sometimes contradictory, making tradeoffs even more difficult. [51] For example, one objective of an environmental quality agency may be to reduce river pollution. On the other hand, an objective of a public utilities agency might be to construct electronic plants on these same waterways, thus increasing thermal pollution in the rivers. These objectives are in direct opposition, making tradeoff analysis extremely difficult. This criticism of PPB is summarized by the following statements:

> PPBS as presently administered does not illuminate trade-offs among broad objectives. PPBS analysts do not ask whether it is better to spend an additional dollar on education or on clean air, but rather ask: given the goal of achieving clean air, what is the best alternative way of doing it among the considered proposals and what are the marginal improvements in air quality associated with the extension of marginal programs?[52]

> Never in all the oft-paraphrased list of particulars is it made clear how PPBS would both force us to ask and, curiously, help us at the same time to answer such questions as whether we should concentrate on an underprivileged child's education, health, or parents' welfare. Actually, persons less bedazzled than White House speech writers should have known that PPBS methods can neither identify nor solve such problems.[53]

Response: As stated earlier, unrealistic expectations have often been demanded of program budgeting. PPB in the federal government was unreasonably intended to facilitate tradeoffs among the vast bureaucratic departments. Large-scale analyses of tradeoffs require special consultant study efforts as they are not a normal part of an on-going budgetary process. Program budgeting and the Budget Analysis should not be expected to resolve this vast and complex question.

Program budgeting and the Budget Analysis can provide data to increase the efficiency of governmental operations as well as provide data for such a tradeoff study. Such a complex study requires outside consultants for a one-time massive effort involving great expense, manpower, and time, the results of which can then be incorporated in the PPB Analysis.

23. *Criticism:* PPB ignores the revenue aspect of budgeting.

One criticism of program budgeting is that it concentrates almost exclusively on the expenditure side of budgeting while ignoring sources of revenue. It offers little help in raising sufficient funds to finance governmental operations.[54]

Response: Program budgeting can be of major assistance in determining future revenue requirements. All programs must provide multiyear plans which include capital improvements projects. Predictions of future revenue needs are therefore included. Sources of revenue for each program are provided in the program budget format (see Appendix). If levels of revenue fluctuate, alternatives can be reviewed. This criticism is not valid since program budgeting does identify present revenue sources. Separate analysis (the need for a fiscal model projecting revenues and expenditures has already been described and included in this budgetary process) can more comprehensively cover revenue questions. Again, this is not a legitimate on-going function of a PPB or the Analysis, but, as stated, is a subject for study in another work which would then be incorporated in the Budget Analysis for evaluation.

On the whole, the criticisms discussed above illustrate a lack of understanding of the inherent structural integrity and comprehensiveness of the PPB and the Budget Analysis system. A correctly implemented PPB and associative annual Budget Analysis would, especially when co-joined with fiscal and land-use models, negate the basically invalid assumptions underlying most of these criticisms.

NOTES

1. Allen Schick, "Systems Politics and Systems Budgeting," *Public Administration Review* 29 (March-April 1969): 150.

2. Murray L. Weidenbaum, "Program Budgeting—Applying Economic Analysis to Government Expenditure Decisions," *Policy Analysis in Political Science*, ed. Ira Sharkansky (Chicago: Markham Publishing Co., 1970), p. 396.

3. "Is PPBS All That Good?" *Armed Forces Management* 14 (April 1968): 32, cited by Stephen J. Knezevich, *Program Budgeting (PPBS)* (Berkeley, Calif: McCutchan Publishing Corp., 1973), p. 273.

4. Ida R. Hoos, *Systems Analysis in Public Policy: A Critique* (Berkeley, Calif.: University of California Press, 1972), pp. 66-67.

5. Ibid., p. 243.

6. Jerome B. McKinney and Edward S. Kiely, "Has Success Spoiled PPB?" *The Federal Accountant* 22 (September 1973): 61.

7. William H. Anderson, *Financing Modern Government* (Boston: Houghton-Mifflin Co., 1973), p. 78.

8. McKinney and Kiely, op. cit., pp. 57 and 60.

9. Felix A. Nigro and Lloyd G. Nigro, *Modern Public Administration* (New York: Harper and Row, 1973), p. 350; John Rehfuss, *Public Administration as Political Process* (New York: Charles Scribner's Sons, 1973), p. 170.

10. Hoos, loc. cit.

11. Leonard Merewitz and Stephen H. Sosnick, *The Budget's New Clothes: A Critique of Planning-Programming and Budgeting-Cost Analysis* (Chicago: Markham Publishing Co., 1971), p. 5.

12. Anderson, loc. cit.

13. Hoos, op. cit., p. 245.

14. Schick, op. cit., pp. 149-150.

15. Merewitz and Sosnick, op. cit., p. 70.

16. Knezevich, op. cit., p. 142.

17. Robert B. Denhardt, "Organizing the Budget Function," *Municipal Finance* 43 (May 1971): 168.

18. Nigro and Nigro, op. cit., p. 350; John Rehfuss, loc. cit.

19. Hoos, op. cit., p. 74.

20. Robert A. Levine, *Public Planning: Failure and Redirection* (New York: Basic Books, Inc., 1972), p. 189.

21. McKinney and Kiely, loc. cit.

22. Charles E. Lindblom, "The Science of 'Muddling Through'," *Public Administration Review* 19 (Spring 1959): 79-88, cited by Charles L. Schultze, *The Politics and Economics of Public Spending* (Washington, D.C.: The Brookings Institution, 1968), p. 52.

23. *Program Budgeting in State and Local Governments: The Practitioner's View* (UCLA: Institute of Government and Public Affairs, 1972), p. 4.

24. Anderson, op. cit., p. 85.

25. Aaron Wildavsky, "The Political Economy of Efficiency: Cost-Benefit Analysis, Systems Analysis, and Program Budgeting," *Public Administration Review*, 26 (December 1966): 305; Anderson, op. cit., p. 78.

26. Nigro and Nigro, loc. cit.

27. Werner Z. Hirsch, Sidney Sonenblum, and Ronald Teeples, *Local Government Program Budgeting: Theory and Practice* (UCLA: Institute of Government and Public Affairs, 1973), p. 151.

28. Robert D. Lee, Jr., and Ronald W. Johnson, *Public Budgeting Systems* (Baltimore: University Park Press, 1973), pp. 219-226.

29. Aurora T. Payad and Mohamen Chouari, "PPBS: Perspectives and Prospects for Local Governments," *Philippine Journal of Public Administration* 16 (October 1972): 471.

30. Robert E. Millward, "PPB: Problems of Implementation," *American Institute of Planners Journal*, 34 (March 1968): 93; S. Kenneth Howard, *Changing State Budgeting*, (Lexington, Ky.: Council of State Governments, 1973), p. 159.

31. Merewitz and Sosnick, op. cit., p. 273.

32. Hoos, loc. cit.

33. Levine, op. cit., p. 145.

34. McKinney and Kiely, op. cit., p. 59.

35. James C. Snyder, "Financial Management and Planning in Local Government," *Atlanta Economic Review* 23 (November-December 1973): 47.

36. Allen Schick, *Budget Innovation in the States* (Washington, D.C.: The Brookings Institution, 1971), p. 203.

37. Wildavsky, loc. cit.

38. Haldi Associates, Inc., *A Survey of Budgetary Reform in Five States* (Lexington, Ky.: Council of State Governments, 1973), p. 27.

39. Ibid.

40. Hirsch, Sonenblum, and Teeple; op. cit., p. 184.

41. Ibid., p. 127.

42. Merewitz and Sosnick, loc. cit.

43. Payad and Chouari, loc. cit.

44. Knezevich, op. cit., p. 274.

45. Hoos, op. cit., p. 72.

46. *Program Budgeting in State and Local Governments: The Practitioner's View*, op. cit., p. 18.

47. Howard, op. cit., p. 117.

48. Stanley B. Botner, "PPBS: A Tool for Smaller Cities?" *Municipal Finance* 43 (May 1971): 178.

49. Graham Watt, Remarks prepared for the Conference on Regional Accounts Meeting, 1971, cited in *Program Budgeting in State and Local Governments: The Practitioner's View*, loc. cit.

50. Weidenbaum, loc. cit.

51. Lindblom, loc. cit., cited by Schultze, op. cit., pp. 37-42.

52. Anderson, op. cit., p. 78.

53. Hoos, op. cit., p. 70.

54. Howard, loc. cit.

6

BUDGETARY FISCAL MODELS

As incredible as it may seem, legislative bodies have historically deliberated over operational budgets on a year-to-year basis without any discussion of their impact relative to either future overall expenditures or revenue sources. Thus, costly new programs or departments have been, and are still being, created without any fiscal analysis as to future revenue sources or aggregate budgetary effect.

In recent years, many cities have experienced the sudden termination of federal grants or programs, and in many such cases, local city councils have felt obligated to continue these programs with alternative sources of funding. This step can result in a severe strain on limited local revenue sources. When combined with sudden and substantial inflationary or wage increases, an emergency situation can develop. To respond to these circumstances, the cities should have a built-in contingency capability.

In order to meet these fiscal crises, a budgetary fiscal model with contingency funding alternatives should be a part of the budgetary process. In the absence of such an alternative plan, abortive attempts have often been made to cover deficits (i.e., indiscriminate across-the-board cuts of 5 to 10 percent by each department). This approach represents the crudest, "meat-ax" alternative which a legislative body can propose in response to fiscal requirements. Without a PPB and a preplanned set of priorities, a rational decision-making policy in emergencies is very unlikely, as lower priority programs cannot be identified for reduction or elimination. And fiscal emergencies arise more often than cities or states would like to admit. The case of New York City's financial plight is due to a lack of political restraint. As the city had no fiscal contingency plan, its crisis was met by the immediate layoff of city employees. Needless to say, New York's budgetary process indicates a complete disregard for municipal responsibility relative to budgetary procedures and an independent budget review process.

The program budget is a prerequisite to a budgetary fiscal model. All identification of future expenditures and revenues are extrapolated from program budget projections, department by department. The budgetary fiscal model would include federal monies, state monies, and revenue from all other sources, including bonded indebtedness. These expenditure and revenue curves would be plotted along a time continuum. Should a gap be identified, new programs should not be initiated. Rather, a course of action to alleviate the potential deficit circumstance, either through tax increases, program reductions, or a delay of new programs, should be undertaken.

As mentioned, should a cutback in existing programs be necessary, the programmatic structure identified in a program budget would serve as the primary base for establishing a system of priorities. In other words, in such an event, the PPB almost automatically, through its program identification, establishes the basis of a priority system. Reductions can be made on a selective basis, with a clear understanding of what savings are involved and what the price of these savings would be in foregone benefits or output.

The role of the Budget Analysis would be to ascertain if any program or department would strain the overall revenue sources in the near future.

FISCAL MODEL REVIEW

In San Diego, the auditor and comptroller, the Department of Financial Management, and the Legislative Analyst Office are presently attempting to develop a budgetary fiscal model. There are basic variables which can significantly affect the reliability of the model. For example, incorrect estimates of the assessed valuation of property, as determined annually by the county assessor, can materially alter the results of a budgetary fiscal model. Naturally, the same would apply to inflation, federal grants, state subventions, and the like. The sophisticated development of a budgetary fiscal model would track these exogenous variables and make all assumptions explicit. This fiscal model would also establish an alternative set of funding sources or program reductions, should it fall short of accurate estimation.

The methodology generally utilized in budgetary fiscal models is linear regression analysis[1] based on population indices. The linear regression model, also known as the least-squares method (i.e., a mathematical method for calculating the overall average correlation between two variables), assumes that the level of service would increase at a constant rate relative to population growth. In making forecasts via a budgetary fiscal model, one must keep in mind that a five-year period would create sufficient uncertainty as to set the uppermost limit for such a fiscal model.

Since most municipalities do not prepare a budgetary fiscal model beyond one fiscal year, one may ask if the effort is worthwhile—especially in light of the question of forecasting reliability.

The benefits of this fiscal model appear to outweigh the difficulties cited for several reasons: (1) the discipline of examining costs and revenues over a five-year period automatically sets into motion analysis of revenues and programs over that time period, as well as long-range evaluative justification of the program, and (2) the early warning signal of a deficit, which a budgetary fiscal model could trigger, sets up alternative actions at the earliest possible time.

Several studies of state and local tax revenue projections have been made. One such study conducted by McLoone, Lupo, and Mushkin (1966) attempted to review the purpose and extent of long-range revenue estimation in the United States on the state, city, and county levels. A major finding was that "of the respondents, 32 countries and 87 cities make long-range revenue projections; 57 counties and 105 cities do not."[2]

The majority of the cities in the study projected revenues for a five- to six-year period. "Of the cities reporting, 73 use revenue projections for advance capital budgeting. Fifty-seven use them for general planning purposes; and 42, for advance planning of operating budgets. Two cities have made comprehensive projections in connection with their urban-renewal programs, and one emphasized the role of revenue projections in planning changes in the revenue structure."[3]

The methodology most widely used was a straight-line extrapolation of past trends. Most of the revenue projections were substantially below actual collections. These attempts at revenue estimation point to the recognized need for such projections. Major decisions were based on the projections, and yet, a relatively historical and unsophisticated method was used to attain the figures.

In this report, Kansas was cited as one of the first states to "undertake long range projections on a systematic and comprehensive basis."[4] Apparently, the approach to estimation in Kansas is not as systematic and comprehensive as proposed in this text. When queried recently, the Budget Office in Kansas reported that, although Kansas has been estimating its revenues since 1954, they are not consistently projected for a constant time frame. Also of significance are the facts that the gross projections are based on historical trends and that the estimates are made on an informal basis and are used only in the event of a potential fiscal crisis.

The historical trend methodology is only of limited value when projecting revenues and expenditures. Yet, cities continue to rely on this technique. It is indeed true that:

The current projection practice of allowing previous patterns of revenues and expenditures to largely determine projections is inadequate for making long-range estimates. When making projections for more than one year into the future, this extrapolation technique becomes meaningless. Such a technique does not take into account underlying economic, demographic, and social changes in the community that impact upon the City's financial status.[5]

Forecasts such as these are based on the notions of a particular forecaster as to what is reasonable. This method assumes that there is a link between a certain time period and expenditures. For example, using this method, the analyst might reason that since there was a 2-percent increase in an expenditure item in one year there will be a 2-percent increase the next year. The method will work relatively well if the factors that caused last year's increases continue to exist in the coming year. For example, if sanitation expenditures rise proportionately (i.e., 2 percent) with population trends (also 2 percent) and the population continues to increase at this rate, sanitation expenditures can be expected to increase at an equal rate, and the method will make predictions that will approximate the actual amounts. However, should the population rate change, the method will prove inaccurate. What is required is a method that links the marginal increments of sanitation expenditures to its determinants, not to time. This is provided for in a well-designed budgetary fiscal model.

To discover the current status of budgetary fiscal models, ten cities in California were contacted:[6] San Francisco, San Jose, Los Angeles, Long Beach, Sunnyvale, Berkeley, Oakland, Fresno, San Bernardino, and Sacramento. Of the ten cities, four have some type of fiscal model, two are working on the preparation of a model, three have none, and one relied on the data output of a fiscal model in the past but will no longer utilize a model. Upon followup, it was found that of the four cities with a fiscal model only one city had the model proposed in this text. It appears that most cities are relying on historically based trends rather than on a more sophisticated method.

Los Angeles has a budgetary fiscal model, but it does not utilize as advanced a projection method as that outlined in this text. During Los Angeles' councilmanic discussion of the 1973-1974 budget, the possibility of projecting the revenue/appropriation gap was discussed. It was recognized that "some knowledge of the probable size of such 'gaps' would be helpful in preparing to counter them."[7] For this reason, a study of a five-year projection of trends was conducted by the Finance Specialist Office.

The fact that Los Angeles is faced with a chronic revenue gap, as are most cities in California, is evident.

> The chronic nature of the insufficiency of current revenues is emphasized by the fact that appropriations have been increasing at a rate of about 11% per year compared with a natural growth rate in revenue yields of only about 4%. The problem appears to reflect in large part the fact that the natural growth of the City's revenue yields lags behind the growth of the economy and demands for local public services, reflected by recent budget appropriations.[8]

If the growth of appropriations is not matched by the natural growth in revenues, measures must be taken each year to fill the gap. In previous years, Los

Angeles has balanced its budget with budgeted Reserve Fund transfers and New Revenue Sources, including newly enacted city revenue measures, major expenditure reductions, federal revenue-sharing, and unbudgeted reserve fund transfers. These maneuvers to balance the budget are typical of the year-to-year budget planning scheme in use by most major cities. However, it became apparent to the Los Angeles budgetary staff that the sources relied on in the past would not be sufficient to curb the effects of increased appropriation levels. A more drastic means of closing the gap would have to be called upon unless a more developed plan of action were provided.

The University of California at Los Angeles and the University of Southern California are currently designing a sophisticated budgetary fiscal model for Los Angeles which, hopefully, will extend the use of the least-squares method to provide more extensive data.

It should be recognized that although Los Angeles does not currently appear to have a fiscal model such as the one this text is advocating, its budget planning is more advanced than that of many other California cities.

Oakland projects its revenues and expenditures over a five-year period. In a report on the Preliminary Budget Recommendations for fiscal year 1974-1975 in Oakland, it was stated that on August 7, 1973, city departments were "directed to submit programmatic changes to the City Manager, involving budget reductions of 10% for FY1974-75, and an additional 6% for FY1975-76."[9] After being submitted, "it was pointed out that most of the reductions which were listed, if implemented, would seriously and deleteriously affect the level of public services in this City."[10]

Consequently, a Long-Range Revenue Task Force was appointed to discuss the possibilities for new sources of revenues. The 1974-1975 proposed budget was balanced by making certain financial planning decisions on additional revenue, including the following: enacting a real estate transfer tax, doubling city parking meter rates, installing more parking meters, and obtaining reimbursement from the Coliseum and School District for after-school programs.[11] Program reductions "having the least calamitous effect"[12] were proposed. In its concluding remarks, the budget states, "The financial situation continues to present a tremendous challenge to determine the future course of the City. Programs were cut back significantly to balance the FY 1974-75 budget and to provide partial relief for the projected FY 1975-76 budget. A further cutback of programs to the extent of the projected deficits would be calamitous."[13] If adopted, the budget will yield no deficit. However, the picture for the future is quite bleak.

In their report, Oakland projected deficits of the following magnitude:

FY 1975-1976	$ (5,351,391)
FY 1976-1977	(15,990,300)
FY 1977-1978	(22,344,800)
FY 1978-1979	(26,460,200)[14]

Deficits in the coming fiscal years are inevitable. Once the deficits are projected, alternative plans of action can be plotted which would eliminate the revenue/expenditure gap. As a partial solution for the apparent FY1975-1976 crisis in Oakland, the following action was proposed:

> In order to meet a portion of this deficit, consideration is being given presently to increasing business license tax revenue of $1,535,000 to $2,335,000. If this action is accomplished, a deficit ranging from $2.0 to $3.8 million remains. Unless other sources of revenue are generated, a property tax rate increase from 27.4c to 34.7c would be required to balance the FY75-76 budget.[15]

A more sophisticated model has been in use for several years in Sunnyvale, California, a city which is very pragmatic in its financial management. Sunnyvale's approach to budget planning is highly quantifiable. This is made possible by their program budget which has been in use since fiscal 1968-1969. The Sunnyvale Council has come to rely on a fiscal planning method and, according to its director, would essentially "be at a loss if it went back to one-year planning."[16] Sunnyvale is a small community compared to metropolitan areas such as Los Angeles or San Francisco, but nonetheless, their effective financial management method can be used by larger cities, or even states.

Sunnyvale is a growing city concerned about its future. It recognizes the need to know more about its community and directs its research accordingly. In an effort to improve objective, rational decision-making, Sunnyvale has incorporated specific quality goals into each of its numerous planned programs:

> A special staff committee took a detailed social resources inventory of the community this past January. Each City department re-examined its goals and objectives in terms of the quality of service it is rendering its citizens, and then translated these in quantifiable objectives to accompany production goals and productivity indices. This whole process was directed toward utilization of a meaningful citizen survey which can help plumb community priorities in terms that will result in specific programs that citizens will support by broad-scale participation and adequate resources. It should sharpen the decision-making process for the City Council as well as clearly outline the difficult choices among the many competing needs which are restricted by financial limitation. This budget is a base from which this whole process can begin.[17]

The quantification of goals and productivity levels, inputs, outputs, and the like forces programs to be run more efficiently and effectively. No one can argue hard data; either the goals are being met or they are not.

Sunnyvale's Resource Allocation Plan is a comprehensive document which could serve as the foundation for a budgetary fiscal model. Each department program is presented in detail. Charts projecting over eight years include such items as work hours, total cost of resources, production units, and unit costs. One example of the thoroughness of their projection can be seen by examining their report on the fire suppression program for their city (see page 13). The quality goals are outlined in detail, and the fiscal year production plan is also stated in highly quantifiable terms.

Not only is each program detailed in this document, but also included are descriptive tables and charts covering the General Operation Fund—Revenues and Expenditures, Operating Expenditures, Summary of Debt Services, Capital Outlay Expenditures, and so on. This document represents a comprehensive, quantifiable approach to budget planning.

The success of such a format is measured by its record of performance. Sunnyvale's financial director, Carl Husby, boasts of no major fiscal problems for eight years. Also, at a time when most cities predict unavoidable decreases in service levels, the Resource Allocation Plan for Sunnyvale states that: "During 1974-75, the City will spend $25,564,066. This budget anticipated that the property tax will remain the same for the next eight years, while service levels will increase slightly."[18] Such claims are rare in these inflationary times. (See the City of Sunnyvale Resource Allocation Analysis on p. 98.)

As can be seen, Sunnyvale has what appears to be an advanced budgetary fiscal model which has proven usable and successful. It should be noted, however, that its model provides no documentation of alternative courses of action in the case of a revenue gap. It may be that Sunnyvale is sufficiently small that it can predict revenues with greater accuracy than a larger metropolitan area. A sophisticated fiscal model, at its best, would include a documented set of alternatives and priorities.

As stated earlier, San Diego has recently incorporated a PPB into its budgetary process. The logical consequence of this change would be to extrapolate PPB data into a fiscal model. The comprehensive approach in terms of long-range expenditures and revenues of the program budget lends itself to the development of a budgetary fiscal model. The program budget states reasons and justifications for each program relative to objective criteria. Thus, priority ranking can be determined. These quantified PPB data form the basis for a budgetary fiscal model relative to a system of priorities and a set of alternatives relative to overall expenditures and revenues.

Unfortunately, cities have utilized budgetary deficits in a political context, especially at the end of a term in office or in an election year. This happened in New York at the end of Mayor Lindsay's term:

> As an example of past budgeteering, Mayor Beame cites a $308 million issue of budget notes, a three-year loan taken out by his predecessor, John V. Lindsay, to balance the 1971-72 budget. Instead of being paid off annually, the notes were dropped into the lap of the incoming mayor. With the budget as strapped as ever, Mayor Beame decided to roll over

City of Sunnyvale
RESOURCE ALLOCATION ANALYSIS

PROGRAM — 349.10 Fire Suppression
FUNCTION — Protective Services
OBJECTIVE — Limit loss of life and property by
fire suppression

Quality Goals
· Reduce deaths, injuries and property loss resulting from fire by 10%
· Be at scene of fire or emergency within 3 minutes 95% of the time
· Assure response and fire suppression capabilities within 5%
· Insure suppression activities maintained losses at minimum level with zero re-kindles
· Reduce injuries and losses resulting from fire by having an informed public, contacting 1/3 of population each year

Fiscal Year Production Plan
· Respond to 2,200 fires, rescues and emergencies
· Ready standby in quarters
· Inspect and maintain apparatus and equipment at 6 stations daily
· Conduct 6,000 inspections of fire protection systems or devices
· Conduct pre-fire planning on 130 target hazards, present fire safety lectures and fire station tours

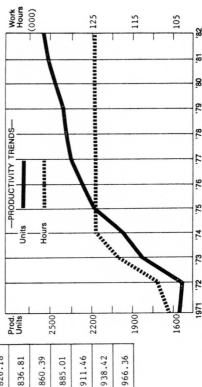

Fiscal Year	Work Hours	Total Cost of Resources	Production Units*	Unit Cost
1970-1971 Actual	105,757	944,694	1,535	615.44
1971-1972 Actual	108,963	1,042,031	1,518	686.45
1972-1973 Actual	117,400	1,297,770	1,830	709.16 ·
1973-1974 Estimated	124,778	1,530,846	2,000	765.42
1974-1975 PROPOSED	124,715	1,781,955	2,200	809.98
1975-1976 Projected	124,715	1,885,346	2,282	826.18
1976-1977 Projected	124,715	1,978,209	2,364	836.81
1977-1978 Projected	124,715	2,076,987	2,414	860.39
1978-1979 Projected	124,715	2,180,674	2,464	885.01
1979-1980 Projected	124,715	2,268,630	2,489	911.46
1980-1981 Projected	124,715	2,359,200	2,514	938.42
1981-1982 Projected	124,715	2,453,586	2,539	966.36

* Emergency responses

SPECIAL NOTES —

the notes as long-term debt. When he introduced his budget in May, one of the means used to balance accounts was a $520 million Stabilization Reserve Corporation, funded by earmarked taxes for the purpose of paying off this sort of debt.

The cumulative effect of such short-term expedients has been to eliminate almost every option the city could use to avoid making cuts in services. City borrowing and taxation have almost reached their natural limit.

One favorite hidden gimmick of the Lindsay years, converting operating expenses into long-term debt by transferring it to the capital budget, has been openly confessed to by the Beame administration. But Mayor Beame, a former accountant and City Controller with a reputation as a fiscal conservative, has been forced to use it even more extensively than Mayor Lindsay. According to city figures, some $728 million of the $1.8 billion capital budget actually went for operating costs like salaries and supplies. The figure for next fiscal year is estimated at $780 million, in a capital budget which will not increase and which includes only $5.1 million for major new construction.[19]

Hopefully, a budgetary fiscal model will preclude or at least call attention to such tactics.

A budgetary fiscal model should not be confused with an economic base study. Although the two projective designs have certain features in common, they differ markedly in the scope of their projections. The objectives of an economic base study are:

"1 - To forecast the *directions* of economic growth
  2 - To enable suitable *public strategies* for economic growth to gain acceptance
  3 - To assist in broadening community *understanding* of the local economy
  4 - To gain an understanding of the *effects* of present economic activity."[20]

An economic base study emphasizes the measurement of the growth of the local economy. For example:

If you have an employment problem, a decline in sales and output in one or more sectors or areas of your city, if new private investment in land and space has ceased or declined; if local property revenues are falling off or inadequate to meet an acceptable level of services and facilities, then you need an economic base study to identify the present and future sources of viability. With the information you develop in a base study you can proceed to plan, program your resources to arrest and reverse the detrimental aspects of the situation.[21]

One might view a budgetary fiscal model as an extension of an economic base study. Knowledge of the financial status of a particular city (i.e., its budgetary revenues and expenditures) depends upon the local economy. An economic base study would necessarily take many variables into consideration that a fiscal model would not deal with or, at most, would consider only to a limited degree. Whereas an economic base study would show the relationship between the city's economy and its present revenue sources, the budgetary fiscal model would project the actual taxable figures. It is far beyond the scope of a budgetary fiscal model to provide the direction and a thorough understanding of local or statewide economic growth.

CRITICISMS OF A BUDGETARY FISCAL MODEL

Ideally, a budgetary fiscal model would project realistic revenues and expenditures into the future, allowing for constructive planning or alternative courses of action. Obviously, this is not a simple task. Much of the current criticism of budgetary fiscal models is understandable, if not legitimate. One major problem is nailing down the inflation rate, which in these times of rapid change is becoming increasingly difficult.

The model's basic methodology of linear regression presents several problems. The method of least-squares relies on correlations of independent and dependent variables, thereby establishing a relationship between them. One limitation is the necessity that the independent variable be accurately projected. Even with a perfect correlation between the variables, the forecast of the dependent variable can only be as reliable as the forecast of the independent variable. A second limitation is the difficulty of predicting exogenous variables, and a third is that the assumption of linearity may not hold if in reality the budgetary item is a department large enough to generate economies of scale. It is beyond the scope of this text to discuss these problems in depth. Let it suffice to say that these limitations can be recognized and that the proposed fiscal model will presumably adjust to these known difficulties and make them explicit.

Another problem is Systematic error: Projections regularly reflect large errors which will throw off final results. Certain revenues can be projected while other revenue items defy projection (i.e., sales tax). It is important to make these assumptions explicit.

In order to make accurate predictions, a fiscal model must be capable of outlining realistic changes that may occur. "The main problem in long-range revenue projection is developing materials that describe and define change—change of factors affecting movement of the base of the major tax sources available to a state or a community. The long-range revenue estimator does not look at how things are, but how they are likely to be, considering the direction and magnitude of change." [22]

Consequently, the model builders need insight in order to project

critical changes in direction and possible magnitude of change. A useful projection must outline in detail its assumptions and procedures, and point out the most likely sources of change. Lack of knowledge about revenue behavior often causes long-range projection to fail. The same result occurs when relationships are not handled with sufficient flexibility, whether they are derived mathematically, historically, or theoretically. The projector must recognize when relationships are shifting, especially in long-range studies. [23]

This approach obviously requires a constant review of all fiscal activities:

Since change is so vital in long-range estimation, events must be under continual observation. Then projections can be adjusted in conformity with unfolding reality and the causes of divergence can be discovered. The long-range projection process is a dynamic one. Even though stable and relevant relationships from the past are projected, special attention must be given to critical or key change. No estimate is, of course, ever final. As new facts appear, estimates should be reviewed; this continuing evaluation is vital to assure projections that correspond to reality. If the updating process is neglected, the projection may lead to very inappropriate policy decisions. [24]

Indeed, some fundamental variables can change significantly and affect the conclusions derived from the model. The successful budgetary fiscal model would take into account exogenous variables which in a very short time could alter its estimates significantly. The budgetary fiscal model can also establish alternative courses of action, should its final estimates fall short.

Of major importance is the fact that long-range planning by a budgetary fiscal model is a projection. Forecasting is a probability statement at best. A model's accuracy depends upon its explicit and implicit assumptions. As conditions change, no simple extrapolation into the future can with great certainty guide policy. One of the greatest dangers of a budgetary fiscal model is to regard it as a factual statement, thereby basing policy decisions solely on it. The output provided by this fiscal model is a projection of the future and should be treated as such. Major policy decisions should be made only after an in-depth exploration of the alternatives provided.

CONCLUSION

The budgetary fiscal model has, as its primary asset, an early warning system and a well-tuned response mechanism (contingency planning capability). As a projective model, it is designed to provide relevant information about the future.

Budgetary fiscal model forecasting provides the foundation for long-range planning. According to Lowry, the essential steps in a planning model are: "1) specification of alternative programs or actions that might be chosen by the planner; 2) prediction of the consequences of choosing each alternative; 3) scoring these consequences according to a metric of goal-achievement; 4) choosing the alternative which yields the highest score."[25]

The author has had personal experience at the state and local governmental levels wherein unplanned, emergency handling of revenue shortages resulted in across-the-board, departmentwide reductions. If there is no built-in establishment of alternatives on a selective basis (i.e., predetermined priorities which allow for reduction at the lower end of the priority scale), the immediate hasty response is simply to reduce all departments equally.

In sum, the entire budgetary process balances community needs and taxable revenues over an extended time period. The budgetary fiscal model identifies and bridges any gap which may arise by preparing a series of alternative actions based on a priority schedule. The countermeasures may include a tax or fee increase, program or departmental reduction or deferment of capital improvement or personnel expenditures, increased request for federal or state monies, or a permutation of the aforementioned responses.

The discipline of projecting the cost of new programs or new departments into a model of aggregate costs can only benefit the decision-making process. Sometimes the total sum of new programs can far outweigh the potential revenue sources at some future date. It is unlikely that many states or cities are following this regimen. More likely, their budgets reflect a year-to-year approach, with little input going beyond the immediate fiscal year.

A budgetary fiscal model seeks to preclude a set of "meat-ax" circumstances by forecasting the eventuality of a fiscal crisis, as well as providing priorities for budgetary reductions and/or identifying new revenue sources for such a contingency. This fiscal model would fit very easily within the budgetary process herein described. Then, any budgetary staff or legislative body could enter the decision-making process with an awareness that a revenue crunch could occur within a given time frame.

NOTES

1. Norman Draper and H. Smith, *Applied Regression Analysis* (New York: John Wiley and Sons, Inc., 1966).

2. Eugene P. McLoone, Gabrielle C. Lupo, and Selma J. Mushkin, *Long-Range Revenue Estimation* (Washington, D.C.: The George Washington University, 1967), p. 38.

3. Ibid., p. 39.

4. Ibid., p. 34.

5. Ken Fabricatore, CMP Program Analyst, City of San Diego Memorandum, to Larry Haden, Financial Management Director, Subject: Prototype Financial Plan, July 19, 1974, p. 3.

6. Legislative Analyst Office survey, November 1974.

7. "1973-74 Budgetary Hearings—Discussion of Need for Five Year Perspective of 'Revenue Gap'," submitted to Council of Los Angeles by Oscar Odegaard, Finance Specialist, October 24, 1973, p. 4.

8. Ibid., p. 4.

9. City of Oakland, "Preliminary Budget 1974-75," submitted to Mayor and Council by Cecil S. Riley, City Manager, May 1, 1974, Oakland, Calif., p. 1.

10. Ibid.

11. Ibid., p. A-14.

12. Ibid., p. A-14.1.

13. Ibid., p. 5.

14. Ibid., p. 3.

15. Ibid.

16. Statement by Carl Husby, Finance Director, Sunnyvale, California, personal interview, November 26, 1974.

17. City of Sunnyvale, "Resource Allocation Plan, 1974-75," submitted by John E. Denver, City Manager, Sunnyvale, Calif., May 21, 1974, p. 11.

18. Ibid., p. iv.

19. *Wall Street Journal*, (Editorial), January 21, 1975.

20. "Analyzing the Economic Base of a City," Francis Hendricks, Municipal Finance Officer's Association of the United States and Canada, Chicago, Ill., September 16, 1965, p. 1.

21. Ibid., p. 2.

22. McLoone et al., op. cit., pp. 43-44.

23. Ibid., p. 49.

24. Ibid., p. 24.

25. Ira S. Lowry, "A Short Course in Model Design, T-3114" (Santa Monica, Calif: RAND Corp., 1965), p. 5.

7

URBAN LAND-USE MODELS

In the previous chapter, attention was drawn to the distinction between a budgetary fiscal model and a general economic model of the private sector. The fiscal model described dealt with local governmental or state revenue and expenditure projections. The general economic model would display economic projections (state, county, or citywide) on primarily private sector activities such as employment, housing starts, industrial inventories, exports, imports, new industry, and sales. The two types of models interrelate to some degree. For example, sales volume will determine the level of local sales tax collected. Many of the indicators, however, in a general economic model would only indirectly affect a budgetary fiscal model. A well-programmed budgetary fiscal model would, of course, incorporate general economic projections where relevant. Thus, it would rely to some degree on local or statewide economic projections as determined by data made available by bank economic research analyses and other research groups.

There is another type of model which a budgetary fiscal model would definitely depend upon. The legislative bodies at both the local and statewide levels can direct the final product of this model (unlike the general economic model's output). Federal economic actions on inflation, federal reserve policy, tax policy, or private sector decisions affecting investment, construction, and the like preclude such state and local government control on general economic conditions.

This model can be characterized as an urban land-use model. As its name indicates, an urban land-use model seeks to guide major policy decisions affecting utilization of land on a regional basis. Decisions on mass transit, location of industrial sites, airport location, zoning, pedestrian malls, urban design, transportation corridors, highway location, quality of environment, et al., would be comprehensively determined within the matrix of an urban land-use model. As stated, because of federal or private preemption, local and state legislators cannot guide major economic variables, but they can influence land-use model decisions for better or worse.

The expenditures and revenues of a budgetary fiscal model would *directly* tie into the determinants of a land-use model as approved by a City Council, County Board of Supervisors, or State Legislative Body.

Land-use decisions directly relate to the budgetary fiscal model revenue and expenditure stream, which is then identified annually in the PPB program expenditure and revenue needs and levels. The schematic illustration on page 106 displays the interrelationships. As seen in the illustration, the PPB and the budgetary fiscal model's expenditure and revenue levels are directly dependent on land-use decisions connected on a time continuum. For example, should a city council approve the zoning for a new community of 50,000 individuals within their city limits, major budgetary capital and operational expenditures will follow (i.e., fire and police stations, schools, roads, libraries, sanitation services, parks, recreational facilities, welfare, senior citizen programs, outreach programs).

A land-use model would indicate the density, timing, and location of population and transportation facilities (i.e., highway, fixed rail, airport location, bus systems, bike paths), as well as the location of industrial sites, port facilities, encouragement of industry by type, and so forth. Thus, land-use decisions literally create expenditures and revenues which subsequently become the inputs to a five-year budgetary fiscal model. The inputs are then itemized in the PPB in a "snapshot" of the incoming fiscal year.

Hence, state or local expenditure/revenue patterns are originally formulated by land-use decisions affecting five-, ten-, fifteen-, and twenty-year time frames. Land-use fiscal requirements are cast in five-year increments in a budgetary fiscal model and are more definitively detailed in the year-to-year PPB.

The land-use model, fiscal model, and PPB interact with the overall economic conditions of the private sector. To simplify the complex interactions between these models, the private sector is viewed as being virtually independent of state and local constraints. As local, state, and federal policies do interact with the decisions of the private sector, a degree of simplification is injected for the purpose of clarity. Thus, the private sector's economic model is differentiated from the urban land-use model and budgetary fiscal model, though decisions made in a land-use model will affect private market investment decisions (i.e., zoning decisions, patterns and modes of transportation, public facility location). Therefore, for heuristic reasons, the models will minimize interactions between the private and public sectors, even though a fully developed model and the real world would require such interactions.

Now, for the first time in this text, we can fully track the expenditure trail from its very inception—the land-use decision. Once the land-use decision(s) is(are) made, the PPB and the budgetary fiscal model calculations become locked in mechanistically. The fiscal circle of the entire public decision-making process is now completely identified.

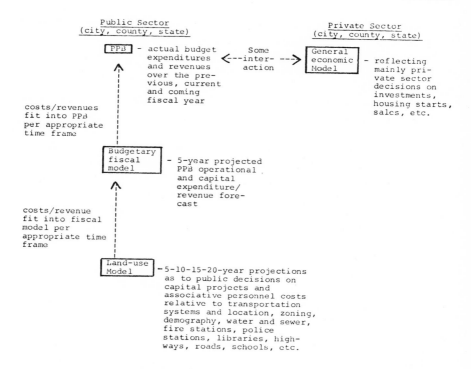

The Legislative Analyst Office in San Diego has been responsible for land-use analyses which would directly affect the city's budgetary fiscal model and PPB. This office recommended against approval of a plan to permit development of a new community of 40,000 residents for numerous reasons. To quote from that analysis:

This report will attempt to address and set criteria for the following parameters:

(1) Population trends and forecasts,
(2) Housing trends and forecasts,
(3) Housing vacancy rates,
(4) Available peripheral lands and new residential development,
(5) Balanced community implementation,
(6) Capital and operating costs,
(7) Related studies which will affect North City West planning,
(8) North City West opportunity cost alternatives of:
   (a) Redevelopment and
   (b) New development located in other geographic areas
   (c) A mix of (a) and (b),
(9) Summary and conclusion.

As can be noted, this report is more inclusive than the identification of various capital and operating costs. This particular approach results from necessary opportunity cost correlations. The concept of opportunity costs (i.e., the comparison of alternative opportunities foregone as a result of the selection of one choice—in this case, North City West) requires a full identification and development of all alternative choices. As a consequence, a complete study would require statistical analysis of various matrices displaying different mixes by competing areas, density patterns, type of housing and income grouping, demographic features, capital inventory, phasing of capital projects, et al.

The need for the population emphasis in this report can be noted in the following quotation from the Urban Observatory:

"(1) When population is increasing, the aggregates of public expenditures and taxes move in the same direction, and
(2) per capita expenditures and taxes increase at a faster rate than population."[1]

The absence of such analyses relative to urban land-use decisions can prove disastrous for the environment as well as the fiscal flow. A condition such as the following could actually prevail:

Otay Mesa, Calif., is a ghastly example of just about everything urban planners try to prevent. Crammed into an isolated corner of San Diego, Otay Mesa is a chaotic subdivision of spanking new $20,000 to $30,000 houses in search of a master plan. The community has no post office, library or fire house and, although it lies miles from the offices of its bread-winners, Otay Mesa offers no public transportation to downtown. The nearest park is beyond most residents' reach, and the nearest schools must now run on double sessions. In 1970, the U.S. Census found 16,200 people in Otay Mesa, although the subdivision was barely three years old. That year there was not a single fire-alarm box in the community.

Unhappily, the trials of Otay Mesa are far from unique. Overcrowded schools, faltering transit and scrambled—or non-existent—services have become endemic to mushrooming megalopolises across the U.S. And as weary taxpayers are fast discovering, correcting existing blight may be less costly than constructing the new sewers and schools that expansion demands. Urban growth, in fact, is beginning to get such a bad name that local government strategists from Cape Cod to the Pacific are starting to plot ways to halt expansion, discourage new building and keep their neighbors few. . . .

In fairness, San Diego planners have made valiant efforts to control the situation in both subdivisions. But the original plan to regulate development in the area went by the boards when local zoning commissioners granted an endless stream of variances. And a ban on new building in Mira Mesa was compromised by the city after being challenged by developers. Things have come to such a pass, in fact, that some San Diego residents are now campaigning for model-cities funds for Otay Mesa—a community that seems well on its way to becoming a model suburban slum.[2]

To forestall such potential fiscal and environmental blights, an urban land-use model (not subject to political changes for expediency) is a *sine qua non*. The responsibility of updating such a land-use model should rest with the Planning and Data Processing Departments. The model would be scrutinized and analyzed by an Environmental Quality Department for its environmental impact, as well as by the independent Legislative Analyst Office for analyses as to planning comprehensiveness and fiscal impacts.

URBAN LAND-USE MODEL REVIEW

Unfortunately, land-use models throughout the United States have not achieved notable success in terms of utilization. Too often, land-use models fall into one of two categories: (1) they are too generalized for definitive decision-making, as they simply express the community's willingness to deal with environmental, fiscal, and population optimization without identifying the mechanism for achieving it; or (2) infinitesimal detail is accumulated wherein literally thousands of equations are programmed for one major category and the total is amassed in mountains of incomprehensible data.

The expensive failures of numerous land-use models are easily explained when one considers their complexity. The determinants (factors which must be given mathematical weight) found within such a model number in the hundreds, if not thousands. As if the quantification within such a model were not sufficiently difficult, qualitative issues must also be evaluated and included within the model's framework. Urban design, for example, can render a tourist or downtown area either a successful, revitalized venture or an empty canyon. Given these considerations, it is easy to see why the end product has produced frustration rather than illumination.

A successfully developed land-use model would have to emphasize urban design utilization. Kevin Lynch and Donald Appleyard instigated such an urban design study for the city of San Diego. The subsequent report detailed not only the urban design qualities of the city, but also brought function into city design by incorporating transportation requirements and environmental physical features.

Again, the lack of a land-use model allowed for numerous abuses as detailed within that report. For example,

> Unfortunately, this historic resource (farming lands) has already been squandered in some places. The most dramatic loss was the conversion of historic Mission Valley in the 1950's into a chaos of highways, parking lots, and scattered commercial buildings. The city should erect an historic monument to that tragic event. It struck a double blow: one directed both at the landscape and at the economy of the center city.[3]

The Appleyard-Lynch study is an excellent beginning point for an urban land-use model. It develops the concept of the historicity of the current landscape, cites the past mistakes made in the natural land base, describes the weather and topographical conditions, and charts the ideal direction for the city in terms of land use. But implementation of this report would require a major technical effort, since it mainly addresses itself to general questions of identifying positive environmental features and potential location sites for future growth. Implementation is left to follow-up analyses and studies. The concept of urban design and the preservation of desirable environmental features should be identified and incorporated with the matrix of a land-use model.

Constantine Doxiadis has elaborated the pitfalls into which American cities have fallen. Unfortunately, the lack of a well-thought-out land-use concept may even work against an attempt at urban improvement. As Doxiadis puts it:

> On the basis of my studies of projects, I am prepared to state that some urban renewal projects are actually working *against* the goals that it was hoped they might achieve. For example, major urban renewal projects in central business districts that tend to increase the density of land use or in some other way attract more people to the area usually do not take into consideration the fact that such projects create additional problems of transportation. Such projects definitely work against the long-term interests of the city and the business community concerned with the prosperity of its central area.[4]

Harry A. Anthony has illustrated another aspect of improper planning:

> I suggest that another wrong planning attitude on the part of the city fathers is to keep pushing for more growth, more development, more population. Beyond a certain size range, cities historically have gone into a decline of quality. San Diego's present metropolitan population of just under one and a half million is almost enough for a good city. Further growth should be considerably slowed down and related to a sound re-

gional plan. Feverish growth may seem good now for business and for politicians, but in the long run it will prove bad for everybody.[5]

The development of a land-use model would involve many technical disciplines. In addition, the model would need built-in flexibility; hence, all assumptions would have to be explicit to allow for changing conditions. The following will give some idea as to the complexity and flexibility needed:

> The development of land use forecasting models requires the integration of a wide range of techniques used in forecasting regional population, employment, incomes, industry structure, housing demand, consumer travel and shopping behavior, residential, industrial and commercial locational decisions, and government housing, investment, transportation and land use policies. The range and depth of interdisciplinary concern indicated by this admittedly partial but imposing list is matched only by the burgeoning volumes of special studies impinging on each of these forecasting problems. A specialist in any one of these areas may consider it presumptuous of economists to endeavor to construct a "model" which must contain implicit or explicit assumptions concerning such a wide range of individual and institutional behavior. The urban land economist must answer, however, that if forecasts are needed which require a complex network of assumptions, he will have served his role if he states the assumptions used in his model and provides a mechanism through which his fellow social scientists can experiment with his "model" under varying assumptions. . . .

> The model builder's dilemma lies in the choice he must make between a model which is theoretically "elegant" and one which is operationally "feasible." Thus the criticism of any urban land use model can be anticipated to be of two sorts: One, the model is too simple to be acceptable on theoretical grounds, or two, the model is too complex to be operational. The model builder's task is to steer his way between the horns of his dilemma and trust that he will not violate his fellow economist's theoretical sensitivities in producing a forecasting model for which data inputs are available and outputs feasible. In addition, he must be mindful of the importance of maintaining sufficient flexibility in the resulting model so that it can accommodate itself to varying assumptions, data inputs, and to changing computer technology.[6]

Only recently have all government levels become more fully aware of the urgent necessity to develop land-use models. In a major report entitled *The Costs of Sprawl*, the federal government concluded that:

> Current pressures upon the nation's finite resources cannot be accom-

modated without better planning and more efficient controls. "Land is our most valuable resource," states Russell Train, former Chairman of the Council on Environmental Quality. Coming to terms with the land is one of the most formidable tasks facing man in this century. Expanding population, urban sprawl, environmental abuses and resource depletion are among the many issues necessitating a critical evaluation of current U.S. state and local land use policies and development practices. . . .

The population of the U.S. is likely to rise by at least 46 million persons between 1970 and 2000, according to the latest revisions of the Census Bureau projection. If 70 percent of the growth occurs in the suburban portions of the nation's metropolitan areas (as occurred from 1960-1970) then suburbs will grow by 32.3 million persons in the three decades from 1970 to 2000, equaling a gain of more than 42 percent from the 1970 sub-urban population. It would be an absolute rise in suburban population equal to 93 percent of that which occurred in 20 years from 1950 to 1970—the period of greatest suburbanization in the nation's history.

Clearly, the particular physical forms in which this large-scale future development occurs will have great implications for both the nature of urban life in America and the total amount of resources required to ac-commodate future growth. Both the criticisms of "suburban sprawl" and its possible advantages indicate that there are probably major dif-ferences in costs and adverse effect on the one hand, and outputs and benefits on the other, between "suburban sprawl" and alternative forms of urban development. It is therefore imperative that public authorities and private developers determine whether such differences really exist, the nature of these differences, and how substantial they are now and might be in the future.[7]

URBAN DESIGN

A comprehensive land-use model is a necessity in formulating an urban de-sign, a planning process which relates people to urban characteristics. An effective urban design project could revitalize the downtown areas of many of our depressed cities.

In Fresno, a shopping mall was constructed which reversed the development trends of the city. This urban design project created a focus for commercial and social activity, pulling business back into the city and encouraging renova-tion of older buildings. The success of the Fresno project is the result of careful analysis of urban relationships and planning. Downtown renewal projects which do not consider the entire urban structure can lead to economic disas-ters. For example, a mall constructed in Riverside, although aesthetically very attractive, has declined continuously since its inception (three main stores on which the mall was dependent have moved) as a result of uncoordinated economic planning and the lack of an overall redevelopment plan.

Incentive bonus zoning is one technique to create urban design amenities such as landscaped plazas, increased light and air view protection, and proliferation of mixed uses in areas where market considerations have resulted in a single type of development. Tradeoffs between increased floor area above the allowed amount in return for provision of the desired amenities can be offered to private developers as an incentive. In San Francisco, bonus incentive zoning resulted in a tradeoff of accessibility, pedestrian movement, light and air protection, and enhancement of views for rapid transit, wider sidewalks, plazas, building setbacks, and observation decks.

Another urban design tool used to preserve urban landmarks is the transfer of development rights. This tool has been utilized to preserve historic landmarks and aesthetic sites.

The successful use of such designing tools again underscores the requirement of a comprehensive urban design plan and land-use model. The city must have a specific goal for its land-use model.

The precise methodology and planned development provided by a comprehensive land-use model will lead to the most effective, least cost alternatives for a city. The Southeastern Wisconsin Regional Planning Commission has described how a completely successful land-use model would be a valuable analytical tool in city decision-making:

> The potential usefulness of a land use plan design model in land use planning is obvious: an operational and flexible plan design model could be used to operate a set of least cost plans for a series of forecast years, ranging from five to 30 years, with each design being developed independent of the others and based only on the initial conditions and forecast requirements. The series of land use plan designs derived from the model will then display the most economic and efficient land use pattern that can be obtained at a particular design year. This, in turn, will aid in making decisions concerning the development of public and private policies regarding the development and use of land in a systematic and efficient way. Furthermore, the model can be well utilized in capital works programming in the time-simulation framework. By running a series of design model runs on a five-year time increment starting from the target year, the proper sequence of capital works programming could be determined. The greatest impact of the plan design model on metropolitan and regional plan making will probably be in establishing a standard, or norm, against which all proposed plans can be evaluated. A final important application of the model relates to the ready estimation of the cost of any suggested plan design constraints.[8]

FAILURE OF URBAN LAND-USE MODELS

The planner should learn from the inadequacies of existing land-use models. To date, there has not been a comprehensive, successful land-use model. The reasons are time constraints and lack of data, knowledge, and financing. To cite a survey on the subject: "There has never been an over-all comprehensive approach to all land, for all uses, using one set of concepts and definitions, in the United States."[9]

In some instances of failure, the purpose of the model, as interpreted by the city or planning commission, unduly restricted its comprehensiveness. Other land-use models did not respond to the complex and multiple process of inter-action characteristic of a land-use model. Often, time deadlines or monetary limitations forced less comprehensive models to be developed.

There should be a balance between the theoretical sophistication of a model and the need for operational feasibility. The requirements for attaining this balance should be recognized at the beginning of the model construction process. The hazards of planning too complex a model without regard for operational feasibility became apparent in the BATSC (Bay Area Transportation Study Commission) study. The original plans were to implement the model in two elaborate phases by utilizing the most advanced state of the art of computer modeling. As the final report on the model concluded: "In actuality, neither the sketch plan model nor the urban simulation model were even implemented; both turned out to be operationally unfeasible when constrained by the data and study time limitations. Fortunately, a less complex back-up model BASS I, was available."[10]

Two other models almost failed because of inadequate planning. The BASS (Bay Area Simulation Study) and PLUM (Project Land Use Model) systems, descriptive models which forecast existing land-use patterns, were not initially structured to account for alternate land-use patterns. However, PLUM was elaborated upon to respond to this need.

The BASS model was not sufficiently funded to permit further necessary refinements. Thus, its potential was not fully actualized; however, its methodology may have been unduly elaborate which would have made any conclusions open to question.

The Boulder Area Growth Study Commission attempted a comprehensive approach to growth and land use, but its model was left incomplete because of time limitations:

Neither the policies nor the scenarios was completed to the satisfaction of the Commission, due to time constraints, even though the policies received a great deal of commission attention. The commission had to face the very difficult decision of either spending more time on the policies and scenarios, in which case the study might never be completed in time, or permitting the consultants to work on them in their imcomplete state, thereby running the risk of varying interpretations and uncoordinated results. The latter course was really the only one open to the Commission. [11]

Similarly, the Southeastern Wisconsin Regional Planning Commission felt that their model was not totally comprehensive: "several deficiencies in the model exist which seriously impair its wide application in land use planning." [12]

The lack of impact or general use of several land-use models has caused a controversy as to their feasibility generally, and many legislators have rejected comprehensive modeling altogether. Unfortunately, as a result of the state of the art and the complexity of the problem, land-use models have not actualized their potential. A workable model must be generated, for there is no real alternative to planning urban growth.

In his article "Requiem for Large-Scale Models," Douglas B. Lee, Jr., elucidates the major ways in which land-use models have failed. He contends that these failures indicate that it is not possible to produce a workable, comprehensive land-use model. His view has been opposed by many who object to his overall condemnation of land-use models on the basis of their lack of success.

Lee's major criticism of land-use models is that the parameters are too complex to be incorporated into an integrated system. He blames the failure of the models on inadequate knowledge of complex urban structures. Along with the complexity of urban issues, Lee cites the error inherent in previous models: "Because the models contain large but unknown amounts of error and they are too complex, and there are no evaluation measures, modelers have little choice except to fudge the models into shape." [13]

Lee's criticism that there are insufficient data on urban infrastructures to allow for incorporation into a model is really a problem of defining and meeting research requirements rather than one of reflecting "innate" flaws. Inadequate urban data would also restrict planning processes without models. With the use of a model, these data inadequacies, at the very least, become more explicit.

To Lee's statement that the large number of undetected errors in land-use models derives from the complexity of the urban problem, one may again answer that the problem is one of explicitly defining the problem areas and inputs rather than of reflecting any inherent defect.

Another of Lee's criticisms is that large-scale models have not produced the fine detail of output which would make them valuable to policy-makers. But exact outputs require very exact inputs. Again, this criticism reflects on the inadequate methodology in planning the model and defining the problem rather than on the concept of modeling itself. Martineau has answered Lee on precisely this argument: "the development of good investigative methodology is an absolute prerequisite to the development of even the most simple theory. In many modeling approaches, this has been totally ignored to the point where many modelers no longer view the model as methodology but instead see their model as an absolute, rigid, infallible embodiment of theory."[14]

Yet another difficulty that Lee identifies centers on the enormous volume of data required for these models. The costly need for data collection in conjunction with their complexity has resulted in major drawbacks, Lee states; thus, he views the success of a comprehensive land-use model as, at best, highly unlikely.

Although Lee's criticisms of existing land-use models are valid, they should not preclude further research into the development of a comprehensive model. The failures of land-use models, to date, can be attributed to imprecise data and research methodologies rather than to any innate inability of a model. Costs associative with data-gathering requirements can only be looked upon as very minor when compared to the enormous social costs and the fiscal impact of improper planning. Friedland shares Lee's view that existing models are inadequate, but attributes its failures to the newness of the concept.[15]

CONCLUSION

At the time this text was being written, the Legislative Analyst Office in San Diego proposed that the city undertake a comprehensive land-use model. The need for such a model and its advantages can be best indicated by reference to the two studies mentioned in this chapter, "Temporary Paradise?" and *The Costs of Sprawl*. The former study, centering on the aesthetics and preservation of environmental qualities, and the latter, indicating economic and psychic benefits summarize both the challenges and the need for land-use models. (The Appendix quotes extensively from *The Costs of Sprawl*.)

In city after city in the United States, the entire economic and environmental base has eroded. This is the result of patchwork responses to urban land-use policies. In contrast, many European cities remain dynamic and still have the humanistic qualities which should belong to every city. In many ways, American cities discourage cultural and aesthetic values. There is an aura of dehumanization in the single-purposed communities which are so totally devoid of any charm or individuality. When urban design deficiencies are coupled with no economic planning and environmental degradation, the city will come to represent the antithesis of those qualities which first brought it into being.

NOTES

1. Legislative Analyst Office, "North City West Analysis," April 15, 1974, pp. 1-3; The Urban Observatory of San Diego, *A Study of Local Government Finance on the San Diego SMSA*, 1972, p. 102.

2. "Banning the Boom," *Newsweek*, August 21, 1972, p. 40.

3. Kevin Lynch and Donald Appleyard, "Temporary Paradise? A Look at the Special Landscape of the San Diego Region," A Report to the City of San Diego, September 1974, p. 5.

4. C. A. Doxiadis, *Urban Renewal and the Future of the American City* (Public Administration Service, 1966), p. 123.

5. Harry A. Anthony, "A Vision of San Diego," *San Diego Magazine*, June 1970, p. 33.

6. Center for Real Estate and Urban Economics, *Jobs, People and Land, Bay Area Simulation Study (BASS)*, 1968, pp. 7-9.

7. Real Estate Research Corporation, *The Costs of Sprawl: Detailed Cost Analysis*, April 1974, p. 26.

8. Southeastern Wisconsin Regional Planning Commission, *A Land Use Plan Design Model, Volume Three—Final Report*, U.S. Department of Housing and Urban Development, April 1973, p. 81.

9. Marion Clawson and Charles L. Stewart, *Land Use Information: A Critical Survey of U.S. Statistics Including Possibilities for Greater Uniformity*, Resources for the Future, Inc. (Baltimore: The Johns Hopkins Press, 1965), p. 1.

10. Stephen R. Rosenthal, Jack R. Meredith, and William Goldner, *Plan Making with a Computer Model: Projective Land Use Model*, Volume I, Institute of Transportation and Traffic Engineering, University of California, Berkeley, February 1972, p. 11.

11. Boulder Area Growth Study Commission, *Exploring Options for the Future: A Study of Growth in Boulder County, Volume I—Commission Final Report*, Boulder, Colo., November 1973, p. 9.

12. Southeastern Wisconsin Regional Planning Commission, loc. cit.

13. Douglas B. Lee, Jr., "Requiem for Large-Scale Models," *Journal of the American Institute of Planners* 39, No. 3 (May 1973): 167.

14. Thomas R. Martineau, "Letters to the Editor," *Journal of the American Institute of Planners*, 40, No. 1 (January 1974): 55.

15. Daniel R. Friedland, "Letters to the Editor," *Journal of the American Institute of Planners*, 40, No. 1 (January 1974): 54.

APPENDIX A

LIBRARY BUDGET

I. FISCAL YEAR 1974-1975

City of San Diego, California **PROGRAM BUDGET**	DEPARTMENT/DIVISION Library			NO. 20.00
Classification	Actual FY 1973	Current FY 1974	Fiscal 1975 Budget Proposed	Final
BUDGET SUMMARY				
OPERATING PROGRAM Staffing (Position-Years) (PEP, YEP, etc.)	289.74 (37.00)	287.02 (7.00)	295.31 (6.00)	
Personnel Expense Salaries & Wages Employee Pensions Injury & Health Ins. Total Personnel	$2,378,053 291,241 51,646 $2,720,940	$2,564,739 365,324 59,532 $2,989,595	$2,655,428 396,307 62,793 $3,114,528	
Non-Personnel Expense Supplies & Services Equipment Purchase Total Non-Personnel	$ 752,825 24,232 $ 777,057	$ 824,110 31,725 $ 855,835	$ 895,232 50,081 $ 945,313	
TOTAL OPERATING Change from Prior Year	$3,497,997 --	$3,845,430 +9.9%	$4,059,841 +5.6%	
CAPITAL IMPROVEMENTS PROGRAM	$ 171,559	$ 573,000	$1,389,000	
TOTAL BUDGET	$3,669,556	$4,418,430	$5,448,841	

FUND SOURCE ANALYSIS

Operating Program General Fund (100)	$3,206,756	$3,451,106	$3,379,534
General Fund (General Revenue Sharing)	--	29,000	284,000
Employee Pension Tax Fund (105) Total Operating	291,241 $3,497,997	365,324 $3,845,430	396,307 $4,059,841
Capital Improvements Program City Funds Capital Outlay (245) Other Bonds (726)	$ 44,818 126,741	$ 433,000 140,000	$1,239,000 150,000
Total City Funded Capital Improvements Funds	$ 171,559	$ 573,000	$1,389,000
TOTAL - ALL FUNDS	$3,669,556	$4,418,430	$5,448,841

Department Goals

To provide a major source of high quality research material and recreational reading for the entire City community; to serve as the public's cultural and intellectual center for individual development, and the continuation of education; to assist the community in social growth, business endeavor, and governmental progress.

City of San Diego, California	DEPARTMENT/DIVISION		NO.
PROGRAM BUDGET		Library	20.00

OPERATING PROGRAM SUMMARY
(Position-Years and Expenditures)

	Actual FY 1973	Current FY 1974	Proposed FY 1975	Final FY 1975
Administration (20.10)	14.00	14.00	14.00	
	$ 229,680	$ 250,331	$ 261,938	
Central Library (20.20)	79.12	70.61	74.78	
	$1,110,078	$1,103,223	$1,196,301	
Extension Division (20.30)	134.40	140.19	143.31	
	$1,581,094	$1,841,455	$1,924,140	
Headquarters (20.31)	11.66	12.66	13.66	
	$ 113,414	$ 142,166	$ 149,330	
Agencies (20.32)	122.74	127.53	129.65	
	$1,467,680	$1,699,289	$1,774,810	
Technical Services (20.70)	54.22	55.72	56.72	
	$ 487,322	$ 559,553	$ 584,593	
Serra Research Center (20.80)	4.00	2.50	2.50	
	$ 33,486	$ 28,969	$ 28,801	
Governmental Reference Library (20.90)	4.00	. 4.00	4.00	
	$ 56,337	$ 61,899	$ 64,068	
TOTALS	289.74	287.02	295.31	
	$3,497,997	$3,845,430	$4,059,841	

City of San Diego, California **PROGRAM BUDGET**	DEPARTMENT/DIVISION Library		NO. 20.00

OPERATING PROGRAM REVENUES/REIMBURSEMENTS

	Actual FY 1973	Current FY 1974	Proposed FY 1975	Final FY 1975
Central Library (20.20)				
Library Fines	$ 27,020	$ 28,242	$ 29,565	
Charges for Lost and Damaged Books	6,092	6,372	6,844	
All Other Library Charges	7,852	6,688	2,394	
Rents and Commissions	18	--	6,306	
Sub-Total Central Library	$ 40,982	$ 41,302	$ 45,109	
Extension Division (20.30)				
Agencies				
Library Fines	73,054	76,358	79,935	
Charges for Lost and Damaged Books	4,233	4,428	4,756	
All Other Library Charges	12,810	10,912	3,906	
Rents and Commissions	27	--	9,894	
Sub-Total Extension Division	$ 90,124	$ 91,698	$ 98,491	
Serra Research Center (20.80)				
County Grants	$ 45,434	$ 38,500	$ 40,700	
Governmental Reference Library (20.90)				
County Contribution	$ 28,186	$ 27,300	$ 29,715	
TOTALS	$204,726	$198,800	$214,015	

PROGRAM DETAIL

Administration Program (20.10)

Need - The administration of the 31 separate Library Department facilities (including branches and bookmobiles) requires the centralized administrative, clerical, fiscal, personnel, supply, and public information support provided by the Administration Program.

Objectives - To reduce full-time personnel turnover; to increase the number of purchase requisitions and letter orders written per position-year; to increase the number of supply and duplication requests filled per position-year. To maintain a high level of information dissemination to the public through the broadcast and publication of library-oriented news events and the exhibition of public displays; and to develop cost-benefit analysis as a management tool.

Authority - Municipal Code, Chapter II, Article 2, Division 2, Section 22.0201; Article 2, Division 18, Section 22.1801.

FM-1008 (REV. 11-73)

City of San Diego, California	DEPARTMENT/DIVISION	NO.
PROGRAM BUDGET	Library	20.00

General Description - The City Librarian gives general direction to and provides general planning for the department; the Assistant City Librarian provides supervision over day-to-day departmental operations. The administration staff performs administrative analysis; financial, payroll and personnel work; materials and equipment requisitions; supply handling, storage and distribution; mail distribution and messenger service general direction over custodial care and security; children's service coordination; and public information duties. The increase in Non-Personnel Expense for FY 1975 reflects additional expenditures for vehicle operation and photocopy services, price increases for office supplies, drafting and photographic supplies.

	Actual FY 1973	Current FY 1974	Proposed FY 1975	Final FY 1975
Input				
Staffing (Position-Years)	14.00	14.00	14.00	
Personnel Expense	$166,269	$186,335	$190,377	
Non-Personnel Expense	63,411	63,996	71,561	
TOTAL	$229,680	$250,331	$261,938	
Output				
Percent of full-time termina- tions to total full-time equivalent positions	29.34%	29.00%	28.00%	
Purchase requisitions and letter orders written per position- year	1,078	1,100	1,122	
Supply and duplication re- quests filled per position-year	5,660	5,773	5,888	
Releases prepared for broad- cast and publication	786	880	880	
Exhibits prepared	84	90	90	

Central Library Program (20.20)

Need - A comprehensive collection of research and information resources is needed by the community to facilitate the pursuit of information. The effectiveness and efficiency of such a program is maximized by a centralized facility.

Objectives - To achieve a higher per capita attendance figure; to initiate the recording of patron unfilled needs and complaints per capita; to maintain the amount of library materials available per capita; to increase the circulation of library materials per capita; to initiate the recording of materials used in the library besides those circulated in order to gauge collection use; and to increase the answering of information, reference and research questions.

Authority - Municipal Code, Chapter II, Article 2, Division 2, Section 22.0201; Article 2, Division 18, Section 22.1801.

General Description - The Central Library includes five adult-oriented sections, a children's section, a young adults' collection, a rare books collection (Wangenheim Room), and supportive services, supplemented by a full depository of United States and State of California documents. The staff selects materials in anticipation of public use, and assists the public in obtaining the most benefit from these resources. The proposed budget includes the addition of 4.17 position-years to continue the Directory and Information Service, and to handle the increased workload for the Art, Music, and Recreation Section. The increase in Non-Personnel Expense for FY 1975 reflects price increases for books, periodicals, and binding.

City of San Diego, California **PROGRAM BUDGET**	DEPARTMENT/DIVISION Library			NO. 20.00
	Actual FY 1973	Current FY 1974	Proposed FY 1975	Final FY 1975
Input				
Staffing (Position-Years) (PEP, YEP, etc.)	79.12 (25.00)	70.61 (4.00)	74.78 (3.00)	
Personnel Expense Non-Personnel Expense TOTAL	$ 831,470 278,608 $1,110,078	$ 769,322 333,901 $1,103,223	$ 819,432 376,869 $1,196,301	
Output				
Attendance, per capita	NA	NA	NA	
Patron unfilled needs and complaints, per capita	NA	NA	NA	
Library materials available, per capita	2.02	2.05	2.05	
Total circulation	790,543	806,392	812,198	
Materials circulated, per capita	1.06	1.07	1.08	
Materials used in the library besides those circulated, per capita	NA	NA	NA	
Information, reference and research questions, per capita	1.06	1.07	1.08	

Extension Division Program (20.30)

Need - Easy access to library service is needed by the entire community.

Objectives - To initiate the maintenance of per capita attendance figures at each agency; to initiate the recording of patron unfilled needs and complaints, per capita; to maintain the amount of library materials available, per capita; to increase the circulation of library materials, per capita; to initiate the recording of materials used in the branches besides those circulated, per capita; to increase the per capita answering of information and reference questions.

Authority - Municipal Code, Chapter II, Article 2, Divsion 2, Section 22.0201; Article 2, Division 18, Section 22.1801.

General Description - The Extension Division Program consists of a division headquarters (located at the Central Library), 25 branches, three bookmobiles and a bookmobile headquarters (located at the University Heights Branch). The branches are itemized under Extension Division Agencies below. The bookmobiles made a total of 24 scheduled stops in those areas of the City located outside the service areas of branch libraries. In addition to reading and informational resources, programs relating to books and reading are provided for adult, young adult and juvenile groups. The increase in Non-Personnel Expense for FY 1975 reflects increased expenditures for vehicle operation, binding, books, periodicals, and equipment outlay.

City of San Diego, California **PROGRAM BUDGET**	DEPARTMENT/DIVISION Library			NO. 20.00
	Actual FY 1973	Current FY 1974	Proposed FY 1975	Final FY 1975

Input

Staffing (Position-Years)	134.40	140.19	143.31	
(PEP, YEP, etc.)	(3.00)	(-0-)	(-0-)	
Personnel Expense	$1,199,133	$1,443,768	$1,495,145	
Non-Personnel Expense	381,961	397,687	428,995	
TOTAL	$1,581,094	$1,841,455	$1,924,140	

Output

Attendance, per capita	NA	NA	NA	
Patron unfilled needs and complaints, per capita	NA	NA	NA	
Library materials available, per capita	1.14	1.16	1.16	
Total circulation	2,826,103	2,882,701	2,970,156	
Materials circulated, per capita	3.79	3.80	3.81	
Materials used in branches besides those circulated, per capita	NA	NA	NA	
Information and reference questions, per capita	.60	.61	.62	

City of San Diego, California	DEPARTMENT/DIVISION		NO.
PROGRAM BUDGET		Library	20.00

Extension Division Headquarters Program Element (20.31)

General Description - Provides general supervision and supportive services for the library extension agencies. The proposed budget includes the addition of 1.00 position-year to provide for vacation and sick leave relief.

	Actual FY 1973	Current FY 1974	Proposed FY 1975	Final FY 1975
Input				
Staffing (Position-Years) (PEP, YEP, etc.)	11.66 (1.00)	12.66 (-0-)	13.66 (-0-)	
Personnel Expense	$111,530	$137,263	$147,912	
Non-Personnel Expense	1,884	4,903	1,418	
TOTAL	$113,414	$142,166	$149,330	
Output				
Outgoing book bags (est. 40 books per bag) and miscellaneous materials	25,763	27,875	29,597	
Incoming book bags (est. 40 books per bag) and miscellaneous materials	32,275	34,663	36,673	
Daily telephone requests delivered to branches	16,524	17,500	18,500	
New branches opened or being planned	10	8	7	

Extension Division Agencies Program Element (20.32)

General Description - The Extension Division Program is accomplished through its 25 branches and three bookmobiles. The FY 1975 Capital Improvements Program includes $140,000 for furniture and book purchases for the Mira Mesa Branch; $103,000 for furniture and book purchases for the Rancho Bernardo Branch; $70,000 to purchase land for the South Bay Branch; $536,000 to construct the University Community Branch; and $540,000 to construct, furnish and provide books for the 43rd and Logan Branch. The proposed operating budget includes the addition of 2.12 position-years to staff the San Carlos Branch on a full-year basis.

	Actual FY 1973	Current FY 1974	Proposed FY 1975	Final FY 1975
Input				
Staffing (Position-Years) (PEP, YEP, etc.)	122.74 (2.00)	127.53 (-0-)	129.65 (-0-)	
Personnel Expense	$1,087,603	$1,306,505	$1,347,233	
Non-Personnel Expense	380,077	392,784	427,577	
TOTAL	$1,467,680	$1,699,289	$1,774,810	

City of San Diego, California **PROGRAM BUDGET**	DEPARTMENT/DIVISION Library		NO. 20.00

OUTPUT

	Position-Years	Total Expense	Circulation	Circulation Per Capita
1. Rancho Bernardo (Temporary) 11510 Poblado	2.33	$ 36,783	14,057	3.5
2. La Jolla 1006 Wall Street	7.11	92,222	193,913	7.3
3. University Community (Temporary) 3328 Governor Drive	2.67	41,412	21,824	5.5
4. North Clairemont 4616 Clairemont Drive	9.94	122,763	243,075	9.0
5. Clairemont 2920 Burgener Blvd.	7.00	91,875	185,839	6.7
6. Pacific Beach 4606 Ingraham Street	7.28	93,044	209,853	5.1
7. Ocean Beach 4801 Santa Monica Avenue	4.83	67,533	120,536	4.9
8. Point Loma 2130 Poinsettia Drive	7.17	91,677	183,796	4.3
9. Balboa 4255 Mt. Abernathy	4.38	65,021	175,507	6.5
10. Linda Vista 6960 Linda Vista Road	3.94	59,145	81,591	3.6
11. Serra Mesa 3440 Sandrock Road	7.22	94,350	166,998	6.4
12. Mission Hills 925 West Washington Street	2.67	41,738	78,621	4.5
13. University Heights 4193 Park Boulevard	2.67	41,705	62,918	3.9
14. North Park 3795 - 31st Street	5.11	70,065	143,143	6.4
15. College Heights 4710 College Avenue	5.46	74,406	105,033	3.4
16. Benjamin (Allied Gardens) 5188 Zion Street	7.17	92,272	166,788	9.8
17. San Carlos 7265 Jackson Drive	7.00	89,229	200,097	9.0 (est)
18. Oak Park 2802 - 54th Street	2.67	42,258	47,475	3.1
19. East San Diego 4089 Fairmount Avenue	5.11	70,167	125,064	4.0
20. Normal Heights-Kensington 4121 Adams Avenue	2.67	41,233	75,049	5.1
21. Paradise Hills 5922 Rancho Hills Drive	2.67	41,746	63,796	4.3
22. Skyline Hills 480 South Meadowbrook	2.67	43,228	64,766	4.2
23. Logan Heights 811 South 28th Street	3.47	53,806	24,437	1.6
24. Valencia Park 101 - 50th Street	3.89	59,692	38,672	1.4
25. San Ysidro East Park Avenue and San Ysidro Blvd.	2.55	37,848	18,623	.6
26. Bookmobiles	10.00	119,592	158,685	NA
TOTALS	129.65	$1,774,810	2,970,156	

City of San Diego, California	DEPARTMENT/DIVISION	NO.
PROGRAM BUDGET	Library	20.00

Technical Services Program (20.70)

Need - Books and other library materials must be purchased, cataloged and prepared for circulation.

Objectives - To purchase books with bond issue and capital outlay funds for current and new branches; to further the completion of a revision to the Periodical Holdings File, while handling titles currently received; to maintain the number of volumes bound or rebound; to increase the number of materials mended; to classify, catalog and process books for current and new branches; to handle an increased per capita circulation at the Central Library; and to begin recording the percentage of overdue materials recovered for the library system.

Authority - Municipal Code, Chapter II, Article 2, Division 2, Section 22.0201; Article 2, Division 18, Section 22.1801.

General Description - Personnel in this division purchase books and other library materials which have been selected by various Central Library sections and Extension Division branches. Materials are received, tallied with invoices, classified, cataloged and physically prepared for public use. Existing library materials are mended or prepared for shipment to a commercial bindery. A Circulation Section checks out books at the Central Library, handles registration records, and recovers overdue books for the entire library system. The position increase for FY 1975 is provided to assist in the overall processing of volumes in the Order and Catalog Sections. The increase in Non-Personnel Expense for FY 1975 reflects additional expenditures for photocopy services to reduce the backlog in handling overdue notices.

	Actual FY 1973	Current FY 1974	Proposed FY 1975	Final FY 1975
Input				
Staffing (Position-Years)	54.22	55.72	56.72	
(PEP, YEP, etc.)	(8.00)	(2.00)	(2.00)	
Personnel Expense	$449,795	$516,999	$535,265	
Non-Personnel Expense	37,527	42,554	49,328	
TOTAL	$487,322	$559,553	$584,593	
Output				
Volumes ordered for existing agencies	93,309	102,145	108,364	
Volumes ordered for new agencies, not yet open	13,926	15,170	16,094	
Magazine titles currently received	2,196	2,260	2,260	
Number of volumes bound or rebound	24,900	25,000	25,000	
Number of materials mended	7,204	7,500	7,800	
Volumes added to existing agencies	75,857	81,000	86,265	
Volumes added to new agencies not yet open	18,012	19,000	20,235	
New titles added	11,371	12,000	12,660	

FM-100B (REV. 11-73)

City of San Diego, California **PROGRAM BUDGET**	DEPARTMENT/DIVISION Library		NO. 20.00
	Actual FY 1973	Current FY 1974	Proposed FY 1975	Final FY 1975

	Actual FY 1973	Current FY 1974	Proposed FY 1975	Final FY 1975
Title transactions	35,777	38,000	40,356	
Volumes withdrawn	60,756	60,000	60,000	
Total circulation	790,543	806,392	812,298	
Circulation per capita, at Central Library	1.06	1.07	1.08	
Percentage of overdue materials recovered for entire library system	NA	NA	NA	

Serra Research Center Program (20.80)

Need - The public needs additional library resources to supplement the City library system.

Objectives - Short-range plans are determined by the Executive Committee of the Serra Regional Library System.

Authority - State of California Education Code, Section 27111-27146, and Administrative Code, Title 5, Chapter 2; Joint Powers Agreement, July 5, 1967, (City Clerk Document 713880).

General Description - Under the 1964 Public Library Services Act, the State of California and twelve public and county libraries in San Diego and Imperial Counties are organized into the library cooperative called the Serra Regional Library System. The Serra Research Center, located in the City's Central Library Building, is financed by this system.

The Research Center uses the San Diego Public Library's resources to answer research questions, and to supply books that are not available to member libraries. If answers or books are unobtainable from the San Diego Public Library, the Center calls on the State Library in Sacramento or the Southern California Regional Resource Center at the Los Angeles Public Library.

	Actual FY 1973	Current FY 1974	Proposed FY 1975	Final FY 1975
Input				
Staffing (Position-Years)	4.00	2.50	2.50	
Personnel Expense	$33,224	$28,719	$28,551	
Non-Personnel Expense	262	250	250	
TOTAL	$33,486	$28,969	$28,801	
Output				
Author, title & record requests:				
Received	10,749	11,716	12,770	
Filled by Serra	6,266	7,029	7,662	
Forwarded to other libraries	3,480	3,749	4,086	

City of San Diego, California **PROGRAM BUDGET**	DEPARTMENT/DIVISION	Library		NO. 20.00

	Actual FY 1973	Current FY 1974	Proposed FY 1975	Final FY 1975
Subject requests:				
Received	606	650	700	
Filled by Serra	551	592	637	
Forwarded to other libraries	·55	58	63	
Materials sent	933	1,000	1,200	
Photocopied pages sent	193	257	342	
Reference requests:				
Received	1,651	1,675	1,725	
Answered	1,608	1,631	1,679	
Forwarded to other libraries	43	44	46	
Materials sent	1,115	1,550	2,155	
Photocopied pages sent	2,602	3,500	4,500	
Photocopy requests:				
Received	383	550	825	
Photocopied pages sent	1,928	2,750	4,125	
Forwarded to other libraries	52	74	111	

Governmental Reference Library Program (20.90)

Need - City and County employees require specialized library resources for operational and planning purposes, and for professional development.

Objectives - To maintain or increase the amount of library materials available, per City-County employee; to maintain or increase the usage of library materials; to maintain or increase the answering of information and reference questions.

Authority - 1966 Agreement with the County of San Diego.

General Description - The Governmental Reference Library is located in the County Administration Building. It is jointly supported by the County and the City, and is staffed by the City Library. The collection consists of books, periodicals, reports, surveys, pamphlets, and other materials which pertain to government operations.

	Actual FY 1973	Current FY 1974	Proposed FY 1975	Final FY 1975
Input				
Staffing (Position-Years)	4.00	4.00	4.00	
(PEP, YEP, etc.)	(1.00)	(1.00)	(1.00)	
Personnel Expense	$41,049	$44,452	$45,758	
Non-Personnel Expense	15,288	17,447	18,310	
TOTAL	$56,337	$61,899	$64,068	
Output				
Library materials available, per City-County employee (full-time equivalent)	2.5	2.5	2.5	
Total circulation	57,054	58,081	58,499	
Materials circulated, per City-County employee (full-time equivalent)	4.0	4.0	4.0	
Information and reference questions, per City-County employee (full-time equivalent)	2.0	2.0	2.0	

FM-100B (REV. 11-73)

City of San Diego, California POSITION AND SALARY SCHEDULE		DEPARTMENT/DIVISION LIBRARY					NO. 2000	
Salary Rate		Position Title	Position Years			Current Budget	FISCAL 1975	
Current	Final		Current Budget	Proposed Budget	Final Budget		Proposed	Final
2010		ADMINISTRATION DIVISION						
		FULL-TIME POSITIONS						
U/C		CITY LIBRARIAN	1.00	1.00		22,526	22,603	
U/C		ASST CITY LIBRARIAN	1.00	1.00		18,938	19,001	
43.5		ASSOC ADMIN ANALYST	1.00	1.00		14,788	15,034	
42.5		SUPV LIBRARIAN	1.00	1.00		15,171	15,242	
39.5		SENIOR LIBRARIAN	1.00	1.00		13,257	13,457	
39.0		PUB INFORMATION OFF	1.00	1.00		12,587	12,632	
35.1		PRINCIPAL CLERK	1.00	1.00		10,711	10,711	
32.6		SENIOR STENOGRAPHER	1.00	1.00		9,367	9,579	
29.6		INTER STENOGRAPHER	1.00	1.00		7,887	7,961	
28.1		INTERMEDIATE CLERK	1.00	1.00		7,283	7,491	
28.1		INTERMEDIATE TYPIST	2.00	2.00		14,960	14,982	
24.1		JUNIOR CLERK	1.00	1.00		5,913	6,107	
24.1		JUNIOR TYPIST	1.00	1.00		5,814	6,003	
		UNUSED SICK LEAVE				945	1,002	
		2010 TOTAL	14.00	14.00		160,147	161,805	
2020		CENTRAL LIBRARY DIV						
		FULL-TIME POSITIONS						
45.5		PRINCIPAL LIBRARIAN	1.00	1.00		17,682	17,682	
42.5		SUPV LIBRARIAN	5.00	5.00		75,855	76,210	
39.5		SENIOR LIBRARIAN	7.00	7.00		92,799	94,199	
36.5		LIBRARIAN	18.89	19.56		214,042	221,048	
33.0		LIBRARY ASSISTANT	1.00	2.00		9,298	18,596	
32.1		SENIOR CLERK	2.00	2.00		18,462	18,478	
28.1		INTERMEDIATE CLERK	.50	3.00		3,641	22,473	
28.1		INTERMEDIATE TYPIST	16.00	16.00		119,680	119,856	
27.5		CUSTODIAN II	1.00	1.00		7,397	7,562	
27.5		GUARD	1.00	1.00		7,947	7,987	
24.1		JUNIOR CLERK	4.00	4.00		23,652	24,428	
		UNUSED SICK LEAVE				3,891	4,334	
		2020 TOTAL FULL TIME	57.39	61.56		594,346	632,853	
		PART-TIME POSITIONS						
36.5		LIBRARIAN	1.22	1.22		13,795	13,787	
19.1		STUDENT WORKER	12.00	12.00		53,352	56,880	
		2020 TOTAL PART TIME	13.22	13.22		67,147	70,667	
		2020 TOTAL F/T & P/T	70.61	74.78		661,493	703,520	
2030		EXTENSION DIVISION						
		FULL-TIME POSITIONS						
45.5		PRINCIPAL LIBRARIAN	1.00	1.00		17,682	17,682	
42.5		SUPV LIBRARIAN	2.00	2.00		30,342	30,484	
39.5		SENIOR LIBRARIAN	15.66	16.00		207,604	215,312	
36.5		LIBRARIAN	30.66	31.00		347,408	350,331	
33.0		LIBRARY ASSISTANT	6.66	7.00		61,924	65,086	
32.1		SENIOR CLERK	1.00	1.00		9,231	9,239	
29.1		BOOKMOBILE DRIVER	6.00	6.00		46,284	47,136	
28.1		INTERMEDIATE CLERK		3.00			22,473	
28.1		INTERMEDIATE TYPIST	49.48	48.50		370,110	363,314	

FM-100D [11-73]

| Salary Rate | | Position Title | Position Years | | | Current Budget | FISCAL 1975 | |
Current	Final		Current Budget	Proposed Budget	Final Budget		Proposed	Final

City of San Diego, California
POSITION AND SALARY SCHEDULE

DEPARTMENT/DIVISION LIBRARY

NO. 2000

Salary Rate		Position Title	Position Years			Current Budget	FISCAL 1975	
Current	Final		Current Budget	Proposed Budget	Final Budget		Proposed	Final
25.1		AUTO MESSENGER	2.00	2.00		12,814	12,998	
24.1		JUNIOR CLERK	3.00	2.00		17,739	12,214	
24.1		JUNIOR TYPIST	2.00	3.00		11,628	18,009	
		UNUSED SICK LEAVE				7,289	7,870	
		2030 TOTAL FULL TIME	119.46	122.50		1,140,055	1,172,148	
		PART-TIME POSITIONS						
36.5		LIBRARIAN	1.00	1.00		11,308	11,301	
19.1		STUDENT WORKER	19.73	19.81		87,719	93,899	
		2030 TOTAL PART TIME	20.73	20.81		99,027	105,200	
		2030 TOTAL F/T & P/T	140.19	143.31		1,239,082	1,277,348	
2070		TECHNICAL SERVICES DIV						
		FULL-TIME POSITIONS						
45.5		PRINCIPAL LIBRARIAN	1.00	1.00		17,682	17,682	
42.5		SUPV LIBRARIAN	1.00	1.00		15,171	15,242	
39.5		SENIOR LIBRARIAN	1.00	1.00		13,257	13,457	
36.5		LIBRARIAN	2.00	2.00		22,662	22,602	
35.1		PRINCIPAL CLERK	2.00	2.00		21,422	21,422	
33.0		LIBRARY ASSISTANT	1.00			9,298		
32.1		SENIOR CLERK	4.00	5.00		36,924	46,195	
28.1		INTERMEDIATE CLERK	1.00	2.00		7,283	14,982	
28.1		INTERMEDIATE TYPIST	27.00	26.00		231,960	194,766	
27.1		BOOK REPAIRER	1.00	1.00		7,467	7,491	
24.1		ASST BOOK REPAIRER	2.00	2.00		12,442	11,902	
24.1		JUNIOR CLERK	.50			2,956		
24.1		JUNIOR TYPIST	11.58	13.08		67,326	78,519	
		UNUSED SICK LEAVE				2,595	2,772	
		2070 TOTAL FULL TIME	55.08	56.08		438,445	447,032	
		PART-TIME POSITIONS						
19.1		STUDENT WORKER	.64	.64		2,845	3,033	
		2070 TOTAL PART TIME	.64	.64		2,845	3,033	
		2070 TOTAL F/T & P/T	55.72	56.72		441,290	450,065	
2080		SERRA REFERENCE CENTER						
		FULL-TIME POSITIONS						
39.5		SENIOR LIBRARIAN	1.00	1.00		13,257	13,457	
28.1		INTERMEDIATE TYPIST	1.50	1.00		11,220	7,491	
24.1		JUNIOR TYPIST		.50			3,002	
		UNUSED SICK LEAVE				145	147	
		2080 TOTAL	2.50	2.50		24,622	24,097	
2090		GOVERNMENTAL REF LIBRARY						
39.5		SENIOR LIBRARIAN	1.00	1.00		13,257	13,457	
36.5		LIBRARIAN	1.00	1.00		11,331	11,301	
28.1		INTERMEDIATE TYPIST	1.00	1.00		7,480	7,491	
24.1		JUNIOR CLERK		1.00			6,107	

FM-100D (11-73)

	City of San Diego, California **TRAVEL BUDGET**	DEPARTMENT/DIVISION Library				NO. 20.00

Trip No.	Meeting Name or Purpose	Destination	No. of Persons	No. of Nights	Fiscal 1975 Budget Proposed	Final
	General Fund					
1	Annual Conference, American Library Association	San Francisco, CA	2	6	$ 744	
2	California State Library Workshop	Sacramento, CA	1	3	159	
3	Workshop in Librarianship	California	1	2	75	
4	Southern California Technical Process Group	California	1	2	75	
5	League of California Cities	Los Angeles, CA	1	3	197	
6	Review Installation of Automated Library Book Ordering System	Houston, Texas and Denver, CO.	1	6	493	
7	Government Business (15 trips)	California	1	–	375	
	Department Total				$2,118	
	(Current Year Total $2,011) (Prior Year Total $1,325)					

Salary Rate		Position Title	Position Years			Current Budget	FISCAL 1975	
Current	Final		Current Budget	Proposed Budget	Final Budget		Proposed	Final

City of San Diego, California
POSITION AND SALARY SCHEDULE

DEPARTMENT/DIVISION: LIBRARY

NO: 2000

Salary Rate Current	Position Title	Current Budget	Proposed Budget	Final Budget	Current Budget	Proposed	Final
24.1	JUNIOR TYPIST	1.00			5,814		
	UNUSED SICK LEAVE				223	237	
	2090 TOTAL	4.00	4.00		38,105	38,593	
	2000 DEPT FULL TIME	252.43	260.64		2,395,720	2,476,528	
	2000 DEPT PART TIME	34.59	34.67		169,019	178,900	
	2000 DEPT GRAND TOTAL	287.02	295.31		2,564,739	2,655,428	

City of San Diego, California
PROGRAM BUDGET

CAPITAL IMPROVEMENTS DETAIL

DEPARTMENT/DIVISION: Library   NO. 20.00

NUMBER	TITLE & DESCRIPTION	COMM. AREA	EXPENDITURE ITEM		REVENUE SOURCE	TOTAL COST $	CURRENT FY 1974	L–LAND PURCHASE FINAL FY 1975	PROPOSED FY 1975	D–DESIGN FY 1976	C–CONSTRUCTION FY 1977	PROJECTED FY 1978	F–FURNISHINGS FY 1979	FY 1980
35-033	74/79 LOGAN HEIGHTS LIBRARY — Acquire site and construct branch library (8,000 sq.ft.) as replacement for existing branch; general vicinity of Imperial Avenue and 28th Street.	38	LAND 100,000 / ENGR & CONSTR 400,000 / FURNISH / Books 105,000 / Furniture 35,000		CAPITAL OUTLAY 440,000 / GAS TAX / BONDS / SEWER / WATER / 200,000 Fed-RS	640,000					40,000	DF 140,000	CF 400,000 / 140,000 400,000	
													Revised estimate – 1974 CIP: $521,000	
35-016	74/76 MIRA MESA LIBRARY — Construct (8,000 sq.ft.) branch library on City-owned land; vicinity Mira Mesa Blvd. and New Salem Street.	6	LAND 400,000 / ENGR & CONSTR 400,000 / FURNISH / Books 105,000 / Furniture 35,000		CAPITAL OUTLAY 540,000 / GAS TAX / BONDS / SEWER / WATER / ASSESS. DISTR.	540,000			DF 140,000	CF 400,000				
													Revised estimate – 1974 CIP: $424,000	
35-014	66/70 RANCHO BERNARDO LIBRARY — Acquire site and construct branch library (8,000 sq.ft.); Bernardo Center Drive and Bernardo Plaza Court.	2	LAND 90,400 / ENGR & CONSTR 400,000 / FURNISH / Books 105,000 / Furniture 35,000		CAPITAL OUTLAY 359,000 / GAS TAX / BONDS 271,400 / SEWER / WATER / ASSESS. DISTR.	540,000			DF 103,000	CF 359,000 / 30,000				
													Revised estimate – 1974 CIP: $514,000	
35-049	74/77 SOUTH BAY LIBRARY — Acquire site and construct branch library (10,000 sq.ft.); vicinity Palm Avenue and Beyer Way.	45	LAND 70,000 / ENGR & CONSTR 530,000 / FURNISH / Books 151,000 / Furniture 42,000		CAPITAL OUTLAY 793,000 / GAS TAX / BONDS / SEWER / WATER / ASSESS. DISTR.	793,000			DF 103,000 / 70,000	CF 389,000 / 198,000	CF 525,000			
													Revised estimate – 1974 CIP: $602,000	
35-011	62/67 UNIVERSITY COMMUNITY LIBRARY — Construct library (10,000 sq.ft.), exact location to be determined.	5	LAND 530,000 / ENGR & CONSTR / FURNISH / Books 151,000 / Furniture 42,000		CAPITAL OUTLAY 496,000 / GAS TAX / BONDS 227,000 / SEWER / WATER / ASSESS. DISTR.	793,000	7,000 / 140,000		L 70,000 / 489,000 / 47,000	DF 198,000	CF 525,000			
													Revised estimate – 1974 CIP: $532,000	
35-023	68/72 43RD & LOGAN LIBRARY — Construct branch library on leased land; vicinity of 43rd Street & Logan Avenue.	43	LAND 400,000 / ENGR & CONSTR / FURNISH / Books 105,000 / Furniture 35,000		CAPITAL OUTLAY 540,000 / GAS TAX / BONDS / SEWER / WATER / ASSESS. DISTR.	540,000	DF 147,000 / 426,000		DFC 536,000 / 540,000					Rescheduled from FY 74;
													Revised estimate – 1974 CIP: $426,000	

*SEE APPENDIX FOR GENERAL EXPLANATORY NOTES AND COMMUNITY AREA MAP

City of San Diego, California
PROGRAM BUDGET

CAPITAL IMPROVEMENTS DETAIL

DEPARTMENT/DIVISION   Library   NO. 20.00

SUMMARY OF MAJOR PROJECT CHANGES

PROJECTS CANCELLED:

San Ysidro Library (35-021)

FISCAL
YEAR
SCHEDULED   AMOUNT   EXPLANATION

FY 1977-79 $494,000   A new library building is not required.
                                  Several alternate plans are being con-
                                  sidered.

FM-3 (11-73)

II. FISCAL YEAR 1973-1974

City of San Diego, California FINANCIAL PLAN		BUDGET SUMMARY			
FUND	NO.	DEPARTMENT/DIVISION			NO.
General	100	Library			20.00
CLASSIFICATION		Actual FY 1972	Current FY 1973	Proposed FY 1974	Final FY 1974
Personnel Man-Years		282.41	289.74	287.02	287.02
Operating Budget					
Personal Services		$2,217,055	$2,389,323	$2,399,418	$2,549,651
Non-Personal Expense		619,909	658,243	731,874	731,874
Equipment Outlay		36,359	27,702	31,725	31,725
Total Operating		$2,873,323	$3,075,268	$3,163,017	$3,313,250
Capital Improvements Budget		$ 223,619	$ 197,000	$ 673,000	$ 573,000
TOTAL APPROPRIATION		$3,096,942	$3,272,268	$3,836,017	$3,886,250

REVENUE SOURCES ANALYSIS

	Actual FY 1972	Current FY 1973	Proposed FY 1974	Final FY 1974
Operating Budget				
General Fund	$2,690,427	$2,874,768	$2,940,817	$3,085,450
General Revenue Sharing	--	--	29,000	29,000
County Grants	45,376	60,900	38,500	38,500
Service Charges	137,520	139,600	154,700	160,300
Total Operating	$2,873,323	$3,075,268	$3,163,017	$3,313,250
Capital Improvements Budget				
Capital Outlay	$ 73,958	$ 70,000	$ 427,000	$ 433,000
Bonds	149,661	127,000	140,000	140,000
Other	--	--	106,000	--
Total Capital Improvements	$ 223,619	$ 197,000	$ 673,000	$ 573,000
TOTAL APPROPRIATION	$3,096,942	$3,272,268	$3,836,017	$3,886,250

Department Goals

The primary goal of the Public Library is to be a major source of information, recreation, and research for the population of the City at large. It is predicated on the notion that in an open society free access to information and knowledge is essential. The library serves as the public's cultural and intellectual center for individual self-development, the continuation of education, social growth, business endeavor, and governmental progress.

It is a goal of the Public Library to serve the whole City community by providing high quality library service to all residents of San Diego who have need for books, learning materials, and information.

The library is oriented toward the general public and not just to students in formal education. Therefore there is some emphasis toward serving the non-student adult who does not have access to other libraries. There is also emphasis toward supplying youth with materials that conform to personal interests that are not encompassed in school or college libraries. The library will continue to provide service to all age groups with distinct programs for reaching and assisting children, young adults, adults, and senior citizens.

FM 100 (1-73)

City of San Diego, California FINANCIAL PLAN		BUDGET SUMMARY	
FUND	**NO.**	**DEPARTMENT/DIVISION**	**NO.**
General	100	Library	20.00

PROGRAM REQUIREMENTS ANALYSIS

Man-Years/Program Expenditures

	Actual FY 1972	Current FY 1973	Proposed FY 1974	Final FY 1974
Administration Division (20.01)	14.00 $ 194,353	14.00 $ 210,344	14.00 $ 212,484	14.00 $ 219,865
Central Library Division (20.02)	78.12 $ 932,260	79.12 $ 942,437	70.61 $ 914,505	70.61 $ 949,342
Extension Division (20.03)	128.65 $1,278,349	134.40 $1,415,602	140.19 $1,516,579	140.19 $1,588,572
Technical Services Division (20.04)	53.64 $ 390,308	54.22 $ 417,308	55.72 $ 442,969	55.72 $ 475,594
Serra Reference Center (20.05)	4.00 $ 30,417	4.00 $ 39,611	2.50 $ 23,309	2.50 $ 24,727
Governmental Reference Library (20.09)	4.00 $ 47,636	4.00 $ 49,966	4.00 $ 53,171	4.00 $ 55,150
TOTALS	282.41 $2,873,323	289.74 $3,075,268	287.02 $3,163,017	287.02 $3,313,250

City of San Diego, California **FINANCIAL PLAN**		**PROGRAM DETAIL**	
FUND	NO.	DEPARTMENT/DIVISION	NO.
General	100	Library	20.00

20.01 Administration Program

<u>Need</u> - The administration of the thirty separate Library Department facilities requires the centralized administrative, clerical, fiscal, budgetary, personnel, supply, and public information support provided by the Administrative Program.

<u>Goals</u> - It is the goal of this program, especially through the offices of the City Librarian and Assistant City Librarian, to provide leadership that enhances a high quality of library services; to provide a working environment that allows the staff to function to the utmost of their abilities; and encourages progressive and systematic program planning.

<u>Authority</u> - Municipal Code, Chapter II, Article 2, Division 2, Section 22.0201; Article 2, Division 18, Section 22.1801.

<u>General Description</u> - The City Librarian gives general direction to the department and the Assistant City Librarian provides supervision over departmental operations. Staff members perform administrative analysis, financial and payroll work, children's service coordination, and provide public information.

Input

	Actual FY 1972	Current FY 1973	Proposed FY 1974	Final FY 1974
Personnel Man-Years	14.00	14.00	14.00	14.00
Personal Services	$132,202	$148,893	$151,821	$159,202
Non-Personal Expense	58,643	56,916	58,050	58,050
Equipment Outlay	3,508	4,535	2,613	2,613
TOTAL	$194,353	$210,344	$212,484	$219,865

Output

	Actual FY 1972	Estimated FY 1973	Estimated FY 1974	Revised FY 1974
Employees hired	197	185	200	200
Purchase requisitions/letters written	553	861	1,040	1,040
Departmental supply requests filled	1,684	1,925	2,137	2,137
Releases prepared for broadcast	759	760	760	760
Releases prepared for publication	120	120	120	120
Exhibits prepared	88	90	90	90

20.02 Central Library Program

<u>Need</u> - Demands by the citizens for a comprehensive collection of informational and research resources made up of books, periodicals, microfilm, recordings, maps, pamphlets, and government publications requires a central source for these materials.

<u>Goals</u> - The Central Library Program provides reading materials in a constantly widening range of subjects and types, in anticipation of demand, and on a level to satisfy the needs of a growing cosmopolitan community.

City of San Diego, California FINANCIAL PLAN		PROGRAM DETAIL	
FUND	NO.	DEPARTMENT/DIVISION	NO.
General	100	Library	20.00

It is a goal of this program to provide a developing major information and research center for the community as a whole, to furnish materials for the cultural, industrial, commercial, professional, and civic groups as well as for individuals; to supplement private, school, and special libraries; to provide a resource center for service to children, young adults, senior citizens, shut-ins, the handicapped, the disadvantaged, and minorities.

Authority - Municipal Code, Chapter II, Article 2, Division 2, Section 22.0201; Article 2, Division 18, Section 22.1801.

General Description - Central Library, opened in 1954, is at 8th and E Streets. It includes five adult-oriented sections and a children's section covering all topics and is supplemented by a full depository of United States and State of California documents. The staff selects materials, within budget limits, in anticipation of public use and assists the public in obtaining the most benefit from these resources. The budget for this program includes: a transfer of 10.00 custodial positions, to Buildings Division for functional consolidation, and increased book and periodical requirements of $22,533.

Input

	Actual FY 1972	Current FY 1973	Proposed FY 1974	Final FY 1974
Personnel Man-Years	78.12	79.12	70.61	70.61
Personal Services	$683,696	$678,311	$622,765	$657,602
Non-Personal Expense	237,589	253,312	282,348	282,348
Equipment Outlay	10,975	10,814	9,392	9,392
TOTAL	$932,260	$942,437	$914,505	$949,342

Output

	Actual FY 1972	Estimated FY 1973	Estimated FY 1974	Revised FY 1974
Materials available:				
General circulating volumes	363,083	377,070	394,200	394,200
Reference volumes	73,713	76,550	80,000	80,000
Bound government documents	40,445	41,750	43,200	43,200
Bound periodicals	60,000	63,170	66,600	66,600
Non-book materials	664,827	688,358	711,157	711,157
Total materials available	1,202,068	1,246,898	1,295,157	1,295,157
Materials circulated	816,299	765,940	804,200	806,390
Materials used in library besides those circulated	669,365	628,070	659,450	666,890
Reference questions	733,750	790,762	806,550	806,550

FM 101 (1-73)

City of San Diego, California FINANCIAL PLAN		PROGRAM DETAIL	
FUND	NO.	DEPARTMENT/DIVISION	NO.
General	100	Library	20.00

20.03 Extension Division Program

Need - To provide easy access to library service in various districts of the City.

Goals - The goal of the Extension Division Program is to provide community library collections that fulfill the basic informational and home reading needs of the area served by each branch. It is a further goal that each community library is to carry a wide range of materials with sufficient depth to satisfy local demands. A goal is to design community libraries with sufficient flexibility to adapt to changes in population and demands for new and different materials and information. Where available, audio-visual materials are to be provided to supplement printed resources.

Authority - Municipal Code, Chapter II, Article 2, Division 2, Section 22.0201; Article 2, Division 18, Section 22.1801.

General Description - There are 24 branches, three bookmobiles, and a division headquarters. The branches include: Rancho Bernardo, La Jolla, University Community, North Clairemont, Clairemont, Pacific Beach, Ocean Beach, Point Loma, Balboa, Linda Vista, Serra Mesa, Mission Hills, University Heights, North Park, College Heights, Allied Gardens (Benjamin), Oak Park, East San Diego, Normal Heights-Kensington, Paradise Hills, Skyline Hills, Logan Heights, Valencia Park, and San Ysidro. San Carlos Branch is due to open in Fiscal Year 1973-74. Funds are in the Capital Improvements Program to construct a new branch in the vicinity of 43rd Street and Logan Avenue, and to design the University Community Library which is now in temporary quarters. Bookmobile stops are at about 20 added locations. Besides providing reading and informational resources, program relating to books and reading are conducted for adult and juvenile groups. The budget for this program includes: an increase of 6.79 positions for new branches and extension support; the elimination of one position for custodial services which will be provided by Buildings Division, and increased book and periodical requirements of $29,958.

Input

	Actual FY 1972	Current FY 1973	Proposed FY 1974	Final FY 1974
Personnel Man-Years	128.65	134.40	140.19	140.19
Personal Services	$ 978,527	$1,101,952	$1,159,800	$1,231,793
Non-Personal Expense	286,312	308,412	346,150	346,150
Equipment Outlay	13,510	5,238	10,629	10,629
TOTAL	$1,278,349	$1,415,602	$1,516,579	$1,588,572

Output

	Actual FY 1972	Estimated FY 1973	Estimated FY 1974	Revised FY 1974
Branches operated	22	24	25	25
Bookmobiles operated	3	3	3	3
Materials available:				
General circulating volumes	641,778	666,500	696,800	696,800
Reference volumes	26,737	27,780	29,000	29,000
Non-book materials	9,671	10,173	11,427	11,427
Total materials available	678,186	704,453	737,227	737,227

City of San Diego, California FINANCIAL PLAN		PROGRAM DETAIL	
FUND	**NO.**	**DEPARTMENT/DIVISION**	**NO.**
General	100	Library	20.00

Output (Cont'd)

	Actual FY 1972	Estimated FY 1973	Estimated FY 1974	Revised FY 1974
Materials circulated	2,906,515	2,796,560	2,936,275	2,882,700
Materials used in branches besides those circulated	216,824	193,000	203,000	215,050
Reference questions	493,450	450,654	459,715	459,715

20.04 Technical Services Program

Need - An organizational unit is necessary to purchase, catalog, prepare, and circulate books and other library materials.

Goals - The Technical Services Program, which is housed in the Central Library, has the primary goal of providing efficient support services to the public service sections and branches of the Library Department. These services include ordering, receiving, classifying, cataloging, and processing new books and other reader materials; repairing and binding existing library materials; and controlling book circulation and recovery of overdue books.

Authority - Municipal Code, Chapter II, Article 2, Division 2, Section 22.0201; Article 2, Division 18. Section 22.1801.

General Description - Personnel in this division purchase books which have been selected by various Central Library sections and branches. Books are received, tallied with invoices, classified and cataloged, and physically prepared for public use. A Circulation Section at Central Library checks out books at the Central Library, handles registration records, and recovers overdue books for the whole system. Book cataloging assistance for new branches requires an increase of 1.50 positions.

Input

	Actual FY 1972	Current FY 1973	Proposed FY 1974	Final FY 1974
Personnel Man-Years	53.64	54.22	55.72	55.72
Personal Services	$358,076	$385,733	$406,070	$438,695
Non-Personal Expense	24,432	24,460	29,243	29,243
Equipment Outlay	7,800	7,115	7,656	7,656
TOTAL	$390,308	$417,308	$442,969	$475,594

Output

	Actual FY 1972	Estimated FY 1973	Estimated FY 1974	Revised FY 1974
Overdue book recovery actions	84,158	89,163	90,000	90,000
Books checked out at Central Library	816,299	765,940	804,200	806,390
New titles added	12,136	12,300	14,000	12,000
Title transactions	38,808	38,850	43,000	38,000
Volumes added	122,182	103,000	115,000	100,000
Volumes withdrawn	63,148	70,317	67,000	67,000

FM 101 (1-73)

City of San Diego, California FINANCIAL PLAN		PROGRAM DETAIL	
FUND	NO.	DEPARTMENT/DIVISION	NO.
General	100	Library	20.00

20.05 Serra Research Center

Need – Under the Public Library Service Act (1964), State of California, twelve public and county libraries in San Diego and Imperial Counties are organized into the library cooperative called Serra Regional Library System. The Serra Research Center located in the City's Central Library Building is financed by the System. The Research Center uses San Diego Public Library resources to supply books that are not available to member libraries and answer research questions not answerable by member libraries.

Goals – The goal of the Serra Research Center is to provide an informational clearing house for members of the System so that all residents of San Diego and Imperial Counties will have equal access to full public library resources.

Authority – State of California Education Code, Sections 27111-27146, and Administrative Code, Title 5, Chapter 2; Joint Powers Agreement, July 5, 1967 (City Clerk Document 713880).

General Description – Staff of the research center receive from System libraries requests to answer questions unanswerable in local libraries. Response is made by using books and other materials from the resources of San Diego Public Library. If answers or books are unobtainable from San Diego Public Library, the Center calls on the State Library in Sacramento or the Southern California Regional Resource Center at Los Angeles Public Library. When needed, books from San Diego Public Library are sent to the inquiring library on loan. Questions and answers are received by telephone or teletype. The major change in this program is the elimination of 1.50 positions due to reductions in the Federal funding which support this program.

Input

	Actual FY 1972	Current FY 1973	Proposed FY 1974	Final FY 1974
Personnel Man-Years	4.00	4.00	2.50	2.50
Personal Services	$29,329	$39,061	$23,059	$24,477
Non-Personal Expense	1,088	550	250	250
Equipment Outlay	--	--	--	--
TOTAL	$30,417	$39,611	$23,309	$24,727

20.09 Governmental Reference Library Division

Need – City and County Officers and employees need informational and research resources in their work for operational and planning purposes.

Goals – The goal of this unique library is to provide professional quality materials in reference and research on governmental problems for staffs of the City and of the County of San Diego.

Authority – 1966 Agreement with County of San Diego.

General Description – The Library is located at the County Administration Building. It is jointly supported by the County and the City and staffed by the City Library. The collection consists of books, periodicals, reports, surveys, pamphlets, and other materials which provide informational and research sources.

City of San Diego, California FINANCIAL PLAN		PROGRAM DETAIL		
FUND	NO.	DEPARTMENT/DIVISION		NO.
General	100	Library		20.00

Input

	Actual FY 1972	Current FY 1973	Proposed FY 1974	Final FY 1974
Personnel Man-Years	4.00	4.00	4.00	4.00
Personal Services	$35,225	$35,373	$35,903	$37,882
Non-Personal Expense	11,845	14,593	15,833	15,833
Equipment Outlay	566	--	1,435	1,435
TOTAL	$47,636	$49,966	$53,171	$55,150

Output

	Actual FY 1972	Estimated FY 1973	Estimated FY 1974	Revised FY 1974
Circulation	54,645	57,000	60,000	58,085
Reference and research questions	30,623	34,986	35,675	35,675
Books and other materials added	4,043	4,200	4,200	4,200

CITY OF SAN DIEGO, CALIFORNIA

POSITION AND SALARY SCHEDULE

FUND		FUNCTION			DEPT. NO.	DEPARTMENT		
100		**GENERAL FUND**			**2000**	**LIBRARY**		

| SALARY RATE | | POSITION TITLE | POSITION QUOTA | | | CURRENT BUDGET | FISCAL 1974 | |
PRE-LIM	FINAL		CURRENT BUDGET	PROPOSED BUDGET	FINAL BUDGET		PROPOSED	FINAL
		2001 ADMINISTRATION DIVISION						
		FULL-TIME POSITIONS						
U/C	U/C	CITY LIBRARIAN	1.00	1.00	1.00	22,131	22,126	22,526
U/C	U/C	ASST CITY LIBRARIAN	1.00	1.00	1.00	18,430	18,538	18,938
43.5	43.5	ASSOC ADMIN ANALYST	1.00	1.00	1.00	14,322	14,388	14,788
42.5	42.5	SUPV LIBRARIAN	1.00	1.00	1.00	14,831	14,771	15,171
39.5	39.5	SENIOR LIBRARIAN	1.00	1.00	1.00	12,849	12,857	13,257
39.0	39.0	PUB INFORMATION OFF	1.00	1.00	1.00	11,054	12,187	12,587
34.5	35.1	PRINCIPAL CLERK	1.00	1.00	1.00	10,101	9,999	10,711
32.0	32.6	SENIOR STENOGRAPHER	1.00	1.00	1.00	8,621	8,695	9,367
29.0	29.6	INTER STENOGRAPHER	1.00	1.00	1.00	7,140	7,260	7,887
27.5	28.1	INTERMEDIATE CLERK	1.00	1.00	1.00	6,550	6,674	7,283
27.5	28.1	INTERMEDIATE TYPIST	2.00	2.00	2.00	13,302	13,730	14,960
23.5	24.1	JUNIOR CLERK	1.00	1.00	1.00	4,530	5,346	5,913
23.5	24.1	JUNIOR TYPIST	1.00	1.00	1.00	5,032	5,250	5,814
		2001 TOTAL	14.00	14.00	14.00	148,893	151,821	159,202
		2002 CENTRAL LIBRARY DIV						
		FULL-TIME POSITIONS						
45.5	45.5	PRINCIPAL LIBRARIAN	1.00	1.00	1.00	16,462	17,282	17,682
42.5	42.5	SUPV LIBRARIAN	5.00	5.00	5.00	74,155	73,855	75,855
39.5	39.5	SENIOR LIBRARIAN	7.00	7.00	7.00	89,943	89,999	92,799
36.5	36.5	LIBRARIAN	18.00	18.89	18.89	195,138	206,486	214,042
33.0	33.0	LIBRARY ASSISTANT	1.00	1.00	1.00	8,720	8,898	9,298
31.5	32.1	SENIOR CLERK	2.00	2.00	2.00	17,090	17,126	18,462
31.5		SUPV CUSTODIAN	1.00			8,808		
29.5		CUSTODIAN III	1.00			8,131		
27.5	27.5	CUSTODIAN II	9.00	1.00	1.00	60,750	6,997	7,397
27.5	27.5	GUARD	2.00	1.00	1.00	14,378	7,547	7,947
27.5	28.1	INTERMEDIATE CLERK		.50	.50		3,337	3,641
27.5	28.1	INTERMEDIATE TYPIST	16.00	16.00	16.00	106,416	109,840	119,680
23.5	24.1	JUNIOR CLERK	4.00	4.00	4.00	18,120	21,384	23,652
		2002 TOTAL FULL TIME	67.00	57.39	57.39	618,111	562,751	590,455
		PART-TIME POSITIONS						
39.5		SENIOR LIBRARIAN	.56			7,195		
36.5	36.5	LIBRARIAN	1.22	1.22	1.22	13,041	13,307	13,795
18.5	19.1	STUDENT WORKER	10.34	12.00	12.00	39,964	46,707	53,352
		2002 TOTAL PART TIME	12.12	13.22	13.22	60,200	60,014	67,147
		2002 TOTAL F/T & P/T	79.12	70.61	70.61	678,311	622,765	657,602

Form BD 1334 (7-72)

CITY OF SAN DIEGO, CALIFORNIA

POSITION AND SALARY SCHEDULE

FUND	FUNCTION				DEPT. NO	DEPARTMENT		
100	GENERAL FUND				2000	LIBRARY		

| SALARY RATE | | POSITION TITLE | POSITION QUOTA | | | CURRENT BUDGET | FISCAL 1974 | |
PRE-LIM	FINAL		CURRENT BUDGET	PROPOSED BUDGET	FINAL BUDGET		PROPOSED	FINAL
2003		EXTENSIUN DIVISION						
		FULL-TIME POSITIONS						
45.5	45.5	PRINCIPAL LIBRARIAN	1.00	1.00	1.00	16,462	17,282	17,682
42.5	42.5	SUPV LIBRARIAN	2.00	2.00	2.00	29,662	29,542	30,342
39.5	39.5	SENIOR LIBRARIAN	15.42	15.66	15.66	198,132	201,341	207,604
36.5	36.5	LIBRARIAN	31.42	30.66	30.66	240,624	335,144	347,408
33.0	33.0	LIBRARY ASSISTANT	4.00	6.66	6.66	34,880	59,261	61,924
31.5	32.1	SENIOR CLERK	1.00	1.00	1.00	8,545	8,563	9,231
28.5	29.1	BOOKMOBILE DRIVER	6.00	6.00	6.00	41,856	42,552	46,284
27.5		CUSTODIAN II	1.00			6,750		
27.5	28.1	INTERMEDIATE TYPIST	46.26	49.48	49.48	307,675	339,680	370,110
24.5	25.1	AUTO MESSENGER	2.00	2.00	2.00	11,092	11,650	12,814
23.5	24.1	JUNIOR CLERK	2.00	3.00	3.00	9,060	16,038	17,739
23.5	24.1	JUNIOR TYPIST	2.00	2.00	2.00	10,064	10,500	11,628
		2003 TOTAL FULL TIME	114.10	119.46	119.46	1,014,802	1,071,553	1,132,766
		PART-TIME POSITIONS						
36.5	36.5	LIBRARIAN	1.00	1.00	1.00	10,690	10,908	11,308
27.5		INTERMEDIATE TYPIST	.67			4,456		
18.5	19.1	STUDENT WORKER	18.63	19.73	19.73	72,004	77,339	87,719
		2003 TOTAL PART TIME	20.30	20.73	20.73	87,150	88,247	99,027
		2003 TOTAL F/T & P/T	134.40	140.19	140.19	1,101,952	1,159,800	1,231,793
2004		TECHNICAL SERVICES DIV						
		FULL-TIME POSITIONS						
45.5	45.5	PRINCIPAL LIBRARIAN	1.00	1.00	1.00	16,462	17,282	17,682
42.5	42.5	SUPV LIBRARIAN	1.00	1.00	1.00	14,831	14,771	15,171
39.5	39.5	SENIOR LIBRARIAN	1.00	1.00	1.00	12,849	12,857	13,257
36.5	36.5	LIBRARIAN	2.00	2.00	2.00	21,682	21,862	22,662
34.5	35.1	PRINCIPAL CLERK	2.00	2.00	2.00	20,202	19,998	21,422
33.0	33.0	LIBRARY ASSISTANT		1.00	1.00		8,898	9,298
31.5	32.1	SENIOR CLERK	4.00	4.00	4.00	34,180	34,252	36,924
27.5	28.1	INTERMEDIATE CLERK	1.00	1.00	1.00	6,550	6,674	7,283
27.5	28.1	INTERMEDIATE TYPIST	27.00	27.00	27.00	179,577	185,355	201,960
26.5	27.1	BOOK REPAIRER	1.00	1.00	1.00	6,839	6,853	7,467
23.5	24.1	ASST BOOK REPAIRER	2.00	2.00	2.00	11,818	11,290	12,442
23.5	24.1	JUNIOR CLERK		.50	.50		2,673	2,956
23.5	24.1	JUNIOR TYPIST	11.58	11.58	11.58	58,270	60,795	67,326
		2004 TOTAL FULL TIME	53.58	55.08	55.08	383,260	403,560	435,850

Form BD 1334 (7-72)

CITY OF SAN DIEGO, CALIFORNIA

POSITION AND SALARY SCHEDULE

FUND		FUNCTION				DEPT. NO.	DEPARTMENT		
100		GENERAL FUND				2000	LIBRARY		
SALARY RATE		POSITION TITLE	POSITION QUOTA			CURRENT BUDGET	FISCAL 1974		
PRE-LIM	FINAL		CURRENT BUDGET	PROPOSED BUDGET	FINAL BUDGET		PROPOSED	FINAL	
2004		TECHNICAL SERVICES DIV (CONTINUED)							
		PART-TIME POSITIONS							
18.5	19.1	STUDENT WORKER	.64	.64	.64	2,473	2,510	2,845	
		2004 TOTAL PART TIME	.64	.64	.64	2,473	2,510	2,845	
		2004 TOTAL F/T & P/T	54.22	55.72	55.72	385,733	406,070	438,695	
2005		SERRA REFERENCE CENTER							
		FULL-TIME POSITIONS							
39.5	39.5	SENIOR LIBRARIAN	1.00	1.00	1.00	12,849	12,857	13,257	
36.5		LIBRARIAN	1.00			10,841			
33.0		LIBRARY ASSISTANT	1.00			8,720			
27.5	28.1	INTERMEDIATE TYPIST	1.00	1.50	1.50	6,651	10,202	11,220	
		2005 TOTAL	4.00	2.50	2.50	39,061	23,059	24,477	
2009		GOVERNMENTAL REF LIBRARY							
39.5	39.5	SENIOR LIBRARIAN	1.00	1.00	1.00	12,849	12,857	13,257	
36.5	36.5	LIBRARIAN	1.00	1.00	1.00	10,841	10,931	11,331	
27.5	28.1	INTERMEDIATE TYPIST	1.00	1.00	1.00	6,651	6,865	7,480	
23.5	24.1	JUNIOR TYPIST	1.00	1.00	1.00	5,032	5,250	5,814	
		2009 TOTAL	4.00	4.00	4.00	35,373	35,903	37,882	
		2000 DEPT FULL TIME	256.68	252.43	252.43	2,239,500	2,248,647	2,380,632	
		2000 DEPT PART TIME	33.06	34.59	34.59	149,823	150,771	169,019	
		2000 DEPT GRAND TOTAL	289.74	287.02	287.02	2,389,323	2,399,418	2,549,651	

Form BD 1334 (7-72)

CITY OF SAN DIEGO, CALIFORNIA
CAPITAL IMPROVEMENT BUDGET DETAIL

2000 LIBRARY DEPARTMENT

PROJECT TITLE	PROJECT NO.	ACTUAL FY 1972	CURRENT FY 1973	PROPOSED FY 1974	FINAL FY 1974
BALBOA BRANCH LIBRARY	35010	78,886			
UNIVERSITY COMMUNITY LIBRARY	35011		40,000	141,000	147,000
SAN CARLOS BRANCH LIBRARY	35013	140,950			
RANCHO BERNARDO LIBRARY	35014		60,000		
NORTH PARK BRANCH LIBRARY PARKING	35022		27,000		
43RD AND LOGAN BRANCH LIBRARY	35023		70,000	532,000	426,000
LINDA VISTA LIBRARY- PARKING	35025	3,783			
TOTAL – ALL PROJECTS		223,619	197,000	673,000	573,000

III. FISCAL YEAR 1972-1973

CITY OF SAN DIEGO, CALIFORNIA

DEPARTMENTAL BUDGET

FUND	FUNCTION		DEPT. NO.	DEPARTMENT	
100	Cultural Programs		20.00	Library	

CLASSIFICATION	FISCAL 1971 ACTUAL EXPENDITURES	CURRENT BUDGET	FISCAL 1973 BUDGET	
			PROPOSED	FINAL
SUMMARY				
POSITIONS	271.70	282.41	289.74	289.74
PERSONAL SERVICES	$2,063,746	$2,231,336	$2,283,003	$2,389,323
NON-PERSONAL EXPENSE	594,635	624,484	658,963	658,243
EQUIPMENT OUTLAY	2,098	34,394	27,702	27,702
TOTAL BUDGET	$2,660,479	$2,890,214	$2,969,668	$3,075,268

BUDGET SUMMARY

Description of Purpose and Functions

The purpose of the Library Department is to provide reading and reference materials and informa-
tional services to the general public. During the current year the department operated
twenty-seven facilities: the Central Library, twenty-two branches, three bookmobiles, and the
Governmental Reference Library. The department is divided into four divisions: Administration,
Central Library, Extension, and Technical Services. In addition, the Governmental Reference
Library serves City and County offices and employees, and is jointly supported by the City and
County.

The Board of Library Commissioners, which is appointed by the Mayor, advises the City Council,
through the City Manager, on all questions of library policy.

The department continues its participation in the cooperative Serra Library System. The Serra
System, which is funded by grants from the State and Federal Governments, provides for enrichment
of book collections and improved library services for readers in communities of member libraries
through financial assistance and inter-library cooperation. The San Diego County Library and all
municipal libraries of San Diego and Imperial Counties are members of the Serra System.

On November 8, 1971 the Library Department instituted a four week, no renewal, book loan period
which replaced the previous two week loan period. Reductions in estimated circulation figures for
the current fiscal year and 1973 reflect this new policy.

FORM BD-1332 (REV. 12-71)

CITY OF SAN DIEGO, CALIFORNIA

DEPARTMENTAL BUDGET

FUND	FUNCTION	DEPT. NO.	DEPARTMENT
100	Cultural Programs	20.00	Library

Significant Work Load Statistics (Department-wide)

	Actual Fiscal 1970	Actual Fiscal 1971	Estimated Fiscal 1972	Estimated Fiscal 1973
Book Stock (on June 30)	991,097	1,066,106	1,132,000	1,211,000
Books per Capita (excl. military)	1.53	1.57	1.60	1.65
Books Purchased	100,721	90,974	98,000	105,600
New Titles Added	14,772	15,706	14,500	15,500
Library Materials Circulated	3,736,346	4,010,061	3,950,000	4,045,000
Change from Prior Year	+3.2%	+7.3%	-1.5%	+2.4%
Circulation per Capita (excl. military)	5.76	5.92	5.67	5.65
Books Cataloged	108,367	100,351	106,000	107,700
Registered Borrowers	254,020	266,062	278,000	290,000
Reference Questions	1,157,211	1,246,596	1,310,000	1,390,000
Change from Prior Year	+2.2%	+7.7%	+5.1%	+6.1%

Change from Current Year (Department-wide)

Total positions are increased 7.33 primarily due to the addition of two new library branches in Fiscal 1973. Additional staffing and normal salary adjustments result in a Personal Services increase of $51,667. Non-Personal Expense is increased by $34,479 primarily due to requirements for the two new branches, additional books and periodicals, increased binding costs, and increased need for office equipment rental. Equipment Outlay is decreased by $6,692. Total requirements of the department are up $79,454 or +2.7%.

ACTIVITY ANALYSIS

20.01 ADMINISTRATION DIVISION

	Actual Fiscal 1971	Current Fiscal 1972	Proposed Fiscal 1973	Final Fiscal 1973
Positions	13.00	14.00	14.00	14.00
Personal Services	$133,929	$140,971	$142,967	$148,893
Non-Personal Expense	52,438	57,488	59,475	58,755
Total Activity Budget	$186,367	$198,459	$202,442	$207,648

Program Description - This division provides planning, direction, and coordination of all library programs; budget control; public relations; and general supervision and clerical support for the library system. It includes the City Librarian's office, Assistant City Librarian's office, the Coordinators of Children's and Young Adult services, and the Library Business office.

CITY OF SAN DIEGO, CALIFORNIA

DEPARTMENTAL BUDGET

FUND	FUNCTION	DEPT. NO.	DEPARTMENT
100	Cultural Programs	20.00	Library

Change from Current Year

Personal Services

No change in positions.

Non-Personal Expense

Reduced requirements for transportation allowance (-$400); postage (-$1,440); and printing reports (-$150) based on experience.	- $1,990
Increased requirements for office supplies based on actual experience during the current year (+$1,405) and the addition of the San Carlos and the University Community Branches (+$1,200).	+ 2,605
Increase in trash disposal service charge for the Central Library and increased costs of custodial supplies (+$564); increase in microfilm requirements based on current year experience and the addition of two new branches (+$558); and increase in memberships (+$250).	+ 1,372
Total	+ $1,987

20.02 CENTRAL LIBRARY

	Actual Fiscal 1971	Current Fiscal 1972	Proposed Fiscal 1973	Final Fiscal 1973
Positions	78.12	78.12	79.12	79.12
Personal Services	$625,341	$637,428	$647,604	$678,311
Non-Personal Expense	247,870	246,241	253,312	253,312
Total Activity Budget	$873,211	$883,669	$900,916	$931,623

Program Description - This division operates the Central Library, selects books and other library materials for the library system, provides Central Library book lending and informational services and sponsors special library services such as lectures, displays, book talks, special music concerts, story hours, and school class visits.

The Central Library includes the Central Children's Room and five adult sections: Art and Music; History and World Affairs; Literature and Languages; Science and Industry, including a depository for U.S. and State Government Documents; and Social Sciences.

Significant Work Load Statistics

	Actual Fiscal 1970	Actual Fiscal 1971	Estimated Fiscal 1972	Estimated Fiscal 1973
Circulation of library materials	761,256	866,940	820,730	817,600
Reference questions	647,235	673,234	679,000	684,000

FORM BD-1333 (REV. 12-69)

DEPARTMENTAL BUDGET

FUND	FUNCTION	DEPT. NO.	DEPARTMENT
100	Cultural Programs	20.00	Library

Change from Current Year

Personal Services

New part-time position required to substitute for professional personnel due to sick and vacation leave.   + 1.00 Librarian

Non-Personal Expense

Book and periodical requirements increased due to the addition of new titles and increased unit costs.   + $11,685

Reduced need for miscellaneous contractual services based on experience.   - 2,000

Reduction in repair and upkeep of equipment based on experience.   - 1,400

Miscellaneous adjustments: water and sewer service charge (-$550); motive equipment rental (-$500); binding (-$164).   - 1,214

Total   + $ 7,071

20.03 EXTENSION DIVISION

	Actual Fiscal 1971	Current Fiscal 1972	Proposed Fiscal 1973	Final Fiscal 1973
Positions	122.94	128.65	134.40	134.40
Personal Services	$ 920,707	$1,015,062	$1,053,684	$1,101,952
Non-Personal Expense	270,593	281,235	308,412	308,412
Total Activity Budget	$1,191,300	$1,296,297	$1,362,096	$1,410,364

Program Description - This division provides community library services through branch libraries and bookmobiles. This is accomplished by providing assistance to library patrons and by encouraging the reading of books through story hours, school class visits, booklists, displays, and book talks.

This budget includes funds for the operation of two new branch libraries. The interim University Community Branch is expected to open January 1, 1973 in leased facilities, and the scheduled opening date for the new San Carlos Branch is March 1, 1973.

CITY OF SAN DIEGO, CALIFORNIA

DEPARTMENTAL BUDGET

FUND	FUNCTION	DEPT. NO.	DEPARTMENT
100	Cultural Programs	20.00	Library

Significant Work Load Statistics

Branch Circulation	Actual Fiscal 1970	Actual Fiscal 1971	Estimated Fiscal 1972	Estimated Fiscal 1973
Balboa	--	--	95,000	93,000
Benjamin	216,796	226,042	221,000	218,000
Clairemont	235,864	247,097	239,000	236,000
College Heights	163,479	167,469	164,000	162,000
East San Diego	137,095	142,753	135,000	133,000
La Jolla	202,602	214,070	209,000	206,000
Linda Vista	88,898	105,572	99,000	98,000
Logan Heights	25,049	25,729	24,000	24,000
Mission Hills	80,729	83,569	79,000	78,000
Normal Heights - Kensington	77,711	79,937	79,000	78,000
North Clairemont	299,729	311,261	308,400	304,250
North Park	153,607	161,618	159,000	156,000
Oak Park	62,052	58,371	57,000	57,000
Ocean Beach	121,360	133,452	131,000	130,000
Pacific Beach	213,645	231,017	224,000	221,000
Paradise Hills	74,799	74,454	71,000	70,000
Point Loma	191,251	200,394	192,000	189,000
San Carlos	--	--	--	100,000
San Ysidro	15,300	15,560	15,000	15,000
Serra Mesa	207,586	220,064	213,000	210,000
Skyline Hills	72,880	81,419	77,000	76,000
University Community	--	--	--	39,000
University Heights	66,561	73,297	68,000	67,000
Valencia Park	48,938	46,519	46,000	46,000
Bookmobile I	84,130	89,861	74,000	73,000
Bookmobile II	--	30,621	63,000	62,000
Bookmobile III	86,396	76,362	42,000	42,000
Total	2,926,457	3,096,508	3,084,400	3,183,250

FORM BD-1333 (REV. 12-69)

CITY OF SAN DIEGO, CALIFORNIA

DEPARTMENTAL BUDGET

FUND	FUNCTION	DEPT. NO.	DEPARTMENT
100	Cultural Programs	20.00	Library

Change from Current Year

Personal Services

Staffing for new San Carlos Branch scheduled to
open March 1, 1973. Staffing level determined
by branch staffing formula, which is based
primarily on circulation statistics.

+ 0.42 Senior Librarian
+ 0.92 Librarian
+ 1.26 Intermediate Typist
+ 0.48 Student Worker

Staffing for the University Community
Branch scheduled to open January 1, 1973. Staffing
Staffing level determined by branch staffing
formula, which is based primarily on circulation
statistics.

+ 0.50 Librarian
+ 0.50 Intermediate Typist
+ 0.34 Student Worker

New part-time position required to substitute
for professional personnel due to sick and
vacation leave.

+ 1.00 Librarian

Required to provide bilingual assistance to San
Ysidro Branch patrons.

+ 0.33 Student Worker

Total

+ 5.75 Positions

Non-Personal Expense

Increase in book fund due to addition of new
titles and increased unit costs (+$15,520); addi-
tional periodicals for new San Carlos and
University Community Branches (+$1,075) and renew-
al of existing periodical titles at increased rates
(+$1,196) for other branches.

+ $17,791

Estimated six month rental for the interim
University Community Branch building.

+   4,050

Increased cost for rebinding books, documents, and
periodicals, based on estimated number of volumes
to be bound and increased unit cost under the
present binding contract.

+   2,883

Increased motive equipment rental rates (+$1,586),
and increased usage (+$229).

+   1,815

Increased requirements for water service charge
(+$310); and book jackets (+$328) due to the addi-
of the two new branches.

+   638

Total

+ $27,177

CITY OF SAN DIEGO, CALIFORNIA

DEPARTMENTAL BUDGET

FUND	FUNCTION	DEPT. NO.	DEPARTMENT
100	Cultural Programs	20.00	Library

20.04 TECHNICAL SERVICES

	Actual Fiscal 1971	Current Fiscal 1972	Proposed Fiscal 1973	Final Fiscal 1973
Positions	53.64	53.64	54.22	54.22
Personal Services	$349,336	$366,223	$367,597	$385,733
Non-Personal Expense	13,677	18,638	22,621	22,621
Total Activity Budget	$363,013	$384,861	$390,218	$408,354

Program Description - The Technical Services Division is responsible for the ordering, classification, cataloging, and conservation of books and other library materials. In addition, the division furnishes various services in support of the registration and book lending activities of the Central Library, branch libraries, and bookmobiles.

Significant Work Load Statistics

	Actual Fiscal 1970	Actual Fiscal 1971	Estimated Fiscal 1972	Estimated Fiscal 1973
Catalog cards produced	490,850	483,995	510,000	525,000
Registrations	89,445	92,833	96,500	100,000
Delinquency actions	101,148	81,686	83,000	85,000
Books and pamphlets repaired and reinforced	6,687	5,824	6,000	6,000

Change from Current Year

Personal Services

New position required due to increased clerical work load in the Order Section.   + 0.58 Junior Typist

Non-Personal Expense

Increased office equipment rental due to acquisition of two new photocopy machines required for production of book catalog cards and duplication of book purchase orders.   + $4,983

Reduced requirements for contractual catalog service.   - 1,000

Total   + $3,983

CITY OF SAN DIEGO, CALIFORNIA

DEPARTMENTAL BUDGET

FUND	FUNCTION	DEPT. NO.	DEPARTMENT
100	Cultural Programs	20.00	Library

20.05 SERRA REFERENCE CENTER

	Actual Fiscal 1971	Current Fiscal 1972	Proposed Fiscal 1973	Final Fiscal 1973
Positions	-0-	4.00	4.00	4.00
Personal Services	$ --	$37,834	$37,332	$39,061
Non-Personal Expense	--	9,000	550	550
Total Activity Budget	$ --	$46,834	$37,882	$39,611

Program Description - The Serra Reference Center, located in the Central Library, is a part of the regional Serra Reference System. The center provides Serra Reference System members with informational services and an inter-library loan program. All expenses incurred in this activity are reimbursed through State and Federal grants.

Change from Current Year

Personal Services

No change in positions.

Non-Personal Expense

Charges for telephone and telegraph will be billed directly to the Serra System's Fiscal Agent (San Diego County) during Fiscal 1973.	- $5,300
Reduction in transportation allowance (-$200), postage (-$2,600), and unclassified materials and supplies (-$350) based on current year experience.	- 3,150
Total	- $8,450

20.09 GOVERNMENTAL REFERENCE LIBRARY

	Actual Fiscal 1971	Current Fiscal 1972	Proposed Fiscal 1973	Final Fiscal 1973
Positions	4.00	4.00	4.00	4.00
Personal Services	$34,433	$33,818	$33,819	$35,373
Non-Personal Expense	10,057	11,882	14,593	14,593
Total Activity Budget	$44,490	$45,700	$48,412	$49,966

Program Description - This section operates an information library for City and County offices and is located in the County Administration Building. The City is reimbursed by the County for one-half of the annual operating costs.

FORM BD-1333 (REV. 12-69)

CITY OF SAN DIEGO, CALIFORNIA

DEPARTMENTAL BUDGET

FUND	FUNCTION	DEPT. NO.	DEPARTMENT
100	Cultural Programs	20.00	Library

Significant Work Load Statistics

	Actual Fiscal 1970	Actual Fiscal 1971	Estimated Fiscal 1972	Estimated Fiscal 1973
Circulation	48,633	46,613	44,870	44,150
Reference questions	21,651	21,549	22,000	22,500

Change from Current Year

Personal Services

No change in positions.

Non-Personal Expense

Book (+$2,295) and periodical (+$507) requirements increased due to addition of new titles and increase in unit costs.	+ $2,802
Miscellaneous adjustments.	⁻ 91
Total	+ $2,711

CITY OF SAN DIEGO, CALIFORNIA

POSITION AND SALARY SCHEDULE

SALARY RATE		POSITION TITLE	POSITION QUOTA			CURRENT BUDGET	FISCAL 1973	
PRE-LIM	FINAL		CURRENT BUDGET	PROPOSED BUDGET	FINAL BUDGET		PROPOSED	FINAL

FUND **100** — FUNCTION **CULTURAL PROGRAMS** — DEPT. NO. **2000** — DEPARTMENT **LIBRARY**

SALARY PRE-LIM	SALARY FINAL	POSITION TITLE	CURRENT BUDGET (QUOTA)	PROPOSED BUDGET (QUOTA)	FINAL BUDGET (QUOTA)	CURRENT BUDGET	PROPOSED	FINAL
2001		**ADMINISTRATION DIVISION**						
		FULL-TIME POSITIONS						
U/C	U/C	CITY LIBRARIAN	1.00	1.00	1.00	20,668	21,871	22,131
U/C	U/C	ASST CITY LIBRARIAN	1.00	1.00	1.00	16,199	17,722	18,430
42.5	43.5	ASSOC ADMIN ANALYST	1.00	1.00	1.00	13,801	13,640	14,322
41.5	42.5	SUPV LIBRARIAN	1.00	1.00	1.00	14,016	14,125	14,831
38.5	39.5	SENIOR LIBRARIAN	1.00	1.00	1.00	12,119	12,297	12,849
38.0	39.0	PUB INFORMATION OFF	1.00	1.00	1.00	11,006	10,528	11,054
33.5	34.5	PRINCIPAL CLERK	1.00	1.00	1.00	9,607	9,620	10,101
31.0	32.0	SENIOR STENOGRAPHER	1.00	1.00	1.00	8,298	8,210	8,621
28.0	29.0	INTER STENOGRAPHER	1.00	1.00	1.00	7,014	6,800	7,140
26.5	27.5	INTERMEDIATE CLERK	1.00	1.00	1.00	6,336	6,238	6,550
26.5	27.5	INTERMEDIATE TYPIST	2.00	2.00	2.00	12,818	12,810	13,302
22.5	23.5	JUNIOR CLERK	1.00	1.00	1.00	4,211	4,314	4,530
22.5	23.5	JUNIOR TYPIST	1.00	1.00	1.00	4,878	4,792	5,032
		2001 TOTAL	14.00	14.00	14.00	140,971	142,967	148,893
2002		**CENTRAL LIBRARY DIV**						
		FULL-TIME POSITIONS						
44.5	45.5	PRINCIPAL LIBRARIAN	1.00	1.00	1.00	16,066	15,678	16,462
41.5	42.5	SUPV LIBRARIAN	5.00	5.00	5.00	70,080	70,625	74,155
38.5	39.5	SENIOR LIBRARIAN	7.00	7.00	7.00	84,833	86,079	89,943
35.5	36.5	LIBRARIAN	18.00	18.00	18.00	187,416	185,850	195,138
32.0	33.0	LIBRARY ASSISTANT	1.00	1.00	1.00	8,894	8,305	8,720
30.5	31.5	SENIOR CLERK	2.00	2.00	2.00	16,152	16,276	17,090
30.5	31.5	SUPV CUSTODIAN	1.00	1.00	1.00	8,463	8,389	8,808
28.5	29.5	CUSTODIAN III	1.00	1.00	1.00	7,767	7,744	8,131
26.5	27.5	CUSTODIAN II	9.00	9.00	9.00	57,609	57,861	60,750
26.5	27.5	GUARD	2.00	2.00	2.00	13,156	13,694	14,378
26.5	27.5	INTERMEDIATE TYPIST	16.00	16.00	16.00	102,544	102,480	106,416
22.5	23.5	JUNIOR CLERK	4.00	4.00	4.00	16,844	17,256	18,120
		2002 TOTAL FULL TIME	67.00	67.00	67.00	589,824	590,237	618,111
		PART-TIME POSITIONS						
38.5	39.5	SENIOR LIBRARIAN	.56	.56	.56	6,928	6,886	7,195
35.5	36.5	LIBRARIAN	.22	1.22	1.22	2,243	12,420	13,041
17.5	18.5	STUDENT WORKER	10.34	10.34	10.34	38,433	38,061	39,964
		2002 TOTAL PART TIME	11.12	12.12	12.12	47,604	57,367	60,200
		2002 TOTAL F/T & P/T	78.12	79.12	79.12	637,428	647,604	678,311
2003		**EXTENSION DIVISION**						

Form BD 1334 (7-72)

CITY OF SAN DIEGO, CALIFORNIA

POSITION AND SALARY SCHEDULE

FUND	FUNCTION				DEPT. NO	DEPARTMENT		
100	CULTURAL PROGRAMS				2000	LIBRARY		
SALARY RATE		POSITION TITLE	POSITION QUOTA			CURRENT BUDGET	FISCAL 1973	
PRE LIM	FINAL		CURRENT BUDGET	PROPOSED BUDGET	FINAL BUDGET		PROPOSED	FINAL
2003		EXTENSION DIVISION	(CONTINUED)					
		FULL-TIME POSITIONS						
44.5	45.5	PRINCIPAL LIBRARIAN	1.00	1.00	1.00	16,066	15,678	16,462
41.5	42.5	SUPV LIBRARIAN	2.00	2.00	2.00	28,032	28,250	29,662
38.5	39.5	SENIOR LIBRARIAN	15.00	15.42	15.42	181,785	189,620	198,132
35.5	36.5	LIBRARIAN	30.00	31.42	31.42	312,360	324,412	340,624
32.0	33.0	LIBRARY ASSISTANT	4.00	4.00	4.00	35,576	33,220	34,880
30.5	31.5	SENIOR CLERK	1.00	1.00	1.00	8,076	8,138	8,545
27.5	28.5	BOOKMOBILE DRIVER	6.00	6.00	6.00	43,494	39,864	41,856
26.5	27.5	CUSTODIAN II	1.00	1.00	1.00	6,401	6,429	6,750
26.5	27.5	INTERMEDIATE TYPIST	44.50	46.26	46.26	285,200	296,296	307,675
23.5	24.5	AUTO MESSENGER	2.00	2.00	2.00	10,768	10,564	11,092
22.5	23.5	JUNIOR CLERK	2.00	2.00	2.00	8,422	8,628	9,060
22.5	23.5	JUNIOR TYPIST	2.00	2.00	2.00	9,755	9,584	10,064
		2003 TOTAL FULL TIME	110.50	114.10	114.10	945,936	970,683	1,014,802
		PART-TIME POSITIONS						
35.5	36.5	LIBRARIAN		1.00	1.00		10,181	10,690
26.5	27.5	INTERMEDIATE TYPIST	.67	.67	.67	4,153	4,243	4,456
17.5	18.5	STUDENT WORKER	17.48	18.63	18.63	64,973	68,577	72,004
		2003 TOTAL PART TIME	18.15	20.30	20.30	69,126	83,001	87,150
		2003 TOTAL F/T & P/T	128.65	134.40	134.40	1,015,062	1,053,684	1,101,952
2004		TECHNICAL SERVICES DIV						
		FULL-TIME POSITIONS						
44.5	45.5	PRINCIPAL LIBRARIAN	1.00	1.00	1.00	16,066	15,678	16,462
41.5	42.5	SUPV LIBRARIAN	1.00	1.00	1.00	14,016	14,125	14,831
38.5	39.5	SENIOR LIBRARIAN	1.00	1.00	1.00	12,119	12,297	12,849
35.5	36.5	LIBRARIAN	2.00	2.00	2.00	20,824	20,650	21,682
33.5	34.5	PRINCIPAL CLERK	2.00	2.00	2.00	19,214	19,240	20,202
30.5	31.5	SENIOR CLERK	3.00	3.00	4.00	24,228	24,414	34,180
26.5	27.5	INTERMEDIATE CLERK	1.00	1.00	1.00	6,336	6,239	6,550
26.5	27.5	INTERMEDIATE TYPIST	28.00	28.00	27.00	179,452	179,340	179,577
25.5	26.5	BOOK REPAIRER	1.00	1.00	1.00	6,570	6,513	6,839
22.5	23.5	ASST BOOK REPAIRER	2.00	2.00	2.00	11,362	11,256	11,818
22.5	23.5	JUNIOR TYPIST	11.00	11.58	11.58	53,658	55,491	58,270
		2004 TOTAL FULL TIME	53.00	53.58	53.58	363,845	365,242	383,260
		PART-TIME POSITIONS						
17.5	18.5	STUDENT WORKER	.64	.64	.64	2,378	2,355	2,473
		2004 TOTAL PART TIME	.64	.64	.64	2,378	2,355	2,473
		2004 TOTAL F/T & P/T	53.64	54.22	54.22	366,223	367,597	385,733

Form BD 1334 (7-72)

CITY OF SAN DIEGO, CALIFORNIA

POSITION AND SALARY SCHEDULE

FUND		FUNCTION				DEPT. NO.	DEPARTMENT		
100		CULTURAL PROGRAMS				2000	LIBRARY		

SALARY RATE			POSITION QUOTA				FISCAL 1973	
PRE-LIM	FINAL	POSITION TITLE	CURRENT BUDGET	PROPOSED BUDGET	FINAL BUDGET	CURRENT BUDGET	PROPOSED	FINAL
2005		SERRA REFERENCE CENTER						
		FULL-TIME POSITIONS						
38.5	39.5	SENIOR LIBRARIAN	1.00	1.00	1.00	12,119	12,297	12,849
35.5	36.5	LIBRARIAN	1.00	1.00	1.00	10,412	10,325	10,841
32.0	33.0	LIBRARY ASSISTANT	1.00	1.00	1.00	8,894	8,305	8,720
26.5	27.5	INTERMEDIATE TYPIST	1.00	1.00	1.00	6,409	6,405	6,651
		2005 TOTAL	4.00	4.00	4.00	37,834	37,332	39,061
2009		GOVERNMENTAL REF LIBRARY						
38.5	39.5	SENIOR LIBRARIAN	1.00	1.00	1.00	12,119	12,297	12,849
35.5	36.5	LIBRARIAN	1.00	1.00	1.00	10,412	10,325	10,841
26.5	27.5	INTERMEDIATE TYPIST	1.00	1.00	1.00	6,405	6,405	6,651
22.5	23.5	JUNIOR TYPIST	1.00	1.00	1.00	4,878	4,792	5,032
		2009 TOTAL	4.00	4.00	4.00	33,818	33,819	35,373
		2000 DEPT FULL TIME	252.50	256.68	256.68	2,112,228	2,140,280	2,239,500
		2000 DEPT PART TIME	29.91	33.06	33.06	119,108	142,723	149,823
		2000 DEPT GRAND TOTAL	282.41	289.74	289.74	2,231,336	2,283,003	2,389,323

Form BD 1334 (7-72)

APPENDIX B

PROGRAM ACCOUNTING
PROCEDURES MANUAL

CITY OF SAN DIEGO

PROGRAM ACCOUNTING PROCEDURES MANUAL

CONTENTS

```
┌─────────────────────────────────────────────────────────────┐
│                      CITY OF SAN DIEGO                        │
│     PROGRAM ACCOUNTING PROCEDURES MANUAL                     │
└─────────────────────────────────────────────────────────────┘
```

CITY OF SAN DIEGO	CHAPTER	SECTION
PROGRAM ACCOUNTING PROCEDURES MANUAL	1	1

SUBJECT	PAGE 1 OF 1
JULY 1, 1974 PROGRAM ACCOUNTING PROCEDURES AND REQUIREMENTS	DATE July 1, 1974

At the direction of the City Council, the City has moved from the traditional organizational budget to a program budget.

To properly reflect the program budgets and expenditures, the City Auditor and Comptroller has undertaken the task of developing the systems, procedures and requirements to accomplish this objective.

The following chapters reflect the changes necessary to achieve the directive of the City Council.

Objectives

The objectives of our program accounting systems are: (1) to properly collect and allocate data on a programmatic basis using the existing systems to the maximum extent possible; (2) to provide meaningful, timely and useful management reports upon which the management of the City may base logical decisions; (3) to assure proper reporting and control of City programs; and, (3) to insure maintenance of the fiscal integrity of all funds and accounts of the City.

Requirements

1. All City departments will be required to report hours worked via labor cards. (See Chapter 2, Section 1.)

2. All City departments will be required to use the City-wide job order numbers. (See Chapter 5, Section 1.)

3. Those departments, maintaining "departmental stores" and desiring the proper allocation to Program/Elements of expenses incurred when supplies are distributed, will use the Auditor and Comptroller's "Stock Material Request." (See Chapter 2, Section 5.)

4. All City departments will, in essence, be full cost (must put a job order number or element number in the job order field of all input documents; i.e., DP's, PO's, etc.)

5. To collect "output" data, departments will be required to submit "Work Unit Reports." (See Chapter 2, Section 2.)

6. To properly collect and record xerox usage all departments having auditrons will use the "Photocopy Usage Report." (See Chapter 2, Section 4.)

CITY OF SAN DIEGO	CHAPTER	SECTION
PROGRAM ACCOUNTING PROCEDURES MANUAL	1	2
SUBJECT	PAGE 1 OF 3	
PROGRAM ACCOUNTING TERMINOLOGY	DATE July 1, 1974	

Program
— A major functional endeavor which fulfills statutory or policy requirements and which is defined in terms of the principle actions required to achieve a significant end objective.

Element
— A subdivision of a program which comprises the specific products that contribute to a program's objectives.

Auditor's Variance Account
- This will be the last element in each department. It will normally be the first two digits of the department number followed by 98; i.e., 0698, 1198, 1598, etc. This account is used for recording actual expenditures for leaves, vacation, holidays, etc., taken by employees of the department. It will also include labor load accounts, comp time expenditure offsets, etc. This account acts as a balancing account for the department.

Object Account
— An expenditure classification referring to the article purchased or service obtained. The lowest level of budgeting and recording expenditures in appropriations in the City of San Diego (referred to as "line item").

Salaries and Wages
— This term is used to replace the present term "Personal Services" (Object Account 1151).

Unused Sick Leave
— The expenditure recorded in all program/elements to charge their proportionate share of Unused Sick Leave (Object Account 1155).

Total Salaries and Wages
- The total of Salaries and Wages (1151) and Unused Sick Leave (1155).

Retirement Contribution
- The City's retirement contributions to the Employees' Pension Fund (Object Account 2150).

Social Security Contribution
- The City's matching Social Security Contribution (Object Account 2152).

Total Pensions
— The total of Retirement Contribution (2150) and Social Security Contributions (2152).

Health and Life Insurance
- The City paid health and life insurance for City employees (Object Account 2424).

Compensation Insurance
- The City's contribution to its Workmen's Compensation Fund (Object Account 2425).

Injury and Health Insurance
- Total of Health and Life Insurance (2424) and Workmen's Compensation Insurance (2425).

Total Personnel Expense
_ This is the grand total of Total Salaries and Wages, Total Pensions, and Total Injury and Health Insurance.

CITY OF SAN DIEGO	CHAPTER 1	SECTION 2
PROGRAM ACCOUNTING PROCEDURES MANUAL	PAGE 2 of 3	
SUBJECT PROGRAM ACCOUNTING TERMINOLOGY	DATE July 1, 1974	

Job Order
— A job order is used to accumulate costs related to a specific project or task. It is a further breakdown of an element but reported in the Job Order Report. This term replaces such terms as work order, cost account, etc. The job order is the lowest level at which dollars are reported.

Operation Account
— An operation account is used primarily in the Work Program System to collect and report position hours and work units.

An operation account may also be used in the Job Order System to break down "Labor" if both a job order number and an operation account number are reported on labor cards by the department. Non-personal costs cannot be used with operation accounts.

Performing Department
— The term used to denote the department doing work for someone else.

Benefiting Department
— The department receiving the benefit of the work being done by the performing department.

Benefiting Agency
— Same as a Benefiting Department except that it is a non-City entity.

Load
— See Labor Load.

Labor Load
— The percentage factor by which Salaries and Wages (Object Account 1151) is increased to reflect the actual usage of such items as vacation, sick leave and scheduled holidays. Each department has a rate developed and monitored by the Auditor and Comptroller's Department.

Overhead
— Overhead is the percentage factor added to Salaries and Wages (Object Account 1151) in the Job Order System when the job order is billable to another fund, outside agency, or person.

Period Ending
— The Period Ending date reflects the last date any expenditures, encumbrances, work units, etc., were recorded in the report. Any data received by the Auditor's department after that date is reflected in the next report.

A Period Ending may be the end of a pay period, the end of the last pay period of a month, or an end of a calendar month.

Output
— See Work Unit.

CITY OF SAN DIEGO	CHAPTER	SECTION
PROGRAM ACCOUNTING PROCEDURES MANUAL	1	2

SUBJECT

PROGRAM ACCOUNTING TERMINOLOGY

PAGE 3 OF 3

DATE
July 1, 1974

Work Unit
— A work unit is a measurable unit of output accomplished by the use of a department's resources.

A work unit can be any definable and measurable item: i.e., tons of asphalt laid; miles of streets paved; number of reports prepared; number of citations issued; number of permits issued, etc.

Labor Distribution System
— The Labor Distribution System is a system that takes the labor reported via labor cards and the payroll of all City employees and properly allocates that payroll (and related City costs) expenditures over all departments, programs and elements of the City.

Position Hours
— This term is used to replace the present term "man hours"

```
                          CITY OF SAN DIEGO
   PROGRAM ACCOUNTING PROCEDURES MANUAL
```

CITY OF SAN DIEGO	CHAPTER	SECTION
PROGRAM ACCOUNTING PROCEDURES MANUAL	2	1
SUBJECT	PAGE 1	OF 1
LABOR CARDS (DP-16A & B and DP-17A & B)	DATE July 1, 1974	

Labor Cards will be used by all City departments for the reporting of position hours expended on a particular job order or program/element. They will be filled out on a daily or biweekly basis (there will not be a month end card for biweekly users). A department may have some employees use daily cards and others use biweekly cards, depending on their need.

The position hours reported will be used to allocate to Appropriations and the Cost System the employer related expenses. These expenses are Salaries & Wages, Unused Sick Leave, Overtime, City's Retirement Contributions, City's Social Security Contributions, Compensation Insurance, and City Paid Health and Life Insurance.

A department may select one of two available labor types. Type 1 requires the use of only a job order number. Type 2 requires the use of a job order number and an operation account number.

If a department does not elect to set up their own job order numbering structure, they may use their Program/Element number to record position hours, excepting the City-wide job order numbers which all departments must use (see Chapter 5, Section 1).

Attached are examples of the two labor types for Daily and Biweekly Labor Cards.

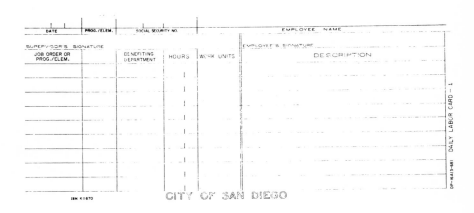

CITY OF SAN DIEGO

CITY OF SAN DIEGO

SUPERVISOR'S SIGNATURE					EMPLOYEE'S SIGNATURE																
JOB ORDER NO.	OPER. ACCT.	BENEFITING DEPARTMENT	HOURS	WORK UNITS	FRI	SAT	SUN	MON	TUE	WED	THU	FRI	SAT	SUN	MON	TUE	WED	THU			

PERIOD ENDING — DEPT./AC — SOCIAL SECURITY NO — EMPLOYEE NAME

CITY OF SAN DIEGO

BI-WEEKLY LABOR CARD-2

DP-1781(3-68)

SUPERVISOR'S SIGNATURE					EMPLOYEE'S SIGNATURE
JOB ORDER NO.	OPER. ACCT.	BENEFITING DEPARTMENT	HOURS	WORK UNITS	DESCRIPTION

CITY OF SAN D 90

DAILY LABOR CARD – 2

DP-1681(3-68)

CITY OF SAN DIEGO	CHAPTER	SECTION
PROGRAM ACCOUNTING PROCEDURES MANUAL	2	2

SUBJECT	PAGE 1 OF 1
BIWEEKLY WORK UNIT REPORT (AC-301)	DATE July 1, 1974

The Biweekly Work Unit Report will be used by departments to record their work units (output) completed; i.e., tons of asphalt laid; miles of streets paved; number of reports prepared; number of citations issued; number of permits issued, etc.

An operation account must be established for each work unit (output) reported. Each operation account may be used with or without a job order number depending upon the type of information a department desires.

Attached are examples of the Biweekly Work Unit Report.

> NOTE: An operation account structure for work units (output) should be developed by each department. When drafted they should be submitted to the Accounting Systems Section, Auditor and Comptroller's Department for review. If assistance in developing work unit (output) structures is desired contact the Accounting Systems Section.

THE CITY OF SAN DIEGO, CALIFORNIA
OFFICE OF CITY AUDITOR AND COMPTROLLER
BIWEEKLY WORK UNIT REPORT

DEPARTMENT TITLE: _POLICE_

PERIOD ENDING: _7_ / _18_ / _74_

DEPT. NO.: _____
(1-4)

#	JOB ORDER 18-23	OPERATION ACCOUNT 26-29	WORK UNITS 38-43		#	JOB ORDER 18-23	OPERATION ACCOUNT 26-29	WORK UNITS 38-43
1		1001	20 0		31			
2		1005	50 5		32			
3		2016	101 3		33			
4		2023	937 2		34			
5		3112	500 0		35			
6		4027	33 6		36			
7					37			
8					38			
9					39			
10					40			
11					41			
12					42			
13					43			
14					44			
15					45			
16					46			
17					47			
18					48			
19					49			
20					50			
21					51			
22					52			
23					53			
24					54			
25					55			
26					56			
27					57			
28					58			
29					59			
30					60			

TOTAL UNITS PAGE: _1_ OF _1_ | 16 47 6 |

PREPARED BY:	DATE:	APPROVED BY:	DATE:

(THIS SECTION FOR AUDITORS USE ONLY)						BATCHED BY:	DATE:
BATCH DATE 1-6	BATCH NO. 8-11	T Y P E 14	UNITS 20-28	DEPT. 30-33	C O D E 80		
		U			*	KEYPUNCH:	DATE:

AC-301 (3-74)

BIWEEKLY WORK UNIT REPORT

DEPARTMENT TITLE: __Police__   PERIOD ENDING: __7 / 13 / 74__

DEPT. NO.: __1500__

#	JOB ORDER	OPERATION ACCOUNT	WORK UNITS		#	JOB ORDER	OPERATION ACCOUNT	WORK UNITS
1	1510	1112	12 7		31			
2	65234	1940	300 0		32			
3	78104	1529	27 0		33			
4	15001	1623	536 6		34			
5	15125	1740	20 1		35			
6					36			
7					37			
8					38			
9					39			
10					40			
11					41			
12					42			
13					43			
14					44			
15					45			
16					46			
17					47			
18					48			
19					49			
20					50			
21					51			
22					52			
23					53			
24					54			
25					55			
26					56			
27					57			
28					58			
29					59			
30					60			

TOTAL UNITS PAGE: __1__ OF __1__ | 895 9 |

PREPARED BY:	DATE:	APPROVED BY:	DATE:

(THIS SECTION FOR AUDITORS USE ONLY)							
BATCH DATE	BATCH NO.	T Y P	UNITS	DEPT	C O D E	BATCHED BY:	DATE:
1-5	6-11	11	20-28	30-33	35		
		U				KEYPUNCH:	DATE:

AC-301 (3-73)

BIWEEKLY WORK UNIT REPORT

DEPARTMENT TITLE: Police   PERIOD ENDING: 7 / 13 / 74

DEPT. NO.: 1500

#	JOB ORDER 18-25	OPERATION ACCOUNT 26-29	WORK UNITS 30-43		#	JOB ORDER 18-25	OPERATION ACCOUNT 26-29	WORK UNITS 30-43
1		3101	50.0		31			
2	153100	310+	730.0		32			
3		3107	100.0		33			
4		3108	480.0		34			
5	153200	3202	5.0		35			
6		3203	1.0		36			
7		3204	900.0		37			
8		3205	1.0		38			
9		3306	1.0		39			
10		3107	10.0		40			
11		3308	950.0		41			
12	153300	3309	20.0		42			
13					43			
14					44			
15					45			
16					46			
17					47			
18					48			
19					49			
20					50			
21					51			
22					52			
23					53			
24					54			
25					55			
26					56			
27					57			
28					58			
29					59			
30					60			

TOTAL UNITS PAGE: 1 OF 1   3248.0

PREPARED BY:	DATE:	APPROVED BY:	DATE:

(THIS SECTION FOR AUDITORS USE ONLY)							
BATCH DATE 1-5	BATCH NO. 8-11	TYPE 11	UNITS 2P-23	DEPT. 11-32	CODE 50	BATCHED BY:	DATE:
		U			*	KEYPUNCH:	DATE:

AC-301 (3-74)

CITY OF SAN DIEGO	CHAPTER	SECTION
	2	3

PROGRAM ACCOUNTING PROCEDURES MANUAL

PAGE 1   OF 1

SUBJECT

EQUIPMENT RENTAL SYSTEM

DATE

July 1, 1974

The Equipment Rental System converts the mileage reported on Equipment Cards to the expenditures reflected in the Job Order and Appropriation Systems.

Equipment Rental Cards are completed by employees in the field and the cards are forwarded to Data Processing through the Auditor & Comptroller.

The major changes in the Equipment System for FY 1975 are:

1. The reports generated by the Equipment System will be as of the final pay period in a calendar month.

2. The possession charge will be prorated on a biweekly basis.

3. Each equipment charge will have to have a job order.

4. The Equipment Card will be a Daily/Biweekly Card.

				EMPLOYEE'S SIGNATURE:															
DATE OR PERIOD ENDING	EQUIP NO. (17-20)		SOCIAL SECURITY NO. (23-31)	SUPERVISOR'S SIGNATURE:															
PROG./ELEM. 34-37	JOB ORDER NUMBER 40-45	48-5:	MILES OR HOURS 54-59	STOP START SPEEDOMETER READING	FRI	SAT	SUN	MON	TUE	WED	THU	FRI	SAT	SUN	MON	TUE	WED	THU

TYPE TRANSPORTATION:
☐ R ☐ A ☐ B ☐ C   IBM K12079

AC-213 (REV. 7-74)

THE CITY OF SAN DIEGO-DAILY/BI-WEEKLY EQUIPMENT CARD

				EMPLOYEE'S SIGNATURE:															
DATE OR PERIOD ENDING	EQUIP NO. (17-20)		SOCIAL SECURITY NO. (23-31)	SUPERVISOR'S SIGNATURE:															
PROG./ELEM. 34-37	JOB ORDER NUMBER 40-45	48-5:	MILES OR HOURS 54-59	STOP START SPEEDOMETER READING	FRI	SAT	SUN	MON	TUE	WED	THU	FRI	SAT	SUN	MON	TUE	WED	THU

TYPE TRANSPORTATION:
☐ R ☐ A ☐ B ☐ C   IBM K12079

AC-213 (REV. 7-74)

THE CITY OF SAN DIEGO-DAILY/BI-WEEKLY EQUIPMENT CARD

PROGRAM ACCOUNTING PROCEDURES MANUAL

SUBJECT	PAGE 1 OF 1
BIWEEKLY PHOTOCOPY USAGE REPORTING	DATE July 1, 1974

All City departments using Xerox machines which are owned by the Print Shop (those requiring the use of an Auditron device), must report their usage to the Auditor and Comptroller every two weeks.

The Biweekly Photocopy Usage Report (AC-304) is designed to report the total copies made
by your department and to distribute the cost of those copies out over the various
Program/Elements and Job Orders for which the photocopies were made.

CITY OF SAN DIEGO
CITY AUDITOR & COMPTROLLER

BIWEEKLY PHOTOCOPY USAGE REPORT

DEPARTMENT NUMBER
(8 - 11)
1100

AUDITRON NO.: #49 _____ DATE 07/18/74

DEPT. NAME ___Community Development___

PREPARED BY: _____
                           NAME   PHONE

JOB ORDER OR ELEMENT NO. (17 - 22)	NUMBER OF COPIES (51 - 56)	JOB ORDER OR ELEMENT NO. (17 - 22)	NUMBER OF COPIES (51 - 56)	JOB ORDER OR ELEMENT NO. (17 - 22)	NUMBER OF COPIES (51 - 56)
78001	185				
70023	4				
112086	16				
1110	33				
1143	212				
62125	7				
1151	49				
162061	22				
78104	8				

TOTAL COPIES REPORTED ABOVE   536

ENDING AUDITRON READING   32061

LESS: BEGINNING AUDITRON READING . .   31525

TOTAL COPIES PER AUDITRON   536

DIFFERENCE   0
(EXPLAIN ON REVERSE)

PAGE 1 OF 1

THIS SECTION FOR AUDITORS USE ONLY

DATE (1 - 6)	BATCH NO. (8 - 11)	TYPE (14)	DOC. REF. (19 - 20)	TOTAL COPIES (23 - 28)	OBJ. ACCT. (35 - 38)	CODE (80)	BATCHED BY:	DATE: / /
		E	PC		3236	*	KEYPUNCH:	DATE: / /

AC-304 (3-74)

CITY OF SAN DIEGO	CHAPTER	SECTION
	2	5

PROGRAM ACCOUNTING PROCEDURES MANUAL

PAGE 1 OF 1

SUBJECT
STOCK MATERIAL REQUEST (FORM AC-1389)

DATE
July 1, 1974

Some departments find it convenient and economical to purchase certain materials in bulk (such as stakes for Engineering or fertilizer for Parks). If the appropriate using Program/Element cannot be determined at the time of the initial bulk purchase, the department may create a stockroom in the Auditor's Variance Account. The initial bulk purchase may be by a Stores Requisition, a Request for Direct Payment (DP), or a Purchase Order (PO). As the items are needed for a particular job order the Stock Material Request is completed, and the costs are transferred from the Auditor's Variance Account into the appropriate Program/Element.

The Stock Material Request should be completed only if there has been a departmental stockroom previously set up. The utilization of this procedure is made available for departments that make frequent large bulk purchases, and the issuance of these purchased items cannot be predetermined.

SAMPLE OF A COMPLETED
STOCK MATERIAL REQUEST

08-13-74	100	0622	3303		MR		
DATE	FUND (13-17)	PROG/CLAM (14-21)	OBJ.ACCT. (22-26)		DOCUMENT NO. (17-62)		
AUDITOR COMPTROLLER		STOCKCLERK			EMPLOYEE		
DEPARTMENT NAME		ISSUED BY			RECEIVED BY		
DESCRIPTION	CLASS	STOCK NO.	J.O.NUMBER (27-37)	QUANTITY	PRICE	AMOUNT (38-47)	
			006201	2	10.00	20	00
			078104	3	5.00	15	00

AUDITOR AND COMPTROLLER
STOCK MATERIAL REQUEST
AC-1309 (REV. 7-74)

| 009551 | TOTAL ___ | (35 00) |

CITY OF SAN DIEGO

PROGRAM ACCOUNTING PROCEDURES MANUAL

CITY OF SAN DIEGO	CHAPTER 3	SECTION 1
PROGRAM ACCOUNTING PROCEDURES MANUAL	PAGE 1 OF 1	
SUBJECT	DATE	
WORK PROGRAM STATUS REPORT (DP-102)	July 1, 1974	

The Work Program Status Report (DP-102) is a detailed record by fund and department/ division of actual and budgeted position hours and work units. The report is further broken into program/elements and finally into operation accounts. Each operation account may have position hours, work units, or both, reported for it.

The report is generated on a period basis as of the last pay period in the month. Each report will contain data for two, or sometimes, three biweekly pay periods; except for July and June. The July period report will contain data from the first day of the fiscal year through the last pay period of the month. The June period report will include data through the last day of the fiscal year.

Position hours and work units are received from the Labor Distribution System. Position hours are submitted on labor cards and work units are submitted in the Biweekly Work Unit Report.

The following calculations are made in order to assist the reader in his analysis of the report:

(a) W.U. % Expended $= \dfrac{\text{Work Units YTD}}{\text{Work Units Budgeted}}$

(b) P.H. % Expended $= \dfrac{\text{Position Hours YTD}}{\text{Position Hours Budgeted}}$

(c) P.H. Per Work Unit $= \dfrac{\text{Position Hours}}{\text{Work Units}}$

DP-102

WORK PROGRAM STATUS REPORT

THE CITY OF San Diego, California

DEPT. POLICE   FUND NO. 100   PERIOD ENDED: JULY 18, 1974

ELEMENT AND OPERATION ACCOUNTABILITIES	OPERATION ACCOUNT NUMBER	WORK UNIT DESCRIPTION	CURRENT PERIOD WORK UNITS	CURRENT PERIOD POSITION HOURS	YEAR TO DATE WORK UNITS	YEAR TO DATE W.U. EXP. %	YEAR TO DATE P.H. PER WORK UNIT	YEAR TO DATE POSITION HOURS	YEAR TO DATE P.H. EXP. %	BUDGETED WORK PROGRAM WORK UNITS	BUDGETED WORK PROGRAM P.H. PER WORK UNIT	BUDGETED WORK PROGRAM POSITION HOURS
15.31 TRAFFIC MANAGEMENT												
ACCIDENT REPORTS PROC.	3101	EA. REPORT	53.0	80.0	153.0	1	1.05	160.0	5	12100.0	.25	3020.0
PARKING CITATIONS PROC.	3104	EA. CITATION	750.0	80.0	1238.0	0	.26	320.0	5	320100.0	.02	6000.0
TRAFFIC WARNINGS PROC.	3107	EA. WARNING	106.0	80.0	212.0	0	.37	80.0	4	285000.0	.01	1666.0
MOVING CITATIONS PROC.	3108	EA. CITATION	508.0	80.0	1138.0	1	.28	320.0	5	105000.0	.06	6000.0
TOTAL 15.31				320.0				890.0				16668.0
15.32 TRAFFIC SERVICES												
SAFETY CLASSES VISITED	3202	EA. CLASS	5.0	160.0	15.0	1	21.33	320.0	2	2650.0	5.73	15186.0
SPEECHES	3203	EA. SPEECH			3.0	0	26.67	80.0	2	2680.0	1.42	3797.0
PARKING CITATIONS ISU.	3204	EA. CITATION	1238.0	800.0	1238.0	1	.65	800.0	2	262485.0	.15	37966.0
HIT & RUN CASES	3205	EA. CASE	2.0	160.0	7.0	1	44.57	312.0	2	6124.0	2.48	15186.0
ABAND. VEHICLES APPR.	3206	EA. VEHICLE	1.0	8.0	12.0	1	7.33	88.0	2	2900.0	1.31	3397.0
TOTAL 15.32				1128.0				1600.0				75932.0
15.33 TRAFFIC OPERATIONS												
TRAFFIC WARNINGS	3307	EA. WARNING	10.0	80.0	212.0	0	2.83	600.0	1	96800.0	.69	66857.0
MOVING CITATIONS	3308	EA. CITATION	1000.0	320.0	1138.0	3	.44	500.0	1	46200.0	1.18	54541.0
DRINKING DRIV. ARRESTS	3309	EA. ARREST	25.0	320.0	56.0	1	8.93	500.0	1	6190.0	8.81	54542.0
TOTAL 15.33				720.0				1600.0				175940.0

CITY OF SAN DIEGO	CHAPTER	SECTION
	3	2

PROGRAM ACCOUNTING PROCEDURES MANUAL

SUBJECT	PAGE 1 OF 1
JOB ORDER REPORT (FORM DP-115)	DATE July 1, 1974

The Job Order Report (DP-115) is a summarization of all Detail Transactions for the period by job order. The report is a period report produced as of the last pay period end in a calendar month.

The Job Order Report is divided into two time frames, the first being current period and the second year-to-date. Current period data is comprised of all transactions in the two or sometimes three biweekly pay periods immediately preceding the date of the report. Year-to-date totals reflect all activity from the beginning of the fiscal year to the date of the report.

Detailed breakdown of each job order will be shown. Totals will be at job order, program/element, program, and department levels.

The detail breakdown of each job order will show the following:

A. Summarized Object Accounts

Many of the detailed object accounts used in appropriations fit into broad general classifications. These summarized object accounts are used in the Job Order Report (i.e., Social Security, retirement contribution, insurances, etc., are grouped into Other Personnel Expense).

B. Labor

There are two sample reports attached. In one the labor entry is a single line entry. In the other the labor entry is broken down by operation account. The difference is determined by the labor type chosen for a department. Any department may choose any available labor type, but the labor type will apply to the whole department.

C. Units

Each job order may have a unit of measure shown in it. Each job order is limited to only one unit though. If a unit is to be reported, a Work Unit Report will have to be completed with the appropriate work unit operation account.

D. Calculations

In each job order which shows a unit of measure there will be two calculations done: 1) position hour per work unit, 2) cost per work unit. These calculations will be performed for both the current period and the year-to-date.

115 (REV. 4/74)

THE CITY OF SAN DIEGO, CALIFORNIA
JOB ORDER REPORT

DEPT: POLICE FUND NO. 100 PERIOD ENDING JULY 18, 1974

OPER ACCT	DESCRIPTION	JOB ORDER	TYPE EXPENSE	CURRENT PERIOD UNITS	CURRENT PERIOD DISBURSEMENTS	YEAR TO DATE UNITS	DISBURSEMENTS	ENCUMBRANCES	TOTAL
	1531 TRAFFIC MANAGEMENT								
	SPECIAL EVENTS								
1010	SPORTS ARENA	3102	LABOR	59.2	3329.57	59.2	3329.57		3329.57
1011	STADIUM	3102	LABOR	29.6	1664.78	29.6	1664.78		1664.78
1012	COMMUNITY CONCOURSE	3102	LABOR	14.8	832.39	14.8	832.39		832.39
		3102	OTH PERS		724.93		724.93		724.93
		3102	MILEAGE		70.00		70.00		70.00
		3102	CONTR SR		1190.00		1190.00		1190.00
		3102	MATERIAL		140.00		140.00		140.00
		3102	EVENTS	3.0		3.0			
	TOTAL	3102		103.6	7951.67	103.6	7951.67		7951.67
	MAN HOUR PER WORK UNIT	3102		34.5					34.5
	COST PER WORK UNIT	3102		2650.56					2650.56
	EMERGENCY CONTROL								
3021	FREEWAY	3130	LABOR	37.0	2080.98	37.0	2080.98		2080.98
3047	FIRE	3130	LABOR	7.4	416.20	7.4	416.20		416.20
		3130	OTH PERS		310.69		310.69		310.69
		3130	MILEAGE		30.00		30.00		30.00
		3130	OCCURS	2.0		2.0			
	TOTAL	3130		44.4	2837.87	44.4	2837.87		2837.87
	MAN HOUR PER WORK UNIT	3130		22.2					22.2
	COST PER WORK UNIT	3130		1418.94					1418.94
	TOTAL TRAFFIC MGMT			148.0	10789.54	148.0	10789.54		10789.54

THE CITY OF SAN DIEGO, CALIFORNIA
JOB ORDER REPORT

115 (REV. 4-74)

DEPT: POLICE   FUND NO. 100   PERIOD ENDING JULY 18, 1974

DESCRIPTION	JOB ORDER	TYPE EXPENSE	CURRENT PERIOD		YEAR TO DATE			
			UNITS	DISBURSEMENTS	UNITS	DISBURSEMENTS	ENCUMBRANCES	TOTAL
1531 TRAFFIC MANAGEMENT								
SPECIAL EVENTS	3102	LABOR	103.6	5826.74	103.6	5826.74		5826.74
	3102	OTH PERS		724.93		724.93		724.93
	3102	MILEAGE		70.00		70.00		70.00
	3102	CONTR SR		1190.00		1190.00		1190.00
	3102	MATERIAL		140.00		140.00		140.00
	3102	EVENTS	3.0		3.0			
TOTAL	3102		103.6	7951.67	103.6	7951.67		7951.67
MAN HOUR PER WORK UNIT	3102			34.5				34.5
COST PER WORK UNIT	3102			2650.56				2650.56
EMERGENCY CONTROL	3130	LABOR	44.4	2497.18	44.4	2497.18		2497.18
	3130	OTH PERS		310.69		310.69		310.69
	3130	MILEAGE		30.00		30.00		30.00
	3130	OCCURS	2.0		2.0			
TOTAL	3130		44.4	2837.87	44.4	2837.87		2837.87
MAN HOUR PER WORK UNIT	3130			22.2				22.2
COST PER WORK UNIT	3130			1418.94				1418.94
TOTAL TRAFFIC MGMT			148.0	10789.54	148.0	10789.54		10789.54

CITY OF SAN DIEGO	CHAPTER 3	SECTION 3
PROGRAM ACCOUNTING PROCEDURES MANUAL	PAGE 1	OF 1
SUBJECT	DATE	
PROGRAM/ELEMENT STATUS REPORT	July 1, 1974	

The objectives of the Program/Element Status Report are to summarize and compare in one report the Appropriation Budget, the Allotment, Actual Disbursements, and Work Ouput data in both position hours and costs.

The Program/Element Status Report is divided into two major sections, the "Appropriation" side consisting of Budget, Scheduled To Date, Expended To Date, and Percent Completed, and the "Output" side consisting of Output Unit Title, Position Hours, Position Hour per Work Unit, Work Units, and Cost per Work Unit.

The Appropriation Section of the report shows the total budget for each Program/Element for the year. This will agree with the total budget reflected on all other period budget reports. The Scheduled To Date column reflects the Program/Element's current position regarding its quarterly allotment. This amount is shown next to the Expended to Date, which represents the total Program/Element disbursements and encumbrances to date. The Percentage Completion is a simple ratio of Expended To Date compared to Budget.

The Appropriation Section of the report will be produced for every Program/Element with the data from the Appropriation System.

The Output Section of the report derives its information from the Work Program, Labor, and Job Order Systems. The production of this section of the report is dependent upon a department's use of these systems.

First to appear under the output data is the Output Unit Title. These titles will be the same title as appears in the Work Program Status Report. A Program/Element will be shown with all reported work units.

Position Hours are those hours charged to a job order from the Labor Distribution System. These hours will be an accumulation of all hours reported against a particular job order on labor cards, associated with a particular work unit.

Position Hour per Work Unit is simply a calculation comparing Position Hours to the work units reported on a Work Unit Report. A Work Unit Report must be completed to have work units shown in this Program/Element Status Report.

Under Cost Per Work Unit there may or may not be calculations shown. To have a calculation shown the work unit must be the single work unit reported to a particular job order in the Job Order System. If no calculation is shown the work unit is reported through work program only.

The Program/Element Status Report is a period report and will be produced as of the last pay period end in a calendar month.

CITY OF SAN DIEGO, CALIFORNIA   PROGRAM/ELEMENT STATUS REPORT

DEPT. POLICE

FUND 100   PERIOD ENDED: JULY 18, 1975

PROGRAM/ELEMENT NUMBER	BUDGET	APPROPRIATIONS SCHEDULED TO DATE	EXPENDED TO DATE	% Comp.	OUTPUT UNIT TITLE	OUTPUT DATA POSITION HOURS	POS. HR/ WK. UNIT	WORK UNITS	COST/ WK. UNIT
TRAFFIC MANAGEMENT 1531	186409.00	46602.00	26788.00	14	ACCIDENT REPORTS PROC.	160.0	1.05	153.0	31.52
					PARKING CITATIONS PROC.	320.0	.26	1236.0	7.78
					TRAFFIC WARNINGS PROC.	80.0	.37	212.0	12.64
					MOVING CITATIONS PROC.	320.0	.28	1138.0	8.47
TRAFFIC SERVICES 1532	625369.00	156342.00	84830.00	14	SAFETY CLASSES VISITED	320.0	21.33	15.0	34.26
					SPEECHES			3.0	
					PARKING CITATIONS ISS.	800.0	.65	1239.0	
					HIT & RUN CASES	312.0	44.57	7.0	2423.71
					ABAND. VEHICLES APPR.	88.0	7.33	12.0	353.46
TRAFFIC OPERATIONS 1533	1758447.00	439612.00	111619.00	6	TRAFFIC WARNINGS	600.0	2.83	212.0	200.07
					MOVING CITATIONS	500.0	.44	1138.0	30.41
					DRINKING DRIV. ARRESTS	500.0	8.93	56.0	617.69
AUDITORS VARIANCE ACCT. 1598			3837.00						
TOTAL POLICE DEPT. 1500	7358041.00	1839510.00	588643.00	8					

	CHAPTER	SECTION
CITY OF SAN DIEGO	3	4

PROGRAM ACCOUNTING PROCEDURES MANUAL

PAGE 1 OF 1

SUBJECT

DEPARTMENT/PROGRAM/ELEMENT COMPARISON OF
EXPENDITURES AND REVENUES REPORT

DATE
July 1, 1974

The Comparison of Expenditures and Revenues Report combines the attributes of the Appro-priation Status Report and the Revenue Status Report by providing management with a con-solidated picture of each Program's budget and year-to-date expenditures matched against the estimated revenues the Program is expected to generate and the actual year-to-date revenues received.

Within each Program is a one line statement for each Element's appropriation budget, amount expended to date, the balance available and the percent expended. Appearing opposite this information is a one line summary of each Element's estimated revenue, actual revenue received to date, the amount actuals are over or under the estimate, and the percent received. The final column shows the amount costs are over or under revenues but only for those Elements which have revenues estimated or received.

The revenues reflected in this report are by no means the total revenues received by each fund. They are only the revenues estimated or deposited into specific revenue accounts assigned to those Program/Elements which, as a result of their direct efforts, generate revenues to the fund. There are numerous Elements within the City whose combined efforts may cause revenues to come into the treasury that would not be reflected in this report because each Element's individual entitlement would not be measurable. There are numerous other Elements within the City whose efforts are not intended to produce revenues which naturally would not appear in this report.

The appropriation amounts for each Element are a summary of numerous object accounts and the revenue amounts for each Element are a summary of numerous revenue accounts.

CITY OF SAN DIEGO, CALIFORNIA — DEPARTMENT/PROGRAM/ELEMENT COMPARISON OF EXPENDITURES AND REVENUES

DEPT. POLICE FUND 100 PERIOD ENDED: JULY 18, 1974

PROGRAM/ELEMENT	ACCT. NO.	APPROPRIATIONS BUDGET	EXPENDED	BALANCE	% Exp.	REVENUES ESTIMATED	RECEIVED	OVER OR UNDER (-)	% Rec.	COST OVER/UNDER REVENUE
DEPARTMENTAL ADMINISTRATION	1501	95592	6691	88900	7					
SUPPORT SERVICES BUREAU										
MANAGEMENT	1510	28194	845	27349	3					
RECORDS	1511	32775	5244	27531	16					
COMMUNICATIONS	1512	224580	26949	197631	12					
JAIL	1513	240968	2409	238559	1					
COMMUNITY RELATIONS	1514	16387	327	16060	2					
TRAINING	1515	81936	4096	77840	5		618	618		3478
AUTOMOTIVE MAINTENANCE	1516	98323	7865	90458	8					
LABORATORY	1517	90000		90000	0					
PROPERTY & SUPPLY	1518	6199	681	5518	11					
TOTAL PROGRAM	1510	819362	48421	770941	6		618	618		
PATROL BUREAU										
PATROL ADMINISTRATION	1520	23898	2389	21508	10					
NORTH STATION ADMIN.	1521	28677	1720	26957	6					
SOUTH STATION ADMIN.	1522	28677	3728	24949	13					
CENTRAL PATROL	1523	447796	22389	425407	5	100000	9000	91000-	9	13389
SCHOOL TASK FORCE	1524	14341	1147	13194	8					
NORTHERN PATROL	1525	443388	35471	407917	8	150000	16354	133646-	11	19117
SOUTHERN PATROL	1526	443388	31037	412351	7	250000		250000-	0	31037
BORDER CHECK STA.	1527	47796	59745	11949-	125	50000	439	49561-	1	59306
TOTAL PROGRAM	1520	1477961	157628	1320333	11	550000	25793	524207-	5	
TRAFFIC BUREAU										
TRAFFIC MANAGEMENT	1530	186409	26788	159621	14					
TRAFFIC SERVICES	1531	625369	84830	540539	14					
TRAFFIC OPERATIONS	1532	1758447	111619	1646828	6	500000	25618	474382-	5	86001
TOTAL PROGRAM	1530	2570225	223238	2346987	9	500000	25618	474382-	5	
INVESTIGATION BUREAU										
INVESTIGATION MGMT	1540	24901	2976	21925	12					
CRIMES - PROPERTY	1541	47400	4464	42936	9	200000	9826	190174-	5	5362-
CRIMES - PERSONS	1542	71100	7441	63659	10	200000	2316	197684-	1	5125
JUVENILE	1543	118500	10947	107553	9	50000	63129	13129	126	52182-
FORGERY & AUTO THEFT	1544	237000	15326	221674	6					
NARCOTICS	1545	474000	9633	464367	2	400000	10102	389393-	3	469-
PUBLIC INSPECTIONS	1546	237000	7882	229118	3	50000	29	49970-	0	7853
INVESTIGATIVE SUPPORT	1547	296250	29625	266625	10					
NORTHERN INVESTIGATIONS	1548	474000	30763	443237	7	500000	15428	484572-	3	15335
SOUTHERN INVESTIGATIONS	1549	414750	29765	384985	7	500000	132600	367400-	27	102835-
TOTAL PROGRAM	1540	2394901	148825	2246076	6	1900000	233431	1666569-	12	
AUDITORS VARIANCE ACCT.	1598		3837	3837-						
TOTAL POLICE DEPT.	1500	7358041	588643	6769398	8	2950000	285460	2664540-	10	

CITY OF SAN DIEGO	CHAPTER	SECTION
PROGRAM ACCOUNTING PROCEDURES MANUAL	3	5

SUBJECT	PAGE 1	OF 1
ANNUAL BUDGETED VS. ACTUAL POSITION USAGE BY PROGRAM ELEMENT	DATE	
	July 1, 1974	

This report is designed to display by Program Element the Actual Vs. Budgeted Manpower Usage in both time and costs for a department.

The report lists the Employee Class by Rate and Position Title. For each Position Title a comparison of Budgeted Vs. Actual is shown for both Position Years and Salaries. The current budget for both Position Years and Salaries will correspond to the Position and Salary Schedule. The actual amounts for the fiscal year will come directly from a Program/Element's usage and incurrence of Personnel Salary and Wages.

CITY OF SAN DIEGO, CALIFORNIA
ANNUAL BUDGETED VS. ACTUAL POSITION USAGE BY PROGRAM/ELEMENT
FISCAL YEAR ENDED JUNE 30, 1975

DEPT. POLICE   FUND 100

PROGRAM/ ELEMENT NUMBER	SALARY RATE	POSITION TITLE	POSITION YEARS CURRENT FY 75 BUDGET	POSITION YEARS FY 1975 ACTUAL	SALARIES CURRENT FY 75 BUDGET	SALARIES FY 1975 ACTUAL
1531	50.5	POLICE INSPECTOR	1.00	1.00	22038	21456
	48.4	POLICE CAPTAIN	1.00	1.00	20077	20077
	32.1	SENIOR CLERK	1.00	1.00	9239	8939
	29.6	INTER. STENOGRAPHER	2.00	1.00	15922	7951
	28.1	INTER. TYPIST	4.00	5.00	29964	37455
		TOTAL	9.00	9.00	97241	95888
1532	45.4	POLICE LIEUTENANT	1.00	1.00	17461	17461
	42.9	POLICE SERGEANT	4.00	4.00	62536	62000
	39.9	POLICE OFFICER	19.00	18.00	251427	238194
	32.1	FIELD REPRESENTATIVE	2.00	1.00	18534	9292
	32.1	PKG CONTROL SUPV.	2.00	2.00	19576	19576
	30.1	PARKING CONTROLLER	13.00	12.00	111189	102636
		TOTAL	41.00	38.00	480773	449159
1533	45.4	POLICE LIEUTENANT	3.00	3.00	52383	52383
	42.9	POLICE SERGEANT	13.00	13.00	202342	201519
	39.9	POLICE OFFICER	79.00	82.00	1045407	1035306
		TOTAL	95.00	98.00	1301032	1339107
		TOTAL POLICE	1290.00	1290.00	3867195	3843360

CITY OF SAN DIEGO	CHAPTER 3	SECTION 6
PROGRAM ACCOUNTING PROCEDURES MANUAL	PAGE 1	OF 1
SUBJECT ANNUAL BUDGETED VS. ACTUAL POSITION USAGE BY DEPARTMENT	DATE July 1, 1974	

The Annual Budgeted vs. Actual Position Usage by Department Report differs from the Annual Budgeted vs. Actual Position Usage by Program Element Report only in that the by Department Report shows positions on a department only level. (See Annual Budgeted vs. Actual Position Usage by Program Element.)

CITY OF .. SAN DIEGO, CALIFORNIA
ANNUAL BUDGETED VS. ACTUAL POSITION USAGE BY DEPARTMENT
FISCAL YEAR ENDED JUNE 30, 1975

DEPT. POLICE

FUND 100

PERIOD ENDED: JUNE 30, 1975

PROGRAM/ ELEMENT NUMBER	SALARY RATE	POSITION TITLE	POSITION YEARS		SALARIES	
			CURRENT FY 75 BUDGET	FY 1975 ACTUAL	CURRENT FY 75 BUDGET	FY 1975 ACTUAL
1500		POLICE CHIEF	1.00	1.00	29389	29300
		DEPUTY POLICE CHIEF	1.00	1.00	24321	24329
		SECY TO POLICE CHIEF	1.00	1.00	9692	9392
	52.4	ASST. POLICE CHIEF	4.00	4.00	96384	95000
	50.4	POLICE INSPECTOR	6.00	7.00	132234	154273
	48.4	POLICE CAPTAIN	15.00	15.00	301155	294116
	46.5	SENIOR ADMIN. ANALYST	1.00	.50	18268	9134
	45.4	POLICE LIEUTENANT	36.00	36.00	626292	626202
	42.9	POLICE SERGEANT	108.00	105.00	1666055	1620360
	39.9	POLICE OFFICER	302.00	298.00	3927510	3875490
	32.1	SENIOR CLERK	5.00	5.00	40155	46155
	29.6	INTER. STENOGRAPHER	10.00	9.00	76570	70983
	28.1	INTER. TYPIST	15.00	14.00	102570	95732
	24.1	JUNIOR TYPIST	25.00	31.00	145350	180234
		TOTAL POLICE	530.00	527.50	7205546	7132200

CITY OF SAN DIEGO
PROGRAM ACCOUNTING PROCEDURES MANUAL

CITY OF SAN DIEGO	4		1
PROGRAM ACCOUNTING PROCEDURES MANUAL	PAGE 1	OF	1
SUBJECT	DATE		
BUDGET STATUS REPORT (FORM DP 104)	July 1, 1974		

The Budget Status Report is designed to reflect the status of each Program/Element budget in the same format as the annual budget submitted by each department. It contains line item amounts for each object account in each Element with summary totals at the Program and Department level.

Current period expenditures activity as well as year-to-date totals are provided for in addition to the total budget, the unencumbered balance of the budget and the percent of the budget expended.

The purpose of the Budget Status Report is to provide a means of monitoring the current year expenditure budget as finalized on the Annual Budget Request (DP-103) and, when necessary, taking corrective action to curtail expenditures or request a budget adjustment. This report provides a means of analyzing the objects of expenditure within each Element and presents detailed financial data to enable management to project future appropriation requirements.

In addition, to presenting the budget status of the appropriated funds to operate each department, the Budget Status Report provides information on the manpower necessary to carry out the various programs by showing the budgeted Position Years in each Element and the current period and year-to-date utilization of personnel in each Element, Program, and Department.

For a detailed analysis of the transactions making up the current period activity you should consult the Appropriation Ledger.

DF-104 (7/74)

THE CITY OF SAN DIEGO, CALIFORNIA

BUDGET STATUS REPORT

Police Department   FUND NO. 100   PERCENT OF YEAR COMPLETED   PERIOD ENDING July 31, 1974

ELEMENT AND OBJECT ACCOUNTABILITIES	ACCT. NO.	CURRENT PERIOD			YEAR TO DATE			% BUD EXP	TOTAL BUDGET	UNENC BAL OF BUDGET
		DISBURSED	ENCUMBERED	TOTAL DISB & ENC	DISBURSED	ENCUMBERED	UCB TOTAL DISB & ENC			
Traffic Mgmt.	15.31									
Position Years		.75		.75	.75		.75	8	9.00	8.25
Personnel Exp.										
Salaries & Wages	1151	8,323.92	84.08	8,408.00	8,323.92	84.08	8,408.00	8	105,100.00	96,692.00
Unused Sick Lv.	1155	243.62	2.46	246.08	243.62	2.46	246.08	8	3,076.00	2,829.92
Total Sal. & Wages		8,567.54	86.54	8,654.08	8,567.54	86.54	8,654.08	8	108,176.00	99,521.92
Retir. Contr.	2150	356.40	3.60	360.00	356.40	3.60	360.00	8	4,500.00	4,140.00
Soc. Sec.	2152	396.00	4.00	400.00	396.00	4.00	400.00	8	5,000.00	4,600.00
Total Pensions		752.40	7.60	760.00	752.40	7.60	760.00	8	9,500.00	8,740.00
Workmen's Comp.	2424	19.80	.20	20.00	19.80	.20	20.00	8	250.00	230.00
Health & Life	2425	19.80	.20	20.00	19.80	.20	20.00	8	250.00	230.00
Total Insurance		39.60	.40	40.00	39.60	.40	40.00	8	500.00	460.00
Total Personnel		9,359.54	94.54	9,454.08	9,454.08	94.54	9,454.08	8	118,176.00	108,721.92
Non-Personnel										
Transportation	3210	100.00		100.00	100.00		100.00	5	2,000.00	1,900.00
Telephone	3212	1,500.00		1,500.00	1,500.00		1,500.00	13	11,203.00	9,703.00
Utilities	3241	200.00		200.00	200.00		200.00		31,030.00	30,830.00
Office Supplies	3301	200.00		200.00	200.00		200.00	10	2,000.00	1,800.00
Total Suppl & Ser.		1,800.00		1,800.00	1,800.00		1,800.00	4	46,233.00	44,433.00
Equipment	4540	22,000.00	22,000.00	22,000.00	22,000.00	22,000.00	22,000.00	100	22,000.00	
Total Outlay		22,000.00	22,000.00	22,000.00	22,000.00	22,000.00	22,000.00	100	22,000.00	
Total Non-Per		1,000.00	22,000.00	23,800.00	1,800.00	22,000.00	23,800.00	3	68,233.00	44,433.00
Total	15.31	11,159.54	22,094.54	33,254.08	11,159.54	22,094.54	33,254.08	18	166,409.00	153,154.92
Traffic Mgmt.	15.31									
Traffic Services	15.32									
Position Years		1.64		1.64	3.28		3.28	8	41.00	37.72
Personnel Exp.										
Salaries & Wages	1151	18,156.74	183.40	18,340.14	36,496.88	183.40	36,680.28	8	458,503.50	421,823.22
Unused Sick Lv.	1155	484.18	4.89	489.07	973.25	4.89	978.14	8	12,226.76	11,248.62
Total Sal & Wgs.		18,640.92	188.29	18,829.21	37,470.13	188.29	37,658.42	8	470,730.26	433,071.84
Retir. Contr.	2150	2,420.90	24.45	2,445.35	4,866.25	24.45	4,890.70	8	61,133.80	56,243.10
Soc. Sec.	2152	1,936.72	19.56	1,936.26	3,893.00	19.56	3,912.56	8	48,907.04	44,994.48
Total Pensions		4,357.62	44.01	4,401.63	8,759.25	44.01	8,803.26	8	110,040.84	101,237.58

CP 134127M
7

BUDGET STATUS REPORT

DEPT Police Department   FUND NO. 100   PERCENT OF YEAR COMPLETED   PERIOD ENDING July 31, 1974

ELEMENT AND OBJECT ACCOUNTINGS	ACCT. NO.	CURRENT PERIOD			YEAR TO DATE			UCB	% BUD EXP	TOTAL BUDGET	UNEXP BAL OF BUDGET
		DISBURSED	ENCUMBERED	TOTAL DIS & ENC	DISBURSED	ENCUMBERED	TOTAL DIS & ENC				
Workmen's Comp.	2424	242.08	2.45	244.53	386.61	2.45	489.06	8	6,113.38	5,624.24
Health & Life	2425	968.36	9.78	978.14	1,946.50	9.78	1,956.28	8	24,453.52	22,497.24
Total Insurance		1,210.44	12.23	1,222.67	2,433.11	12.23	2,445.34	8	30,566.90	28,121.48
Total Personnel		24,208.98	244.53	24,253.51	48,662.49	244.53	48,907.02	8	611,338.00	562,430.98
Non-Personnel										
Office Supplies	3301	500.00	5.00	505.00	6,720.00	5.00	6,725.00	48	14,031.00	7,306.00
Total Non-Per		500.00	5.00	505.00	6,720.00	5.00	6,725.00	48	14,031.00	7,306.00
Total Traffic Services	15.32	24,708.98	249.53	24,958.51	55,382.49	249.53	55,632.02	9	625,369.00	569,736.98
Traffic Oper.	15.33									
Position Years					7.40		7.40	8	95.00	87.40
Personnel Expense										
Salaries & Wages	1151				102,296.52		102,296.52	8	1,278,706.50	1,176,409.98
Unused Sick Wa.	1155				2,727.91		2,727.91	8	34,098.84	31,370.93
Total Sal. & Wge					105,024.43		105,024.43	8	1,312,805.34	1,207,780.91
Retir. Contr.	2150				13,639.54		13,639.54	8	170,494.20	156,845.66
Soc. Sec.	2152				10,911.63		10,911.63	8	136,395.36	125,483.73
Total Pensions					24,551.17		24,551.17	8	306,889.56	282,338.39
Workmen's Comp.	2424				1,363.95		1,363.95	8	17,049.42	15,685.47
Health & Life	2425				5,455.81		5,455.81	8	68,197.68	62,741.87
Total Insurance					6,819.76		6,819.76	8	85,247.10	78,427.34
Total Personnel					136,395.36		136,395.36	8	1,704,942.00	1,568,546.64
Non-Personnel										
Transportation	3210								1,000.00	1,000.00
Postage	3211								2,000.00	
Telephone	3212	100.00		100.00	500.00		500.00	25	12,000.00	1,000.00-
Spec. DPTL Ex.	3217		405.00	405.00		405.00	1,300.00	108	405.00	1,000.00-
Photocopy	3236						405.00	5	8,405.00	8,000.00
Utilities	3241	2,000.00		2,000.00	3,000.00		3,000.00	23	13,000.00	11,000.00
Laundry Serv.	3270								500.00	500.00
Office Supplies	3301								11,500.00	
Ammunition	3318	20,000.00		20,000.00	20,000.00		20,000.00		2,000.00	20,000.00-
Safety Awards	3322								100.00	2,000.00
Books	3360								100.00	
Total Supl. & Ser		22,100.00	405.00	22,505.00	23,500.00	405.00	34,905.00	7	50,505.00	1,000.00

BUDGET STATUS REPORT

DEPT. Police Department

FUND NO. 100 PERCENT OF YEAR COMPLETED

PERIOD ENDING July 31, 1974

ELEMENT AND OBJECT ACCOUNTLIES	ACCT. NO.	CURRENT PERIOD				YEAR TO DATE				BUDGET STATUS	
		DISBURSED	ENCUMBERED	TOTAL DISB. & ENC.	DISBURSED	ENCUMBERED	TOTAL DISB. & ENC.	% BUD EXP	TOTAL BUDGET	UNENC BAL. OF BUDGET
Equipment	4540	53.00	299.00	352.00	900.00	299.00	1,199.00	34	3,000.00	1,801.00
Total Outlay		53.00	299.00	352.00	900.00	299.00	1,199.00	34	3,000.00	1,801.00
Total Non-Per		22,153.00	704.00	22,857.00	24,400.00	704.00	38,104.00	71	53,505.00	2,801.00
Total Traffic Oper.	15.33	22,153.00	704.00	22,857.00	160,795.36	704.00	174,499.36	10	1,758,447.00	1,571,347.64

BUDGET STATUS REPORT

DEPT: Police Department   FUND NO. 100   PERIOD ENDING July 31, 1974

ELEMENT AND OBJECT ACCOUNTABILITIES	ACCT. NO.	CURRENT PERIOD DISBURSED	CURRENT PERIOD ENCUMBERED	CURRENT PERIOD TOTAL DISB & ENC	YEAR TO DATE DISBURSED	YEAR TO DATE ENCUMBERED	YEAR TO DATE TOTAL DISB & ENC	% BUD EXP	BUDGET STATUS TOTAL BUDGET	UNENC BAL OF BUDGET
Total Traffic Bureau	15.30									
Position Years		2.39		2.39	11.63		11.63		145.00	133.37
Personnel Exp.										
Salaries & Wages		26,480.66	267.48	26,748.14	147,117.32	267.48	147,384.80	8	1,842,310.00	1,694,925.20
Unused Sick Lv.		727.80	7.35	735.15	3,964.78	7.35	3,952.13	8	49,401.60	45,449.47
Pensions		5,110.02	51.61	5,161.63	34,062.82	51.61	34,114.43	8	426,430.40	322,315.97
Insurance		1,250.04	12.63	1,262.67	9,292.47	12.63	9,305.10	8	116,314.00	107,008.90
Total Personnel		33,568.52	339.07	33,907.59	194,417.39	339.07	194,756.46	8	2,434,456.00	2,239,699.54
Non-personnel										
Supplies & Serv.		24,400.00	410.00	24,810.00	32,020.00	410.00	32,430.00	29	110,769.00	78,339.00
Outlay		53.00	22,299.00	22,352.00	900.00	22,299.00	23,199.00	93	25,000.00	1,801.00
Total Non-per.		24,453.00	22,709.00	47,162.00	32,920.00	22,709.00	55,629.00	41	135,769.00	80,140.00
Total Traffic Bureau	15.30	58,021.52	23,048.07	81,069.59	227,337.39	23,048.07	250,385.46	10	2,570,225.00	2,319,839.54

BUDGET STATUS REPORT

DEPT. Police Department   FUND NO. 100   PERIOD ENDING July 31, 1974   PERCENT OF YEAR COMPLETED

ELEMENT AND OBJECT ACCOUNT TITLES	ACCT. NO.	CURRENT PERIOD			YEAR TO DATE				BUDGET STATUS	
		DISBURSED	ENCUMBERED	TOTAL DISB & ENC	DISBURSED	ENCUMBERED	TOTAL DISB & ENC	% BUD EXP	TOTAL BUDGET	UNENC. BAL OF BUDGET
Auditors Variance Account	15.98				.03		.03			.03
Position Years										
Personnel Exp.										
Salaries & Wages	1151	172.13-		172.13-	1,469.53		1,469.53			1,469.53
Unused Sick Lv	1155				34.69		34.69			34.69
Total Sal. & Wgs.		172.13-		172.13-	1,504.22		1,504.22			1,504.22
Retir. Contr.										
Soc. Sec.	2150				124.19		124.19			124.15
Total Pensions	2152				68.19		68.19			68.19
					192.38		192.38			192.38
Workmen's Comp.	2424				135.72		135.72			135.72
Health & Life	2425				138.14		138.14			138.14
Total Insurance					273.86		273.86			273.86
Total Personnel		172.13-		172.13-	1,970.46		1,970.46			1,970.46
Non-Personnel										
Office Supplies	3301	23.14		23.14	1,218.00		1,218.00			1,218.00
Cleaning Supplies	3311	5.98-		5.98-	649.13		649.13			649.13
Total Supl. & Serv.		17.16		17.16	1,867.13		1,867.13			1,867.13
Total Non-per		17.16		17.16	1,867.13		1,867.13			1,867.13
Total										
Auditors Variance Account	15.90	154.97-		154.97-	3,837.59		3,837.59			3,837.59

BUDGET STATUS REPORT

CITY OF SAN DIEGO, CALIFORNIA

DEPT. Police Department   FUND NO. 100   PERCENT OF YEAR COMPLETED   PERIOD ENDING July 31, 19

ELEMENT AND OBJECT ACCOUNTING	ACCT. NO.	CURRENT PERIOD			YEAR TO DATE			% BUD EXP	BUDGET STATUS	
		DISBURSED	ENCUMBERED	TOTAL DISB.& ENC.	DISBURSED	ENCUMBERED	TOTAL DISB.& ENC.		TOTAL BUDGET	UNENC. BAL OF BUDGET
Total Police Dept.	1500									
Position Years		53.84		53.84	103.84		103.84	8	1,298.00	1 19.
Personnel Exp.										
Salaries & Wages		30,598.00	15,468.75	46,066.75	293,906.85	15,468.75	309,375.60	8	3,867,195.00	3,557,819
Unused Sick Lv.		1,420.00	365.15	1,785.15	6,937.89	365.15	7,303.04	8	91,288.00	83,984
Pensions		12,342.12	2,025.75	14,367.87	38,475.40	2,025.00	40,500.40	8	506,255.00	445,754
Insurance		3,691.17	2,882.75	6,573.92	54,772.29	2,882.75	57,655.04	8	720,688.00	663,032
Total Personnel		48,051.29	20,741.65	68,792.94	394,092.43	20,741.65	414,834.08	6	5,185,426.00	4,770,591
Non-Personnel										
Supplies & Serv.		24,400.00	8,796.10	33,196.10	167,125.94	8,796.10	175,922.04	12	1,466,017.00	1,290,094
Outlay		1,286.00	22,299.00	23,585.00	189,680.40	22,299.00	211,979.40	30	706,598.00	494,618
Total Non-per.		25,686.00	31,095.10	56,781.10	356,806.34	31,095.10	387,901.44	18	2,172,615.00	1,784,713
Total Police Dept.	1500	73,737.29	51,836.75	125,574.04	750,898.77	51,836.75	802,735.52	10	7,358,041.00	6,555,305

CITY OF SAN DIEGO	CHAPTER	SECTION
PROGRAM ACCOUNTING PROCEDURES MANUAL	4	2

SUBJECT	PAGE 1 OF 1
APPROPRIATION STATUS REPORT (FORM DP-106)	DATE July 1, 1974

The Appropriation Status Report is designed to provide summary management information on the status of each departmental appropriation and allotment in accordance with the requirements of the City Charter, Sections 81 and 89.

The Appropriation Status Report reflects the amounts appropriated, allotted and expended in each department. The amounts are summarized to major object account classification for each allotment level within the department. This means that if your department allots at the department level it would be summarized and appear in the Appropriation Status Report for the department only. If you allot at the program level then each program will be shown in the summary.

The following items shall be reported at each allotment level:

DEPARTMENT OR PROGRAM TITLE & NUMBER

PERSONNEL EXPENSE
    SALARIES & WAGES (Total regular Salaries & Wages (including Comp Time earned & Labor Load)).
    UNUSED SICK LEAVE (Total Employer's Contribution to Unused Sick Leave)
    OVERTIME (Total Overtime Salaries & Wages Paid)
    TOTAL SALARIES & WAGES (Total of above)

    OTHER PERSONNEL EXP. (Total Employer Contribution to Retirement, Social Security, Workmen's Compensation & Health & Life Insurance)

TOTAL PERSONNEL EXP. (Total of above)

TOTAL NON-PERSONNEL EXP. (Total Supplies, Services & Outlay)

TOTAL PROGRAM OR DEPARTMENT (Total of above depending on the Allotment Level(s)).

Overtime Salaries & Wages paid is reflected on this report and you should be aware that the Appropriation Status Report is the only report to display paid overtime. In addition to this item, the amount allotted, the amount unallotted and the unencumbered balance of the allotment shows only on the Appropriation Status Report.

For a more detailed picture of the amounts for each element and object account you should consult the Budget Status Report.

CP 106 (1/74)

DEPT POLICE DEPT.

APPROPRIATION STATUS REPORT
THE CITY OF SAN DIEGO, CALIFORNIA

FUND NO. 100   PERIOD ENDING, JULY 31, 1974   PERCENT OF YEAR COMPLETED: 008

DESCRIPTION	ACCT NO	AMOUNT APPROPRIATED	ALLOTTED	ACTIVITY TO DATE — DISBURSED	ACTIVITY TO DATE — ENCUMBERED	TOTAL DISB & ENCUMB	% YR REQD	UNENC BALANCE OF ALLOTMENT	UNALLOTTED	UNENC BALANCE OF APPROPRIATION
TRAFFIC BUREAU	15.30									
PERSONNEL EXPENSE										
SALARIES & WAGES		1842 310 00	460 578 00	147 117 32	267 48	147 384 80	8	313 193 20	3 224 042 00	1 694 925 20
UNUSED SICK LEAVE		49 401 60	12 350 40	3 944 78	7 35	3 952 13	8	8 398 27	37 051 20	45 449 47
OVERTIME										
TOTAL SALARIES & WAGES		1891 711 60	472 928 40	151 062 10	274 83	151 336 93	8	321 591 47	1 418 783 20	1 740 374 67
OTHER PERSONNEL EXPENSE		542 744 40	135 696 10	43 355 29	64 24	43 419 53	8	92 266 57	407 058 30	499 324 87
TOTAL PERSONNEL EXPENSE		2434 456 00	603 614 50	194 417 39	339 07	194 756 46	8	413 858 04	1 825 841 50	2 239 699 54
TOTAL NON-PERSONNEL EXP.		135 769 00	60 000 00	32 920 00	22709 00	55 629 00	41	4 371 00	75 769 00	80 140 00
TOTAL TRAFFIC BUREAU	15.30	2570 225 00	668 614 50	227 337 39	23048 07	250 385 46	10	418 229 04	1 901 610 50	2 319 839 54
INVESTIGATION BUREAU	15.40									
PERSONNEL EXPENSE										
SALARIES & WAGES		1555 050 00	393 763 00	124 404 00		124 404 00	8	264 359 00	1 166 287 00	1 430 646 00
UNUSED SICK LEAVE		7 814 00	1 953 00	625 12		625 12	8	1 327 88	5 861 00	7 185 98
OVERTIME				312 15		312 15		312 15-		312 15-
TOTAL SALARIES & WAGES		1562 864 00	390 716 00	125 341 27		125 341 27	8	265 374 73	1 272 148 00	1 437 522 73
OTHER PERSONNEL EXPENSE		295826 00	74 207 00	23 746 08		23 746 08	8	50 460 92	222 619 03	273 079 92
TOTAL PERSONNEL EXPENSE		1859 690 00	404 923 00	149 087 35		149 087 35	8	315 835 65	1 494 767 00	1 710 602 65
TOTAL NON-PERSONNEL EXP.		196 919 00	49 230 00	157 523 16	230 36	157 753 52	80	108 523 52-	147 689 00	39 165 52-
TOTAL INVESTIGATION BUREAU	15.40	2056 609 00	514 153 00	306 610 51	230 36	306 840 87	15	207 312 13	1 642 456 00	1 749 765 13
AUDITORS VARIANCE ACCT.	15.98									
PERSONNEL EXPENSE										
SALARIES & WAGES				1 469 52		1 469 53		1 469 53-		1 469 53-
UNUSED SICK LEAVE				3469		34 69		34 69-		34 69-
OVERTIME										
TOTAL SALARIES & WAGES				1 50422		1 504 22		1 504 22-		1 504 22-
OTHER PERSONNEL EXPENSE				46624		456 24		456 24-		456 24-
TOTAL PERSONNEL EXPENSE				1 97046		1 970 46		1 970 46-		1 970 46-
TOTAL NON-PERSONNEL EXP.				1 86713		1 867 13		1 867 13-		1 867 13-
TOTAL AUDITORS VARIANCE ACCT.	15.93			3 63759		3 837 59		3 837 59-		3 837 59-

CF 10a (7/77)

APPROPRIATION STATUS REPORT
THE CITY OF SAN DIEGO, CALIFORNIA

DEPT: POLICE DEPT.   FUND NO. 100   PERIOD ENDING JULY 31, 1974

DESCRIPTION	ACCT NO	AMOUNT APPROPRIATED	ACTIVITY TO DATE			PERCENT OF YEAR COMPLETED		OOB	APPROPRIATION STATUS		
			AUDITED	DISBURSED	ENCUMBERED	TOTAL DISB & ENCUMB	% APPR TO PLAN		UNEXPD BALANCE OF ALLOTMENT	UNALLOTTED	UNEXPD BALANCE OF APPROPRIATION
POLICE DEPARTMENT	15.00										
PERSONNEL EXPENSE											
SALARIES & WAGES		3 867 195 00	966 799 00	293 594 70	15 458 75	309 053 45	8		657 735 55	2 900 395 00	3 558 131 55
UNUSED SICK LEAVE		91 288 00	22 822 00	6 937 89	365 15	7 303 04	8		15 518 96	68 456 00	83 334 96
OVERTIME				312 15		312 15			312 15-		312 15-
TOTAL SALARIES & WAGES		3 958 483 00	939 621 00	300 844 74	15 833 70	315 678 64	8		672 942 35	2 966 862 00	3 641 804 35
OTHER PERSONNEL EXPENSE		1 226 943 00	305 735 00	93 247 69	4 907 75	93 155 44	8		205 579 56	920 208 00	1 128 787 55
TOTAL PERSONNEL EXPENSE		5 185 426 00	1 295 356 00	394 082 43	20 741 65	414 834 03	8		381 521 92	3 339 070 00	4 770 591 92
TOTAL NON-PERSONNEL EXP.		2 172 615 00	543 154 00	356 806 34	31 095 10	387 901 44	18		155 252 56	1 629 461 00	1 284 713 55
TOTAL POLICE DEPARTMENT	15.00	7 358 041 00	1 839 510 00	750 898 77	51 836 75	802 735 52	10		1 016 774 48	5 518 531 00	6 555 305 48

CITY OF SAN DIEGO

PROGRAM ACCOUNTING PROCEDURES MANUAL

CITY OF SAN DIEGO	CHAPTER	SECTION
	5	2
PROGRAM ACCOUNTING PROCEDURES MANUAL	PAGE 1 of 1	
SUBJECT	DATE	
CHANGES TO THE JULY 1, 1973 CHART OF OBJECT ACCOUNT NUMBERS	July 1, 1974	

The CMP Project has necessitated some modification to the Chart of Accounts now in use. Please note the following changes:

New Object Acct. No. (7/1/74)		Change From Existing (7/1/73)
	Personnel Expense	
1151	Salaries & Wages	Title Change
1155	Unused Sick Leave	New Account
2150	Retirement Contribution	3450
2152	Social Security Contribution	3452
2424	Compensation Insurance	No Change
2425	Employee Group Insurance	No Change
	Non-Personnel Expense	
3600	Contingencies - UR	2100
3601	Power Reserve - UR	2101
3602	Fire Program - UR	2102
3212	Telephone & Telegraph	2212
3210	Transportation Allowance	2215
3241	Gas, Light and Power Service	2241
3242	Street Light and Traffic Signal	2242
3244	Water Service - Including Hydrant Rental	2244
3245	Alternate Paying Agents' Fees	2245
3246	Sewer Service Charge	2246
3282	Data Processing Services	2292
3227	Transfers - Cash	2299
3411	Rental of Lands and/or Buildings	2411
3401	Rent to Owners (Leased Housing Authority Only)	2412
3430	Petty Cash Advance Auditors	2430
3488	Equipment Depreciation	2435
3613	Rental of Automotive, Construction and Shop Equipment	2613
3614	Tab Equipment	2614

CITY OF SAN DIEGO	CHAPTER	SECTION
	5	3
PROGRAM ACCOUNTING PROCEDURES MANUAL	PAGE 1a OF 14	
SUBJECT	DATE	
CHART OF DEPARTMENT/PROGRAM/ELEMENT NUMBERS	July 1, 1974	

The Chart of Department Level and Program/Element Numbers that follows is
as complete as can be complied at this time. This chart does not reflect
any reorganization that may be implemented July 1, 1974.

In the Title section of the chart, the first level of indentation indicates
Program level, while the second level of indentation identifies the Element
level.

*FIRE STATION
LOCATION MODEL*

FIRE DEPARTMENT

The responsibilities of the Fire Department are to: extinguish fires promptly, provide emergency assistance, and fire prevention.

Department No. 16.00
Budget Page   155

	Amount	*Positions*
Actual FY 1972	$10,036,711	692.00
Current FY 1973	10,421,727	670.00
Proposed FY 1974	10,885,095	687.75
Proposed Increase	463,368(4.4%)	17.75(2.6%)

ANALYSIS AND RECOMMENDATIONS

1. The Legislative Analyst Office recommended during the CIP Budget Meeting that no expenditures for fire stations be allocated until a computerized location system had been reviewed. As numerous fire stations are being newly created and relocated, a strong possibility exists that one or several of the stations might not be required. The computerized system would determine the exact response time needs for the immediate area. Should the study determine that less stations are required major savings would result in CIP and operational expenditures. The personnel increases of 17 man-years in the fire fighting program reflects the expanded CIP program as the additional man-years are necessary to staff the additional fire stations.

The City Manager's Office has concurred with our Office's CIP recommendation as to determining optimal, computerized locations before allocations are made on specific sites for proposed main and satellite stations. *This is a major recommendation as it impacts on the CIP expenditures and on-going annual operational costs as reflected in the increase of 17 man-years in the fire fighting program and the CIP expenditure of $1.5 million.* In addition, our Office has been informed by the Fire Department that the Uniform Fire Information Reporting System project of the Fire Department results in a computerized system with inputs, such as time response. This will allow better record keeping abilities, and be of assistance in a computerized location system for fire stations. The Uniform Fire Information Reporting System, however, will not in itself enable the Fire Department to locate Fire Stations.

2. AB 2066 requires the Chief Fire Official of each city to gather statistical fire information and submit this data to the State Fire Marshall. The Fire Department is requesting two additional man-years, one clerical and one fire engineer, to perform this data collection and comply with the state requirement.

The uniform fire incident reporting system will cost the City an estimated $50,000 non-personal costs annually. This is the cost of operating the system and does not include the required man-years. The cost of this program is due to State mandate (SB2066) whose effective date is January 1, 1974. *The Legislative Analyst Office therefore recommends that the Legislative Representative initiate legislation, in conjunction with the League of California Cities, which would amend and clarify the provisions of SB90 to allow local governments reimbursements for all new State-mandated programs whose operative date is after January 1, 1973.*
Currently SB90 requires that the State reimburse local governments the full costs of those programs which result from new state-mandated programs enacted after January 1, 1973.

3. Also, in regard to the creation of new stations, we believe it is imperative that the Planning Department provide the Council with planning and development information. (See recommendation 5, Page 64, Planning Department, Budget Hearing, May 21.)

4. We would also like to urge Council to adopt our recommendation of last year relative to the Fire Department establishing a fire inspection fee schedule. This proposed recommendation will result in a $250,000 annual savings to the City. It reflects the user fee principle which our Office has strongly advocated.

5. The City Manager's Office has accepted our Office's recommendation concerning improvements to existing stations which are scheduled to be abandoned (notably equipment purchases including air conditioners, awnings, etc.). As a result, the proposed Fire Department operating budget does not include such expenditures.

6. The Fire Department prepares an 800'' scale map book showing the City street system and fire hydrant location which is continuously updated to reflect new subdivision activity and also prepares a large wall map which is given to all fire stations. These maps are prepared at the La Jolla fire station by seven trained firemen (2 Fire Captains, 2 Engineers and 3 Firemen). The estimated manhours per year is 4,000 - 5,000.

The program budget of the Fire Department does not break out the Mapping

Program nor its costs. Salaries would amount to approximately $27,500 and the printing and associated costs to $6,600 for a total annual cost of $34,100.

The Legislative Analyst Office does not believe that this Mapping program represents the most efficient use of man-years or the most effective Mapping Program; *therefore, we recommend that the present mapmaking program of the Fire Department be made a responsibility of a centralized map making unit.*

During the 1973 Budget Review our Office recommended that the City mapping programs be analyzed for the purpose of achieving a more unified and efficient mapping program. The Committee Report on Review of Mapping Needs of City Departments was released February, 1973. Basically the Committee recommended centralizing the major mapping programs under the Public Works Department.

The Legislative Analyst Office concurs with this recommendation as it would centralize the major mapping program and provide quality material for use by Departments at a reduced cost.

The Legislative Analyst Office further recommends that a fee schedule be utilized for private distribution as well as a departmental reimbursement of cost to the Public Works Department so as to cover all costs of this mapping program.

CITY of SAN DIEGO

MEMORANDUM

November 29, 1973

Phil Steed, Legislative Analyst's Office

R. C. Phillips, Fire Department

FIRE STATION LOCATION PROGRAM

The Fire Station Location Program conducted by the Fire Department was undertaken in the following phases.

PHASE I - DESCRIBING THE AREA

    A. Census tracts were drawn on maps to facilitate incident reporting.

    B. Focal points were established at:

        1. Target hazards - schools, hospitals, petroleum storage, lumber yards, high rise structures, hazardous processing areas, etc.

        2. Geographical centers of groups of like occupancies - dwellings, apartments, small retail stores, etc.

    C. Fire Demand Zones (FDZs) were established around each focal point. The size of the FDZ was limited to the time required to travel from the focal point to any point on the FDZ perimeter. Thirty seconds was used in most cases. There were a total of 1,181 FDZs.

    D. The structural content of each FDZ was analyzed and evaluated as to its fire protection needs. Fire potential and risk were considered.

    E. A response time for each FDZ was determined. The basis used was the correlation of "flashover time" and response time. The hypothesis used was if the Fire Department is not able to commence extinguishment operations prior to flashover, the life and property loss will be excessive. (See enclosures 1, 2, 3) Response times assigned initially were:

        1. Principal business district - 1½ minutes

        2. Target hazards - 3 minutes

        3. Residential - 5 minutes

        4. Undeveloped areas - 6 plus minutes

F. Station sites were located on the maps. The 34 existing stations and 166 potential sites were used.

G. The link system was then constructed:

1. Nodes were placed at focal points, station sites, and at all intersections that a fire apparatus traveling from a station site to a focal point would pass.

2. The nodes were then linked together and the distance between each node was measured in hundredths of miles. The speed with which a fire apparatus could reasonably be expected to respond between each link was also determined. Posted speed limits were used as a basis and adjusted by actually timing fire apparatus responses throughout the City. There were in excess of 4,000 links.

PHASE II - PATH PROGRAM

A. All of the above data was coded and placed on key punch cards.

B. Cards were organized into checked and corrected card files.

C. The Path Program was run by Data Processing. It produced an output report that displayed the actual path and response time required from each proposed site to every focal point in the system.

D. The Path Program was analyzed, corrected, recoded, and re-run by Data Processing.

PHASE III - LOCATION PROGRAM

A. The number of Fire Department incidents and the number of responses made into each zone last year was determined.

B. The response level deviation file was developed. This file shows the number of engine companies that should respond to each FDZ on a first alarm.

C. The response time deviation file was developed. This file shows the response time that was assigned to each FDZ.

D. A control card was produced that governed the response time standard used, the stations seeded (required to be included in the solution), whether the response time deviation file and the response level deviation file would be used.

E. The above data was coded and placed on key punch forms.
    Together with the output from PATH, this information was
    then run on the computer.

    1. The first run was made using no seeds, a three minute
        standard time, and the response level deviation file.

    2. Output from the first run made it apparent that a three
        minute standard could not be obtained without a large
        number of additional stations. It was decided to go to
        a four minute standard. This would mean that the prin-
        cipal business district standard would be 2 minutes,
        4 minutes for target hazards, 6 minutes for residential
        areas, and 6 plus minutes for undeveloped areas.

F. Using this 4 minute standard, the next run showed that to
    cover all zones in the City within the required time would
    take 105 fire stations. Additional runs were made at
    5, 6, 7, 8, 9, 10 and 11 minutes. (See graph, enclosure #4).

G. The next runs were made seeding stations 1, 28 and 35. The
    station sites that showed on the previous runs were analyzed
    and sites that did not appear in any solutions were elimi-
    nated. This was done because the computer was going "cyclic"
    on some runs and we were advised by Data Processing personnel
    that the number of sites should be reduced to eliminate the
    problem.

H. Different configurations of station locations were then run.
    These outputs were analyzed, taking into account the number
    of FDZs covered, and uncovered, and the number of responses
    occurring within the FDZ the last year.

I. Additional runs were made and analyzation continued to be
    made until the final solution was reached.

J. The final solution showed 33 as the minimum acceptable number
    of stations.

K. The final solution was then used to determine the minimum
    number of truck companies needed. Response times of 3, 7, and
    10 minutes were used. The same analyzing process used for
    station locations was used. The final solution indicated 11
    truck companies minimum.

This is a general description of the station location process. If there
is additional information needed, please contact me.

                                    R. C. Phillips
                                    Assistant Chief
                                    Fire Department

RCP/mry
Encls.

CITY of SAN DIEGO
MEMORANDUM

FILE NO.:

DATE : January 21, 1974

TO : Honorable Mayor and Council

FROM : Michael Babunakis, Legislative Analyst

SUBJECT: Recommended Fire Station Location Model

Our Office in the Fiscal Year 1973-74 CIP Analysis of the Fire Department identified major revisions from year to year in the proposed station expenditures indicating: (1) uncertainty as to goals, (2) a lack of adequate response time, and (3) a lack of location data for effective planning. For these reasons, it was recommended that a Fire Station Location Model be created prior to CIP expenditures of the Fire Department. This recommendation was accepted. Several methods for such a computerized undertaking were examined resulting in the final selection of Public Technology Incorporated (PTI) to assist City personnel in conducting a computerized Fire Station Location Model. (See enclosed.)

We are happy to report that preliminary results of the Fire Station Location Model indicate: (1) substantial savings to the City; specifically, the capital improvement program based upon the recommended Fire Station Location Model will result in an estimated, one-time CIP savings of approximately $800,000 and annual, recurring operational savings of approximately $1 million as compared to the original 1965 Master Plan of the Fire Department, (2) improved response times or the average response time will be decreased by approximately 30 seconds when compared with existing coverage, and

(3) increased zone coverage as an additional 12% of all fire
demand zones will be covered within Fire Department time constraints (this represents a 33% reduction in zones uncovered
with time constraints).

   Further benefits of this methodology may be expected if a
locational study were performed on a biannual basis. This would
necessitate maintenance of the street network file by traffic
engineering, Community Development, and other appropriate departments or divisions. Because this model can be extended to the
location of other public facilities (i.e., libraries, parks,
hospitals, etc.) with similar monetary savings and improved
efficiency the Legislative Analyst Office recommends that similar
locational models be performed prior to the adoption of departmental master plans for capital improvements when such facilities
provide services based on response or travel times or geographic
service areas.

   Finally, we are most pleased to report that this recommendation represents such a fine result in terms of fiscal savings,
increased fire protection coverage and response time.

                                        Michael Babunakis

MB/PS/dma

ANALYSIS OF THE BUDGET
STATE OF CALIFORNIA
FISCAL YEAR 1970-71

Department of Motor Vehicles

DEPARTMENT OF MOTOR VEHICLES

Items 234, 235 and 236 from the Motor Vehicle
Fund, Motor Vehicle License Fee Fund,
and the Harbors and Watercraft Revolv-
ing Fund   Budget page 1223

Requested 1970–71	$64,562,780
Estimated 1969–70	64,426,747
Actual 1968–69	59,497,332
Requested increase $136,033 (0.02 percent)	
Total recommended reduction	$8,857,223

SUMMARY OF MAJOR ISSUES AND RECOMMENDATIONS

1. We recommend that the price for vehicle registration information be be raised from $7 per thousand to $25 per thousand and the budget be reduced $857,268.

2. The charge for individual items of vehicle registration information be raised to $1 and the budget reduced by $86,710.

3. The driver improvement programs be discontinued, the budget reduced $4,047,601 and the man-year allocation reduced 405.2 man years.

4. The price per item for driver's license information be raised to $1 and the budget reduced by $3,832,200.

5. The price per item for financial responsibility information be raised to $1 and the budget reduced by $33,444.

6. The Department of Motor Vehicles conduct a survey of states with EDP systems to determine the potential utilization of the computer to provide service to field office operations.

GENERAL PROGRAM STATEMENT

The Department of Motor Vehicles is part of the Business Transportation Agency along with the Department of Public Works and the California Highway Patrol which, together, facilitate a cooperative approach to the development of a safe and effective highway system. The department's objectives are to: (1) identify ownership of vehicles through registration, (2) promote highway safety through the licensing and control of drivers, (3) protect the public through licensing and regulation of occupations and businesses related to the manufacturing, sale, transporting or disposal of vehicles, and (4) promote financial security following accidents. Programs designed to achieve these objectives are (1) vehicle licensing and titling, (2) driver licensing and control, (3) occupational licensing and control, (4) security following accidents, (5) Department of Motor Vehicles Associated Services and (6) administration.

ANALYSIS AND RECOMMENDATIONS
VEHICLE LICENSING AND TITLING

The purpose of this program is to register vehicles, collect fees and record vehicle transactions. Program elements include: (1) vehicle

Transportation Agency   Items 234–236

Department of Motor Vehicles—Continued

ownership, registration documentations and certificate issuance, (2) vehicle fee collection, (3) vehicle record and file maintenance, (4) vehicle information and sale of records and (5) use tax computation and collection.

The department requests $32,404,164 for the program for fiscal year 1970–71, an increase of $1,517,873 over the current year. The increase is attributed to wage and salary increases and increased operating expense. The requested man-year allocation is 2,915.1, a 3.3 man-year reduction from the current authorized level. The department estimates that it will register approximately 13,776,000 vehicles, a 3.2 percent increase over the current year, and will collect approximately $265,-931,000 in fees, an increase of $10,827,000. Program elements about which we have questions are discussed below.

Vehicle Information and Sale of Records

We recommend that the department raise the price for vehicle registration information from $7 per thousand to $25 per thousand and that the budget be reduced by $857,268 to reflect the increased revenue.

The department for several years has provided, (1) vehicle registration, (2) driver's license and (3) financial responsibility information to both governmental and nongovernmental entities. The information falls into two categories; information in bulk and individual information item requests regarding a specific driver or vehicle.

Bulk Sale of Vehicle Registration Information

Table 1 indicates the volume of information provided, both fee and gratis.

Table 1
Vehicle Registration Information Sales

Individual requests	Actual 1968–69	Estimate 1969–70	Estimate 1970–71
Fee requests _____	331,112	327,500	333,500
No fee requests _____	592,057	611,200	632,600
Total _____	923,169	938,700	966,100
Bulk sales _____	44,459,170	46,015,200	47,625,800

The gratis requests are by governmental agencies.

As Table 1 indicates, during fiscal year 1968–69, the department sold 44,459,170 items in bulk from the registration files. It transferred the information from its EDP system to magnetic tape at a charge sufficient only to cover the direct costs ($1 per thousand). Information included name, make, year and model of every registered vehicle. The department does not regulate the use of the mailing lists developed from vehicle registration information. The lists may be used for any purpose, may be resold to any person or company and the department does not require copies of material mailed to addresses provided by the motor vehicle records as it did historically when such addresses were provided from the driver's license file.

There are serious questions regarding the wisdom of selling bulk registration information. By providing the names and addresses of millions of Californians the state greatly contributes to the increasing

Items 234-236   Transportation Agency

Department of Motor Vehicles—Continued

amounts of unsolicited "junk" mail now being dumped upon them. For this reason we believe the Legislature should give serious consideration to the discontinuance of these bulk sales as a matter of public policy. At the present session, two bills, SB 11 and SB 44 have been introduced with respect to this issue.

If the state is to continue the sale of bulk registration information, we recommend that the price per thousand be raised from $7 to $25. The department has recently taken the position that it properly ought to realize some profit from the sale of its records and accordingly raised the price from $1 to $7 per thousand. Prior to this action, the department investigated the charges levied for similar information by other states. The average charge of those states which sell information is $8.50 per thousand and the charge by state ranges from 47 cents to $25 per thousand. New York, the state most similar to California in terms of population and vehicle registration, charges $25 per thousand. New York, however, has a monopolistic arrangement by which it sells its records to one company only, which in turn sells to various customers. We do not believe the monopoly is necessary since we believe even the $25 is low enough to attract multiple buyers. Table 2 projects the additional potential revenues if the charge per thousand is increased to various levels based on the 1970–71 estimated volume of 47,625,800 items.

Table 2
Current and Projected Revenue for Bulk Sale of
Vehicle Registration Information

Fee per thousand	Total department cost	Total fees	Total net gain
$7	$61,437	$333,382	$271,945
10	61,437	476,260	414,823
15	61,437	714,390	652,953
20	61,437	952,520	891,083
25	61,437	1,190,650	1,129,213

The Department of Motor Vehicles is in the process of spending approximately $110 million for one of the most advanced EDP systems in the world. It can provide more information faster and more economically than any other state motor vehicle department in the country. The department provides far more information than any other state motor vehicle department and the information is in a much more usable form. We believe that the sale of information should help amortize the cost of automation and that the state is justified in charging these profitmaking organizations $25 per thousand.

Sale of Individual Items from the Registration Files

We recommend that the department increase the charge per individual items of vehicle registration information to $1 and that the budget be reduced by $87,710 to reflect the increased revenue.

At the present time, the department sells three types of information (1) vehicle registration, (2) driver's license and (3) financial responsibility, of which only the sale of driver's license information produces profit. The sale of vehicle registration and financial responsibility

Department of Motor Vehicles—Continued

information does not produce enough revenue to offset the cost of producing it so that in effect, the purchasers of driver's license information subsidize the purchases of vehicle registration and financial responsibility information.

The department estimates that it will sell approximately 333,500 individual items of vehicle registration information. The cost per item to the department for providing this information is 74 cents, but it charges only 40 cents per item, for a total estimated loss in fiscal year 1970–71 of $113,390. Present law provides that the Department of Motor Vehicles may levy a sufficient charge to offset the cost of information. The department has interpreted this to mean that as long as the entire program is creating revenue, each individual program need not be self-supporting.

We believe that the present rate for vehicle registration information should be increased for two reasons. First, we believe that the purchasers of driver's license information should not be required to subsidize those who obtain vehicle registration information. Second, we believe that since the department has begun a policy of raising the fees for information in order to increase revenue, it should increase all fees, including the fee for individual items of vehicle registration information. In almost every instance those who purchase information from the motor vehicle files, do so because they intend to utilize that information for commercial gain. We, therefore, see no reason why the department should not raise the fee at least to a level that will cover cost. If the fees were increased to $1 per item, the net gain for the estimated sales in fiscal year 1970–71 would be $86,710.

Sale of Information to Private Research Companies

At the present time, there are 11 private research companies located in the Department of Motor Vehicles Building in Sacramento. These companies maintain staffs which have free access to the vehicle registration records and can obtain driver's license information for 40 cents per item. They in turn sell this information for approximately $2 per item. The department theoretically charges these companies for the space they occupy but does not charge a sufficient amount to offset even the cost of the space they rent. The department estimates that the cost for the space is 35 cents per square foot per month, but charges the private research companies only 34 cents per square foot per month.

The department has only a limited amount of floor space available which has been filled to capacity for a number of years. However, the department has no system whereby available floor space is allocated on a competitive basis. These companies provide information to various collection agencies, retail stores and other types of businesses located throughout the state. One of the major problems is the fact that many of the people who deal with these private research companies are under the impression that they are dealing with the Department of Motor Vehicles. In fact, the Department of Motor Vehicles exercises virtually no control over the activities of these research companies.

Items 234–236   Transportation Agency

Department of Motor Vehicles—Continued

We believe there are two alternatives which the state should consider. First, the department could close its files to outside companies and provide information only at a specified charge.

The second alternative would be for the department to lease the space in its building on a competitive basis with the bids beginning at a sufficient level to generate significant revenue for the department. We do not believe any private company should have access to the files free of charge.

DRIVER LICENSING AND CONTROL

The purpose of this program is to license drivers and to promote highway safety by identifying and controlling those drivers who are defined as unsafe. Program elements include, (1) driver's license issuance, (2) postlicensing control, (3) certificate issuance, and (4) information services. The department requests $29,634,371 for the next fiscal year for this program, $1,447,160 less than the estimated expenditure for fiscal year 1969–70. The reduction is primarily attributed to the reduced manpower requirement. The requested man-year allocation is 2,661.6 man-years, a reduction of 474.4 man-years from the currently authorized level. This is largely attributed to increased automation of the driver's license file.

Postlicensing Control

We recommend that the discretionary driver improvement programs be discontinued, that the budget be reduced by $4,047,601 and the man-year allocation be reduced by 405.2 man-years.

The objective of the postlicensing control program is to promote highway safety by identifying and controlling drivers who do not maintain the required standard for safe driving. This element has two parts, that which is mandatory and that which is discretionary. The Vehicle Code requires mandatory actions against drivers convicted of certain major violations such as hit and run, drunk driving, narcotic offenses and manslaughter. The same provisions apply to drivers who fail to satisfy judgments rendered against them as a result of traffic accidents. The customary action is revocation of the driver's license.

The department also has a discretionary program whereby those persons who are classified as negligent drivers by their convictions and/or accident rates are brought into a driver improvement program where an effort is made to change their driving habits.

During the past year, the department has released a study which evaluated various types of driver improvement programs in an attempt to determine which type was most effective in reducing accidents. These programs included various types of group meetings as well as individual meetings. The study concluded that of the methods tested, only "group educational meetings (GEM)" had any downward effect upon the male negligent driver's accident rate, while four programs had some effect upon female negligent drivers. The study concluded that the best program for negligent drivers would be for the male drivers to be subjected to group educational meetings while women should attend one of two types of individual hearings. The report recognized

Department of Motor Vehicles—Continued

that different programs for males and females might not be acceptable and since the number of negligent female drivers is small, suggested that group educational meetings would be acceptable for both. The department has apparently accepted this recommendation and is expanding the group education meetings.

The department is requesting $11,473,710 for its postlicensing control element, $4,257,918 for its mandatory activity and $7,215,792 for the discretionary.

We have serious questions regarding the effectiveness of the entire driver improvement program, particularly the discretionary portion. We question whether enough of the driving population obtain enough benefit from the program to warrant an expenditure at this level. The department informs us that those individuals who are considered negligent drivers constitute 1 percent of the driving population and are responsible for 2 percent of the accidents occurring each year. The number of those affected by the program is further reduced since the study indicates that only one-half of those scheduled for group meetings actually attend. Since the department is shifting the program to group meetings presumably the percentage of those affected by the program will be reduced to one-half of 1 percent of the total drivers. The study also indicated that the accident rate of those who attended group meetings was reduced by 2.2 per 100 accidents. Using this statistic, the program seems to be responsible for reducing the total annual accident rate by only slightly over *.002 percent* (2 hundredths of one percent).

We believe that in some respects the department's driver improvement program is worse than no program because it gives the impression that something is being done to reduce the accident rate when in fact very little is accomplished.

We suggest there are some alternatives to the existing program. At the present time the department sends a warning letter to any individual whose conviction rate indicates he or she is in danger of becoming a negligent driver. If the negligent behavior continues, the individual is then directed to the driver improvement program. An alternative procedure would be for the department to continue to issue the warning notice but to automatically suspend the license of any person who subsequently becomes negligent. The driver's record is approximately 85 percent automated and will be completely automated by December 1970. There would be relatively little effort required since the computer is already programmed to issue warning letters auomatically and could easily be programmed to issue notices of suspension.

We believe that the thrust of the postlicensing control programs should be toward establishing an effective system of notification to judges of the traffic record of all offenders in order that the judicial assessment of punishment may be based on the offender's record. This fact is not now generally in the record submitted to the judge.

We have been unable to pinpoint the exact cost of the discretionary phase of the control program. The department's accounting system is

Department of Motor Vehicles—Continued

still oriented to the old organizational structure rather than to specific programs. The department develops a line item budget first and then simply allocates the amount available to the various program elements. The same is true with the manpower allocation. Specific programs are allotted a given number of man-years but the department is unable to determine the categories of the positions within the programs.

The department has estimated, however, that the approximate cost of the discretionary phase is $7,215,792 of which $3,128,996 represents nonreducible costs such as EDP equipment, rent and pro rata administrative charges. The total reducible amount is therefore $4,047,601. The personnel allocation which could be reduced if the driver improvement program is terminated is approximately 405.2 man-years.

Information Services—Sale of Individual Items—Drivers' License

We recommend the price per item for driver's license information be raised from 40 cents to $1, and the budget be reduced by $3,832,200 to reflect the additional revenue.

As we noted in our analysis of vehicle information and sale of records, the department has for a number of years provided information to private individuals and enterprises for a very low fee. Within the past year, considerable attention was given by the press to the sale of bulk driver's license information. In September 1969, two suits were filed in superior court charging the Department of Motor Vehicles with invasion of privacy for selling driver's license information. As a result of the controversy, the Governor ordered that as of October 31, 1969 the sale of bulk driver's license information be discontinued. The sale of individual items continues.

As we stated earlier, the sale of driver's license information is the only one which produces a net profit. The cost to the department for providing each item is 28 cents while the charge is 40 cents per item. In 1968–69 the department sold 6,139,343 items, in 1969–70 it will sell an estimated 6,262,000 and in 1970–71 a projected 6,387,000. The total estimated profit for this program is $766,440.

Although we have stated that the purchasers of one type of motor vehicle information should not subsidize the users of other types, we are aware of the administrative difficulties in maintaining three price levels, (for driver's license, vehicle registration and financial responsibility). We believe that it is preferable for the price to be set at a level sufficient to pay for the costs of each program and at the same time to realize additional revenue to the transportation program. *We therefore recommend that the price per item for driver's license information be increased from 40 cents to $1 and that the budget be reduced by $3,832,200 to reflect the additional revenue.*

OCCUPATIONAL LICENSING AND REGULATION

The objective of this program is to regulate elements of the motor vehicle industry and is the law enforcement arm of the department. A New Car Dealer's Policy and Appeals Board was established in 1967 for the purpose of giving policy direction to the occupational licensing and regulation program with respect to supervision of new car

Department of Motor Vehicles—Continued

dealers and to provide an administrative appeals forum for the dealers. Program elements include, (1) occupational licensing, and (2) occupational regulation.

The department is requesting $2,977,303 for fiscal year 1970-71, a decrease of $101,081 from the estimated expenditure for the current year. The decreased cost is attributed to the reduced man-year requirement. The proposed man-year level is 215.1, a decrease of 26 man-years from the currently authorized level. This is the result of workload adjustments due to the simplification of certain procedures.

SECURITY FOLLOWING ACCIDENT LAW

The objective of this program is to determine that each driver and/or owner of a motor vehicle involved in a reportable accident demonstrates that he is not at fault or, if at fault, has the ability to satisfy any reasonable judgment for damages against him that may arise from the accident. The department is directed by law to remove from the highway those drivers and their vehicles who have not complied with the Security Following Accident Law.

The department is requesting $3,293,712 for the next year which is a decrease of $86,760 over the current estimated expenditure. The decrease is attributed to salary saving since the requested man-years allocation is 73.4 man years less than the currently authorized level.

The program has two elements, registration and driving privilege control, and information service.

Information Service—Sale of Individual Financial Responsibility Items

During the current year, the department will sell an estimated 54,320 items of financial responsibility information and estimates a volume of 55,740 items for the budget year. The cost to the department for each item is 55 cents. The deficit for fiscal year 1969-70 is estimated to be approximately $8,148, and $8,361 for the next fiscal year.

In line with our recommendations regarding the sale of vehicle registration and driver's license information, we recommend that the charge per item for financial responsibility information be increased from 40 cents to $1 and that the budget be reduced by $33,444 to reflect the increased revenue.

DEPARTMENT OF MOTOR VEHICLES ASSOCIATED SERVICES

The Legislature has directed the department to provide services not directly related to motor vehicles or driver licensing and control. These are the (1) issuance of identification cards, and (2) the registration and fee collection for undocumented vessels which constitute the elements of this program.

The department, upon application, issues photo identification cards to California residents, 18 or older. These cards are accepted by commerical and retail industries as official identification. It is estimated that approximately 55,800 cards will be issued during the next fiscal year.

The department, in conforming to the Governor's Reorganization No. 2, will assume all boat registration functions, authority and respon-

Department of Motor Vehicles—Continued

sibilities by March 1970. Prior to this time, the department acted as an authorized agent of the Department of Harbors and Watercraft to register vessels and collect fees. As a result of the new responsibility, the department's budget for this element has increased from $196,040 in fiscal year 1969-70 to $377,532 for fiscal year 1970-71.

DEPARTMENTAL ADMINISTRATION

The budget request for the administration program is $3,741,897, a reduction of $57,244 below the current expenditure. The undistributed administrative cost is $197,805 with the remainder distributed among the five programs. The elements of the administrative program include the executive, program administration, legal services, fiscal and business management, personnel and training, operations and management analysis, and research and statistics.

Management Reporting and Control (MARC)

During fiscal year 1968-69, the department, in an effort to expand its work measurement program sufficiently to establish departmentwide work standards, hired a consultant firm and began the Management Reporting and Control Program (MARC). The program has been partly operational for nearly two years and will be fully operational by March 1970. The total cost of the program is $536,431.37 which was budgeted from the savings realized from the implementation of the work standards program.

The savings to date resulting from the program are $1,400,000 and the rate of savings is expected to be $2,500,000 annually.

Automated Management Information System (AMIS)

The conversion of Department of Motor Vehicle files to a fully automated system was approved by the Legislature in 1965. The system was scheduled to be fully operational by the end of the 1969-70 fiscal year, at which time the original estimates projected that the cost of operating under the new system would be less than the cost of operating under the existing manual system. Because of problems in converting the various files, the operational date was rescheduled to July 1, 1971. This was necessary because the rate of conversion of the manual driver's license files was slower than had originally been estimated. The department now reports that the conversion problems have been overcome and the driver's license file is 85 percent complete. As a result of improved performance, the expected operational date of the entire system is now scheduled to be December 1, 1970.

The vehicle registration files have been fully converted during the past two years since the original vehicle registration system was processed on a second-generation computer utilizing magnetic tape.

The department estimates that by the end of fiscal year 1972-73, the cost of departmental operation will be less under AMIS than the projected costs under the prior methods of processing. Each year thereafter, savings will increase until the total cost of AMIS implementation will be recovered by 1978. Annual savings in excess of $5 million will accrue for each year following 1978-79. Manpower requirements for the

Transportation Agency   Items 234-236

Department of Motor Vehicles—Continued

department will be significantly reduced following the implementation of AMIS and it is estimated that a cumulative reduction of more than 1,000 man-years will occur when compared to the projection for operating requirements without AMIS.

In our budget analysis for fiscal year 1969–70, we reported that the total projected cost of converting to AMIS was $112,885,169. At that time the department reported that this amount was $11,750,236 above the original estimates. We are now informed by the Department that this overrun estimate through 1974–75 has been revised as of November 28, 1969 and the current additional cost is estimated to be $8,359,544.

The Major Mission of AMIS

As the title implies, AMIS was intended to be a total management information system for the Department of Motor Vehicles. The obvious first task of a system of this magnitude was to accomplish the conversion of the massive files which are a basic part of the Department of Motor Vehicles operation. These files contain the records of over 12,000,-000 registered vehicles and 12,000,000 driver's licenses. Through the use of an on-line, real time computer system utilizing third-generation concepts and large random-access storage units, the information contained in these files is instantaneously available to the public, law enforcement, the courts and other qualified users of driver-control data. When the California Law Enforcement Telecommunication System (CLETS) is operational on April 1, 1970, the DMV computers will be available for a 24-hour, seven-day a week inquiry service and will provide instantaneous information to over 1 000 terminals in the CLETS network.

While there is no question that the AMIS system is providing a valuable service in the maintenance of driver and vehicle records and in the provision of information to law enforcement agencies, we believe that it is now proper for the department to begin determining the extent to which this system can assist in the operation of the 146 DMV field offices. Curently, seven of the large field offices have remote terminals connected to the AMIS system. In the original presentation of the AMIS program to the Legislature, one of the features discussed was the possibility of on-line issuance of drivers licenses. This instantaneous issuance of drivers licenses through a computer system was presented as a major improvement in service to the driving public. However, it appears that there is no advance planning toward the on-line issuance of drivers licenses in the field offices and the department has apparently not pursued this facet of the program as originally presented to the Legislature. We have received data from the department which indicates that such a project would exceed the cost of the present procedure. It is our understanding that a number of other states are experimenting with this application and have successfully issued replacement licenses and renewals, particularly in large population centers. We believe there are many aspects of the field office operations which could be improved through the use of remote terminals.

We therefore recommend that the Department of Motor Vehicles conduct a survey of comparable states with automated systems to determine the potential utilization of the computer to provide on-line issu-

Item 237   Transportation Agency

Department of Motor Vehicles—Continued

ance of drivers licenses or to provide other services to the field offices which could result in a reduction of personnel or a reduction in the number of paper transactions required in the processing of license or vehicle registration information. The results of this survey should be made available to the Joint Legislative Budget Committee by November 1, 1970.

AMIS Budget Request for 1970–71

The total budget request for the AMIS program was $11,709,456 in 1969–70 and the proposed budget for 1970–71 is $12,151,695. This increase of $442,239 includes $128,740 for the proposed installation of new Optical Character Recognition Equipment. Although this equipment was not considered as part of the original AMIS proposal, the cost of converting data to machine readable form for the Department of Motor Vehicles and for other large paper handling departments of the state government has risen dramatically and is a major factor in the total cost of automation. As we discuss under Item 36 of this analysis, the Office of Management Services is coordinating two experimental tests of Optical Character Recognition Equipment. This equipment has the ability to recognize and read typewritten characters on source documents, thereby eliminating the transcription or conversion of basic data to machine readable form. The Department of Motor Vehicles has numerous potential applications for this technique and we urge participation in the tests of OCR to be conducted in the next six months. Because of the potential for very large savings through the use of this technique, we suggest that the funds for OCR equipment be retained in the budget until completion of a study and test by DMV. Therefore, we recommend approval of the budget as proposed.

THE COST OF SPRAWL
(*Excerpt*)

B. MAJOR CONCLUSIONS

Stated in the most general form, the major conclusion of this study is that, for a fixed number of households, "sprawl" is the most expensive form of residential development in terms of economic costs, environmental costs, natural resource consumption, and many types of personal costs. The major economic cost relationships are indicated in Charts 1, 3 and 4. This cost difference is particularly significant for that proportion of total costs which is likely to be borne by local governments. In terms of alternative development patterns for a given site, the study indicates that better planning will reduce all types of costs and their incidence on government but that increasing density will increase some of these costs, though not nearly in proportion to the increased number of households who can live on the site with increased density. These conclusions are explained in somewhat more detail below:

1. *Planned development of all densities is less costly to create and operate than sprawl* in terms of environmental costs, economic costs, personal costs, and energy consumption. These cost differences are particularly significant in terms of those costs borne by local governments.

    a. With regard to total capital costs, planned community development for 10,000 dwelling units saves $15.3 million (four percent) over sprawl development with the same housing mix. Approximately 60 percent of these total costs is consumed by housing, leaving a difference of 8 to 12 percent in non-housing costs. Major cost savings are attributable to the following (see Table 3 and Chart 1):

        • A savings of just under $11 million (approximately 15 percent) in road and utility costs. Cost savings are due to elimination of "leapfrogging" which involves costly road and utility connections between neighborhoods.

        • A savings of over $4 million (or 20 percent) in land costs due to more contiguous, compact development in the planned community.

    b. Planned development is likely to decrease the total capital cost burden to local government by as much as one-third because a larger proportion of land and facilities for open space, roads, and utilities is likely to be provided by the developers.

        • Holding density constant, capital costs borne by government are seven to eight percent less in planned communities compared to sprawl. These savings amounted to over $31 million in the medium density communities and $40 million in the low density communities over a ten year development period.

    c. The on-going operating and maintenance costs of most public or semi-public services—education, recreation, sewage treatment, water supply, general government, police and fire protection—are largely based on population size rather than development pattern or even housing type. For utilities (sewer, water, gas, electricity, telephone) ongoing costs are largely based on consumption of resources and production of wastes; maintenance of pipe and cables is a comparatively small proportion of total cost (see Table 4).

- Savings between planned and sprawl development in operating costs borne by government are five to six percent of total costs, or over $1 million in the tenth year of development.

d. Planned development shows significant environmental advantages over sprawl (Table 5 and Chart 2) through:

- Twenty to thirty percent less air pollution resulting from reduced automobile travel

- Conservation of open space

- Preservation of significant wildlife and vegetation habitats

- Improved site design to minimize noise impacts

- Careful land use design so as to minimize the amount of soil disturbed and paved over (thus lowering slightly the volume of storm water runoff, sedimentation, and water pollution).

e. Contrasting the environmental effects of constructing sprawl communities on a specified site shows that planned development would be superior in a number of ways:

- Fewer miles of road are likely to fall within areas with poor air movement or on poor soils.

- Fewer dwellings will be directly affected by noise and air pollution from expressways and arterial roads.

- Less soil would be eroded as there would be virtually no development on steep slopes or flood plains.

- Less woodland would be cleared, minimizing the adverse effects of development on vegetation and wildlife habitats.

f. Energy consumption, because of reduced automobile travel, will be from 8 to 14 percent less in planned development than in unplanned developments (Table 5 and Chart 2). Water consumption is essentially the same in planned and unplanned developments unless special conservation measures are planned.

g. Various personal costs such as time spent in travel, traffic accidents, and various types of psychic costs are likely to be less in planned development than in sprawl (Table 5). Some particular aspects of this difference are:

- Reduced automobile use and more efficient vehicular circulation in planned developments
- Design of facilities and use of open space to preserve and enhance the visual environment
- Placing facilities in relation to one another in order to increase convenience and to reduce negative impacts as from traffic noise.

2. *Economic and environmental costs (as well as resource consumption are likely to be significantly less at higher densities to house and service a given population* (1,000 households). Some personal costs, however, may increase with increasing density.

a. Total per dwelling unit capital costs (including residential, open space/recreation, schools, roads, utilities and land) range from $48,900 for single-family conventional housing at two units per acre to $20,700 for high-rise apartments at 10 units per gross acre (which is equivalent to 30 units per net residential acre). (See Table 6 and Chart 3)
  - The cost of housing is least for walk-up apartments (5 units per gross acre), being only 37 percent of housing costs at a density of 2 units per gross acre. Housing costs at a density of 10 units per gross acre are somewhat higher than for walk-up apartments, but are still only 47 percent of the housing costs at 2 units per gross acre.
  - Even when all the different types of dwelling units contain the same inside living area, the cost of walk-up apartments is only 57 percent of the cost of single family houses.
  - The cost of roads and utilities for housing at 10 units per gross acre is $6.7 million less than at two units per gross acre (a savings of almost 80 percent).
  - The amount of land required is substantially reduced (even though the cost per gross acre tends to be higher for increased density).

b. Because operating costs for schools, sewage disposal, and water supply are largely based on household population, they are likely to be lower per dwelling unit for denser developments, but this difference disappears when the different densities are adjusted for a constant population. (See Table 7 and Chart 3)
  - However, operating costs per unit for electricity and gas decrease significantly as density increases because less energy is consumed per unit.

c. The total capital costs likely to be borne by local government are reduced as much as 62 percent in denser developments because of the lower costs of roads and public utilities.

- Public operating costs may be reduced by 73 percent.

d. Increased density reduces total environmental costs but increases the concentration of pollution. (Table 8.)

  - Air pollution from natural gas used by residents is reduced by more than half at densities of 10 units per gross acre compared to densities of 2 units per acre. However, the amount of air pollution emitted from this source per acre of development will more than double.

  - Similarly, sediment during construction and water pollution from storm water run-off may be 80 percent less with the denser developments, but the concentration of the pollution will be somewhat greater.

e. Energy and water consumption may be reduced by approximately 40 percent in high density developments (see Table 5).

  - The reduced energy consumption results both from reduced automobile transportation and reduced space heating and cooling requirements.

  - The reduced water consumption results primarily from reduced lawn watering.

f. Some personal costs may increase with denser developments (see Table 8):

  - At higher densities, noise impacts are likely to be more severe and overall satisfaction with the residential environment tends to decrease.

  - On the positive side, higher density living increases leisure time available by reducing household maintenance responsibilities.

  - Psychic costs, such as those associated with a loss of privacy, may increase with higher densities. However, good design can mitigate many of these problems.

3. *Thus, while planning results in cost savings, density is a much more influential cost determinant.* Clearly, the *greatest cost advantages occur when higher density planned developments are constrasted with low density sprawl.* (See Tables 3 and 4 and Chart 1.)

a. Total capital costs for the high-density planned community are 56 percent of those for the conventional low density sprawl development, resulting in a cost savings of $227.5 million for communities with 10,000 housing units.

b. Savings in land costs amount to 43 percent ($12,725,000), with savings of 40 percent for streets ($15,103,000), and 63 percent for utilities ($39,542,000).

c. Operating and maintenance costs in the high density planned community are estimated to be approximately $2 million (11 percent) less per year than the low density sprawl development after completion of the total development. Savings are largely due to less road and utility pipe lengths and reduced gas and electric consumption in the high density community.

d. Compared to low density sprawl, the amount of total capital costs borne by local government may decrease by almost 50 percent for high density planned communities. Operating and maintenance costs borne by local government may decrease by 13 percent.

e. Total air and water pollution and other forms of environmental degradation are similarly reduced. Air pollutants from automobiles are reduced 50 percent and those from space heating and other natural gas uses are reduced 40 percent. Sediment is reduced 30 percent and total storm water runoff 20 percent.

f. Energy consumption is reduced 44 percent and water consumption 35 percent in high density planned communities as compared to low density sprawl communities.

4. When alternative residential developments are considered *for a given site size (e.g., 100 acres), development costs increase with density, but not as rapidly as the increase in the number of dwelling units which can be accommodated.* (See Chart 4.)

a. Exclusive of land and residential costs, capital costs range only between $28,000 and $39,000 per acre. Yet within this range, anywhere from two to ten households per gross acre can be built. Considering total capital costs, five times as many high-rise units as single-family homes can be accommodated on a given site at half the per dwelling unit cost.

b. While density increases from two to ten dwelling units per gross acre (3 to 30 dwelling units per net residential acre), capital costs borne by government almost double (to $2.76 million) and operating and maintenance costs increase 35 percent (to $313,000 per year).

c. For a given site size, air pollution is more concentrated as density increases. The amount of air pollutants from an area developed at 10 units per gross acre is more than double that found in a neighborhood of single-family homes built at two units per acre; emissions from a site with 3.3 units per gross acre would be more than 10 percent greater than at two units per acre.

d. Total energy consumption (excluding transportation) increases approximately 120 percent when the density of a given site increases from two to ten dwelling units per gross acre (an increase of 500 percent). Residential water use will also increase, but again not as rapidly as the number of dwelling units.

e. Many personal costs, particularly those associated with privacy and personal ownership, will increase with increasing densities.

5. *Variation in certain basic study assumptions leads to the following conclusions*:

a. Doubling or tripling the population assumed in the base analysis would allow the community to support additional services—e.g. vocational and other specialized educational services, regional parks, community health clinics, and public transportation. Diseconomies of scale would be experienced with regard to solid waste collection; some operating economies are likely to be realized for schools, police, fire, libraries, government administration. Significant economies (both capital and operating) would be found for solid waste disposal and sewage and water treatment.

b. The effect of extreme site conditions (poor soil, very flat or very steep slopes, absence of ground and surface water sources, high water table, dense or sparse ground cover, extreme climate) will be to either greatly increase development costs or prohibit development altogether. Where planned development minimizes construction in areas poorly suited for development, significant cost savings can occur. In one example of planned and sprawl development on an assumed site, the sprawl community incurred over $2,387,000 in increased costs (beyond those normally incurred under typical site conditions) due to development in areas with fair to poor suitability for construction while the planned community showed much less development in such areas, resulting in only $850,000 in cost increases—a difference of $1.5 million, or $150 per household.

6. Given a constant amount of floor space (200,000 square feet), *shopping center commercial areas will be 20 percent (approximately $1.5 million) less costly to build and service* with roads and utilities than a strip commercial area. (See Table 9.) Savings are largely due to lower land prices per acre in shopping centers than are found for commercial strips. Smaller savings are found for off-site utility and road costs. Environmentally, the strip compares poorly with the shopping center because:

a. The strip is less appealing visually.

b. It takes longer to build (due to incremental construction) thus causing greater sedimentation.

c. The strip configuration encourages multiple stops on shopping trips, thus increasing auto emissions.

d. Traffic accidents are more likely to occur in the strip than the center, which generally has better access control.

7. Although this study provides important basic data about the costs of alternative development patterns, there are some important questions which have not been addressed or are not explored in adequate detail. Some of these questions which are expected to be analyzed in future studies in this series are the various effects at the metropolitan level of alternative development patterns, the costs of replacing facilities which become inadequate to service expanding populations, the effect of including financing costs in the economic cost analyses, and more extensive analysis of cost incidence.

APPENDIX C

EXTRACTS FROM *BUDGET PREPARATION MANUAL*, CITY OF SAN DIEGO

1. Format

The recommended format for FY 1975 should be the same as that used by the California State Department of Finance and by the City of San Diego in the current budget, except for some minor changes.

2. Program Structure

The program structure should logically organize programs into the following classification which provides for three levels of accounting (only the first two levels exist currently):

    I. Department/Division
       A. Program
          1. Program Element

A program should be a group of interdependent, closely related services or activities, contributing to a common objective. Ideally, a program should be clearly delineated, have a minimum of overlapping with other programs, be end-product oriented, and lend itself to quantification. If a program has distinct subobjectives then it should be divided into *program elements*, each with its own subobjective(s). Programs or program elements do not necessarily have to coincide with organizational units; however, they should not encompass more than a single department.

The existing activity structure, or budgetary chart of accounts, should be the basis of the new program structure. Changes should be proposed if they result in needed program consolidation or improved functional accountability.

3. Goals

A goal should be a *broad statement of intended accomplishment of an entire department or major division.* A goal should be viewed as an end state or ideal condition to be attained at some time in the distant future. However, whenever possible, goals should not be stated so broadly that their accomplishment cannot be measured. Since goals are general in nature and cover long time spans, it is useful to divide goals into more specific, short-term objectives.

The most essential characteristic of a goal is that it be community-oriented. That is, it ought to describe *intended effects on citizens and the community.* Examples are:

Recreation: To provide a balanced program of leisure activities for all age groups;

Police: To maintain a peaceful and orderly community by protecting the lives and property of citizens.

4. Objectives

Objectives should be elements of a goal, and accomplishment of an objective should constitute partial fulfillment of a goal. Further, an objective should be a *specific* and *quantitative* statement describing *what* is to be achieved, by *how much*, and within what time frame. The time frame generally should be the next fiscal year.

An objective is not merely an enumeration of what a department or program does but the result, state, or condition to be achieved. Every effort should be made to insure that objectives are results-oriented, rather than means or process-oriented. That is, focus should be on the effect on citizens, instead of activities of employees or administrative functions. Further, objectives should be stated in terms that permit quantitative measurement of their achievement.

The following represents the classification of types of objectives.

A. Objectives which provide quantitative levels to be achieved, e.g., rate of return on investment of at least 3 1/2 percent per annum, reduce the average response time on emergency calls to a maximum of 5 minutes, etc.

B. Objectives which do not provide quantitative levels to be achieved, but which do provide a measure in terms of time and budget constraints, e.g., to process all requests within 24 hours, to reduce the cost of processing to a maximum of 10 dollars per request, etc.

C. Objectives which cannot be expressed in terms of specific levels of quantification, but which can be expressed in terms of full, reduction, maximum, all, etc. Examples are to: reduce property loss from fires, lower fire insurance rates, to respond to all citizen complaints.

D. Objectives which can be expressed in terms of satisfaction or public acceptance of those affected by the services provided, e.g., the performance of a given recreation facility, can be measured in terms of the percentage of people who use the facility who are satisfied, dissatisfied, would like improvements, etc. This objective can be measured through survey and personal interview with recipients of recreation services.

To illustrate what distinguishes a good objective from a poor one, consider the following hypothetical examples. Reasons for poor objectives are given in parentheses.

Good	Poor
• Increase average hourly attendance at recreation facilities by 10% during the next fiscal year	• Promote leisure opportunities which are satisfying, physically healthy, mentally stimulating, aesthetically pleasant, and culturally creative (too general, impossible to measure or determine whether or not achieved)

- Initiate a "family-fun-fitness" program at five recreation centers in next fiscal year

- Increase citizen satisfaction with physical fitness programs, measured by survey of participants

- Provide new recreation programs at various locations (vague; what programs?, which locations?)

- Provide staffing and supervision for physical fitness programs (process-oriented; should be stated in terms of how staffing and supervision affects citizens, e.g. increases participation, reduces accidents, and/or increases satisfaction)

Police Objectives

Good	*Poor*
• Answer all emergency calls within three minutes	• To dispatch police units efficiently to calls for assistance (unspecific)
• Reduce number of accidents on surface streets by category of accident per million miles driven	• Enforce vehicle laws and promote traffic safety (vague, process-oriented; not quantitative)
• To hold per mile operating costs to $ .07	• To maintain and service the departmental fleet of vehicles (unspecific; not quantitative)

5. Output Measures

An output measure should help to evaluate the extent to which an objective is achieved, and ideally should be capable of meaningful quantification. Output measures may generally be defined to include three different types of management indicators:

An *effectiveness measure* is an indicator of how well a program objective is achieved. It focuses on citizen-related effects of programs. Examples are percent of stolen cars recovered, accident loss per 100,000 vehicle miles, and average time to a respond to a complaint.

An *efficiency measure* is an indicator of how economically input (costs or position years) is converted to output (work load or service units), usually expressed as a ratio of input and output. Examples are cost per investigation, number of books circulated per program dollar, and number of inspections per position year.

A *work load measure* is an actual account of work units accomplished, indicating level of work activity. Examples are number of acres mowed, number of fires extinguished, and tons of refuse collected.

The most essential requirement of an output measurement is that it be relevant to an objective. For instance, if an objective is to reduce accidents, then the corresponding output measure should be number of accidents. Other illustrations of the relationship between output measures and program objectives are shown following.

Examples of Output Measurements

Output Measures	Fire Prevention Program	Fire Suppression Program
Effectiveness	• Annual number of fires of various magnitudes (to be defined) • Fire rates per 10,000 population per year • Annual dollar value of property loss due to fire (adjusted for price level changes) • Reduction in number of fires, injuries, lives lost, and dollars of property loss from the base • Average dollar value of property loss per fire	• Average time required to extinguish fires from the time they were first observed, for various classes of fires • Mean time to respond and travel to location of fire by class • Mean loss per fire by classes of fire
Efficiency (Unit Costs) and performance data	• Cost per inspection (by type) • Cost per fire investigation • Cost per plan check • Number of inspections per position year • Number of fire investigations per position year	• Number of fires extinguished (by type) per position year
Basic Work Load Data	• Number of inspections • Number of investigations • Number of plan checks • Number of construction evaluations • Number of fire extinguishers tested, licensed, and certified	• Number of fire responses • Number of inspections (by type) • Number of out-of-service training hours

An actual example which indicates a good understanding of the requirements of a PPB format is provided in the following Fire Department submission for fiscal 1975-1976.

The reader should note the excellent correspondence between the objective statements and the output indices. Ideally, the match between the output and objective statements would indicate a one-to-one relationship wherein the output statement serves as a mechanism for quantification for each of the objective statements.

Department	Program or Program Element	Objective	Output
Recreation	Handicapped Recreation	To increase participation in handicapped recreation and physical fitness programs	Participation rates (e.g., participant-hours)
Library	Central Library	To achieve a higher per capita attendance figure	Attendance per capita
	Extension Division	To increase the circulation of library materials per capita	Materials circulated per capita
Fire	Fire Suppression	To control and extinguish fires	Average loss per fire by occupancy, average response time per fire
	Equipment Maintenance	To insure availability of fire apparatus and equipment as needed	Number of times fire apparatus or equipment is unavailable for service
	Communications	Answer all emergency calls within 3 minutes	Emergency line average wait time
Police	Automotive Maintenance	To increase unit availability time to 95%	Percent availability time
	Field Patrol	To institute crime offense program that results in increasing on-scene apprehensions	Number of crimes interrupted in progress by class
	Traffic	Maintain current level of response and travel time to accident investigation scenes	Response/travel time to accident scene
General Services	Sanitation	To reduce the loss per ton refuse collected	Cost per ton
Building Inspection	Structural Plan Checking	Perform structural plan checks on 3,650 plans having an estimated valuation of $295.4 million	Number of plan checks per work year

Fire Department 16.00 FY 1975-76
Department Goals
To minimize deaths, injuries, and property loss by taking all feasible action to prevent fires, and if they occur, to extinguish them promptly. To perform other life safety and property protection function as needed.

Administration Program (16.10)
Objectives - To lower fire deaths and injuries per 1000 population. To reduce the dollar value of property loss due to fire. To maintain efficiency in departmental operations by not allowing the fire cost per assessed valuation to increase. To develop and implement a new work schedule in Fiscal Year 1976 for fire fighters which will meet Fair Labor Standards Act requirements with the least cost.

Output
Fire deaths per 1000 population
Fire injuries per 1000 population
Dollar value of property loss per assessed valuation
Fire cost per assessed valuation
Projected cost if no changes are made in the work schedule compared to
       cost of adopted plan

Fire Prevention Program (16.20)
Objectives - to reduce by ———% the average loss per fire by occupancy. To maintain the number of plan checks and investigations performed per position hour. To reduce average loss per fire in mercantile occupancies from $——— to $——— by focusing inspection efforts on those occupancies. To reduce the occurrences of fires in mercantile occupancies from ——— to ———.

Output
Number of fires by occupancy
Average loss per fire by occupancy
Number of plans checked
       Plan check per position hour
Number of investigations
       Investigations per position hour
Average loss per fire in mercantile occupancies
Number of fire occurrences in mercantile occupancies

Fire Suppression Program (16.30)
Objectives - To reduce average dollar loss per one and two family dwelling fires by 5%. To reduce the fire insurance commercial rate in South San Diego from rate 5 to 4 and in Penasquitos from rate 7 to rate

6. To reduce the modal response time for the truck company in Southeast San Diego from 6 to 5 minutes. To reduce the modal response time for the Pacific Beach engine company from 4.6 minutes to 4.4 minutes.

Output
Average dollar loss for one and two family dwelling units
Insurance rates South San Diego - Penasquitos
Response time:
  Overall mean
    Pacific Beach mean
  Overall median
  Overall mode
    Southeast San Diego Mode

Equipment Maintenance and Material Program (16.70)
  Objectives - To insure availability of fire apparatus and equipment as needed by reducing down time rates and increasing emergency availability rates. To effect an improvement in the replacement or turn-around time required for fire hose and breathing apparatus from ——— to ———. To improve the emergency refueling capability of the Fire Department from the persent level of ——— to ———.

Output
Down time rates for fire apparatus
Down time rates for other fire equipment
Availability rates (% of times [that] apparatus or equipment is available
    for emergency services on demand)
Turn-around time for fire hose and apparatus
Emergency refueling capability

Fire Communications Program (16.80)
Objectives - To process the increased number of emergency calls while:
    1. maintaining the average dispatch time of one minute.
    2. with no decrease in the dispatcher accuracy rate.
To conduct a feasibility study on the equipment needs for Fire Communications (including computer-aided dispatch). To prepare short and long range plans and recommend decisions based upon the findings of the study.

Output
Average dispatch time
Dispatcher accuracy rate
Number of emergency calls
Number of valid alarms

Average response time
Percent completion of feasibility study

Training Program (16.90)
    Objectives - To effect a 5% reduction in the vehicular accident rate and the on-the-job injury rate by intensified training efforts in those two areas. To prepare and conduct six high rise training exercises in order to assess, evaluate, and improve the capability of fire suppression forces and equipment to adequately cope with high rise fire incidents.

Output
Number of on-the-job injuries per 100 employees
Number of vehicular accidents per 100,000 miles traveled
Number of high rise training exercises
Number of new hires trained
Number of in-service personnel trained

GLOSSARY

Accounting and Resources Management System (ARMS). A program implemented by San Diego County which integrates financial data, personnel and equipment utilization, workload statistics, and other data into one system for improved financial management.

Analysis. A systematic and objective method of examining specific problems and alternative solutions while identifying the cost/benefits of each alternative in order to arrive at an optimal solution.

Authority. A part of the program budget format which cites the legal code sections authorizing the program or program element.

Basic Workload. Measures level of activity, amount of processing, or magnitude of basic workload generally identified in the output statement.

Benefit. The worth or value of the program output, usually expressed in monetary units.

Budget Analysis. Generally originates from an office independent of the authority responsible for the expenditures in the program budget. The PPB provides the systems data required for this budget analysis.

Budgeting. Development, approval, and administration of an annual financial plan. Budgets are short-range segments of adopted programs which set out planned accomplishments during the budget period.

Budget Summary. Itemized expenditures and revenues in summary form for operating and capital improvements programs.

Capital Budget. Includes all expenditures for capital improvements such as new buildings, acquisition of open space, and park development. Capital Improvements are frequently financed by bonds or special funds earmarked for CIP.

Capital Improvement Detail. A description provided for each capital project undertaken. Every project within the detail has a title and brief description indicating the type of project, funding, completion time frame, and the like.

Comparative Analysis. Examines the effectiveness and efficiency of a specific program by comparing that program to similar programs performed in other cities or corporations, et al., in order to establish a basis of comparison as to costs, benefits, etc.

Component. Level of programs subordinate to "element" level and above "task" within the PPBS classification system.

Constraint. A restraint which limits or confines the area of freedom one has in formulating or pursuing programs and objectives.

Cost/benefit Analysis. A technique of analysis which compares costs and benefits of one alternative against those of other alternatives.

Cost/benefit Ratio. An economic indicator computed by dividing program costs by the program benefits. Usually, both the benefit and cost are discounted, so the ratio reflects efficiency in terms of present value of future benefits and costs.

Cost-effectiveness. Systematic examination of an alternative in terms of its advantages and disadvantages as measured by economic cost. The measure of effectiveness is *not* the same as the measure of costs. An index or ratio shows the costs of various alternatives that produce the same degree of effectiveness.

Economic Base Study. Differs from a fiscal model in that its emphasis is placed on the measurement of the overall economic growth of the local economy. This type of study relates to such indices as employment, income, tax bases, vacancy factors, building permits, and economic growth indicators within a particular community or organization.

Effectiveness. The degree to which a program meets its stated objectives.

Effectiveness Measure. An indicator of how well a program objective is achieved and focuses on citizen-related effects of programs.

Efficiency. A measure of how economically input (costs, position-years, etc.) is converted to output.

Efficiency Measure. An indicator of how economically input (costs or position-years) is converted to output (workload or service units), usually expressed as a ratio of input and output.

Fire Station Location Model. A computer model designed to relocate fire stations in San Diego, California, optimizing for response time, costs, fire history, and the like.

Fiscal Control Budgeting. A budgetary system which evolved in the United States between 1911 and 1926 wherein the budget was viewed as the central instrument for administrative control over spending.

Fiscal Model. A model which only identifies expenditures and revenues over an extended time period by utilizing relatively sophisticated models such as linear regression analysis.

Fund Source Analysis. Identifies and itemizes revenue sources for operating or capital improvement programs.

General Description. A brief explanation of the activities of the program or program element which usually includes a historical statement as well as future goals.

Goals. A broad statement of the intended accomplishment of an entire department or major division, an ideal condition to be attained at some point in the future.

Input. A part of the program budget format expressing utilized resources in man-years and expenditure levels in the actualization of the stated objectives, usually indicated over a three-year period.

Land-use Model. A model which seeks to guide major policy decisions affecting utilization of land on a regional basis by indicating the density, timing, and location of population, transportation facilities, open space requirements; the location of industrial sites and port facilities; encouragement of industry by type, zoning, and the like over an extended time frame.

Linear Regression Analysis (least squares method). A mathematical method for calculating the overall, average correlation between two variables; an analysis of the association of one or more independent variables in carrying out a program.

Line-item Budget. A traditional type of budgeting that focuses on categories like supplies, maintenance, and personnel, in terms of their specific expenditure. No program detail is provided in this type of budget.

Management Reporting and Control (MARC). A program aimed at improving management by increasing the effectiveness in the California Department of Motor Vehicles.

Marginal Analysis. An economic technique of analysis which describes the marginal benefit as that last increment of output when compared to one additional unit of cost. Incremental changes in benefit and cost are plotted thus, constructing a curve. An analysis of this curve will reveal how outputs increase or decrease relative to increases in input. Theoretically, when the last unit cost of output equals the last unit cost of input, the process has been maximized and no further inputs should be utilized.

Marginal Cost. In marginal analysis, the change in total cost which is the result of one unit change in output.

Model. A representation of the relationships that define a real-life situation that is under study. The model may be mathematical (an equation), a computer program, a picture, or a verbal description.

Need. As related to the program budget, a need is a statement of the problem which the program is designed to alleviate, phrased so that it is possible to measure its effectiveness. A need does not have to be elaborate.

Objectives. Those goals which are stated in the program budget format by the individual program or elements of a department. They should be elements of an overall goal, and accomplishment of an objective should constitute partial fulfillment of a goal. In the implementation of a PPB, the objective should be a specific and quantitative statement describing what is to be achieved, by how much, and within what time frame.

Operating Budget. Includes all the actual, noncapital costs of running programs. Expenditures are usually financed by the general fund via such means as tax revenues, collection of fees, and licenses.

Operating Program Summary. A summary of man-years and expenditures for each operating program within the department.

Opportunity Cost Analysis. The measurable advantages foregone as a result of the rejection of an alternative use of resources.

Output. As related to the program budget, expresses in quantifiable measurements the degree of workload accomplished by the specific level of input.

Output Measures. An output measure should help to evaluate the extent to which an objective is achieved, and ideally should be capable of meaningful quantification. Output measures may generally be defined to include three different types of management indicators: effectiveness measure, efficiency measure, and workload measure.

Performance Budget. A type of budget which seeks to emphasize workload or output statistics as a measurement of efficiency. This budget is not systems-oriented nor does it identify program needs, objectives, etc. A performance budget may be regarded as a transitional budget falling between a line-item budget and a PPB system. In effect, it is a line-item budget with detailed output or performance statistics.

PPB (Planning and Programming Budget). A type of budget whose format incorporates a description of a program's needs and objectives, a general description, an authority statement, and quantifiable input and output data. This type of budget seeks to divide budgetary expenditures into identifiable programs and program elements. The identification of such program detail permits planning and evaluation on a programmatic basis over an extended time period, as well as the use of analytical techniques such as systems analysis.

Program. A group of interdependent, closely related services or activities contributing to a common objective.

Program Element. A subdivision of a program which satisfies the overall program objective but is regarded as a "subprogram" because of its singular and distinctively identifiable input and output measurements which can be isolated from the overall program.

Resources. Income, personnel, operating expenses, and equipment and capital outlay involved in carrying out a program.

Systems Analysis. A method of analysis which evaluates its subject in its entirety by identifying all external (exogenous) and internal (endogenous) variables and interactions within the overall system.

User Fee Philosophy. The concept of applying a fully reimbursable fee schedule to the users of a public or private service generally considered beyond the normal responsibility of the governing agent.

Work Load Measure. An actual account of work units accomplished, indicating level of work activity.

Zero-based Budgeting. A type of budget wherein every expenditure must be justified from a zero point every year as if a new program or expenditure had just been established, requiring a full rationalization of its need and purported accomplishments.

BIBLIOGRAPHY

Anderson, William H. *Financing Modern Government: The Political Economy of the Public Sector.* Boston: Houghton-Mifflin Co., 1973.

Anthony, Harry A. "A Vision of San Diego," *San Diego Magazine* (June 1970), pp. 30-33, 66-68, 70.

"Banning the Boom," *Newsweek*, August 21, 1972.

Blick, Larry N. "A New Look at Capital Improvements Programming," *Municipal Finance* 42 (November 1969): 110-116.

Botner, Stanley B. "PPBS: A Tool for Smaller Cities?" *Municipal Finance* 42 (May 1971): 173-178.

Boulder Area Growth Study Commission. *Exploring Options for the Future: A Study of Growth in Boulder County*, Volume I, Commission Final Report. Boulder, Colo.: November 1973.

Center for Real Estate and Urban Economics. *Jobs, People and Land: Bay Area Simulation Study (BASS).* Berkeley, Calif.: 1968.

City of Los Angeles. "1973-74 Budgetary Hearings: Discussion of Need for Five Year Perspective of 'Revenue Gap,'" submitted to the Mayor and City Council by Oscar Odegaard. Los Angeles, Calif.: October 24, 1973.

City of Oakland. "Preliminary Budget 1974-75," submitted to the Mayor and City Council by Cecil S. Riley. Oakland, Calif.: May 1, 1974.

City of Sunnyvale. "Resource Allocation Plan, 1974-75," submitted to the Mayor and City Council by John E. Denver. Sunnyvale, Calif.: May 21, 1974.

Clawson, Marion, and Charles L. Stewart. *Land Use Information: A Critical Survey of U.S. Statistics Including Possibilities for Greater Uniformity.* Baltimore: The John Hopkins Press, 1965.

Davis, James W. (ed.). *Politics, Programs and Budgets, A Reader in Government Budgeting.* Englewood Cliffs, N.J.: Prentice-Hall, Inc., 1969.

Denhart, Robert B. "Organizing the Budget Function," *Municipal Finance* 43 (May 1971): 167-172.

Doxiadis, C. A. *Urban Renewal and the Future of the American City.* Chicago: Public Administration Service, 1966.

Draper, Norman, and H. Smith. *Applied Regression Analysis.* New York: John Wiley and Sons, Inc., 1966.

Dror, Yehezkel. "Policy Analysts: A New Professional Role in Government Service," *Public Administration Review* 27 (September 1967): 197-203.

Fabricatore, Ken. "Prototype Financial Plan," City of San Diego Memoranda. San Diego, Calif.: November 1974.

Friedland, Daniel R. "Letters to the Editor," *Journal of the American Institute of Planners* 40 (January 1974), pp. 53-54.

Grossbard, Stephen I. *PPBS for State and Local Officials.* Bureau of Government Research, Research Series No. 15, Kingston, R.I.: University of Rhode Island, 1971.

Haldi Associates, Inc. *A Survey of Budgetary Reform in Five States.* Lexington, Ky.: Council of State Governments, 1973.

Hays, Richard L. "Analysis of the Feasibility of Instituting a PPBS in a Line Agency." Master's dissertation, San Diego State College, 1968.

Hendricks, Francis. "Analyzing the Economic Base of a City." Chicago: Municipal Finance Officers Association of the United States and Canada, September 26, 1965.

Hirsch, Werner A., Sidney Sonenblum, and Ronald Teeples. *Local Government Program Budgeting: Theory and Practice.* UCLA: Institute of Government and Public Affairs, 1973.

Hitch, Charles J., and Roland McKean. *The Economics of Defense in the Nuclear Age.* Cambridge, Mass.: Harvard University Press, 1960.

Holodnak, James. Personal Interview. March 21, 1974.

Hoos, Ida R. *Systems Analysis in Public Policy: A Critique.* Berkeley, Calif.: University of California Press, 1972.

Howard, S. Kenneth. *Changing State Budgeting.* Lexington, Ky.: Council of State Governments, 1973.

Husby, Carl. Telephone interview. November 26, 1974.

Implementing PPB in State, City, and County, A Report on the 5-5-5 Project. State-Local Finances Project of The George Washington University. Washington, D.C.: 1969.

"Introduction to Planning, Programming and Budgeting Systems," *Management Information Services* 1 (September 1969): 1-19.

Kitchen, James, Richard Bigger, and George Babilot. *A Study of Local Government Finance on the San Diego SMSA.* San Diego, Calif.: The Urban Observatory, 1972.

Knapp, David, and Ken Fabricatore. Personal interview. March 20, 1974.

Knezevich, Stephen J. *Program Budgeting (PPBS).* Berkeley, Calif.: McCutchan Publishing Corp., 1973.

Kraemer, Kenneth L. *Policy Analysis in Local Government.* Washington, D.C.: International City Management Association, 1973.

Kraft, Richard H. P. (ed.). *Strategies of Educational Planning.* Tallahassee, Fla.: Educational Systems Development Center, Florida State University, 1969.

Lee, Douglas B., Jr. "Requiem for Large-Scale Models," *Journal of the American Institute of Planners* 39 (May 1973), pp. 163-178.

Lee, Robert D., Jr., and Ronald W. Johnson. *Public Budgeting Systems.* Baltimore: University Park Press, 1973.

Legislative Analyst Office. "North City West Analysis." San Diego, Calif.: April 15, 1974.

———. Telephone survey. San Diego, Calif.: November 1974.

Levine, Robert A. *Public Planning: Failure and Redirection.* New York: Basic Books, Inc., 1972.

Lish, Monty C. "Organizing for a New Approach to Budgeting," *Municipal Finance* 41 (May 1969): 155-162.

Lowry, Ira S. "A Short Course in Model Design," T-3114. Santa Monica, Calif.: The RAND Corporation, 1965.

Lynch, Kevin, and Donald Appleyard. "Temporary Paradise?: A Look at the Special Landscape of the San Diego Region." A report to the City of San Diego, September 1974.

Martineau, Thomas R. "Letters to the Editor," *Journal of the American Institute of Planners* 40 (January 1974): 54-55.

McKinney, Jerome B., and Edward S. Kiely. "Has Success Spoiled PPB?" *The Federal Accountant* 22 (September 1973): 55-66.

McLoone, Eugene P., Gabrielle Lupo, and Selma J. Mushkin. *Long-Range Revenue Estimation.* Washington, D.C.: The George Washington University, 1967.

Merewitz, Leonard, and Stephen H. Sosnick. *The Budget's New Clothes: A Critique of Planning-Programming- and Budgeting—Cost Analysis.* Chicago: Markham Publishing Co., 1971.

Millward, Robert E. "PPB: Problems of Implementation," *American Institute of Planners Journal* 34 (March 1968): 88-94.

Mitchell, Robert A. Personal interview. March 26, 1974.

New York Bureau of Municipal Research. *Making a Municipal Budget.* New York: 1907.

New York Times. August 26, 1965.

Nigro, Felix A., and Lloyd G. Nigro. *Modern Public Administration.* New York: Harper and Row, 1973.

Novick, David. "The Origins and History of Program Budgeting," *California Management Review* 11 (Fall 1968): 7-12.

———. (ed.). *Program Budgeting, Program Analysis, and the Federal Budget.* Cambridge Mass.: Harvard University Press, 1965.

Payad, Aurora T., and Mohamed Chouari. "PPBS: Perspectives and Prospects for Local Governments," *Philippine Journal of Public Administration* 16 (October 1972): 460-473.

Program Budgeting in State and Local Governments: The Practitioner's View. UCLA: Institute of Government and Public Affairs, 1972.

Program Budgeting—The PPBS Task Force. San Diego: Comprehensive Management Planning Program, 1973.

Quade, E. S. *The Systems Approach and Public Policy.* RAND Corp. Paper P-4053. Santa Monica: 1969.

Rabin, Jack. *Planning, Programming and Budgeting for State and Local Governments.* Bureau of Public Administration, The University of Alabama, Citizen Information Report No. 9. Birmingham, Ala.: Commercial Printing Co., 1973.

Real Estate Research Corporation. *The Costs of Sprawl: Detailed Cost Analysis.* Washington, D.C.: April 1974.

Rehfuss, John. *Public Administration as Political Process.* New York: Charles Scribner's Sons, 1973.

Rock, Elliott. "The User's View of Program Budgeting in Local and State Government." Unpublished paper, San Diego State University, 1973.

Rosenthal, Stephen R., Jack R. Meredith, and William Goldner. *Plan Making with a Computer Model: Projective Land Use Model,* I. Berkeley, Calif.: University of California, Institute of Transportation and Traffic Engineering, February 1972.

San Diego Union. March 14, 1974.

Schick, Allen. "A Death in the Bureaucracy: The Demise of Federal PPB," *Public Administration Review* 33 (March-April 1973): 146-156.

———. *Budget Innovation in the States.* Washington, D.C.: The Brookings Institute, 1971.

Schultze, Charles L. *The Politics and Economics of Public Spending.* Washington, D.C.: The Brookings Institute, 1968.

Schwartz, Hal. "Accounting, Resources Management System," *Business Association Review* 11 (Fall 1973): 20-21.

Sharkansky, Ira (ed.). *Policy Analysis in Political Science.* Chicago: Markham Publishing Co., 1970.

Snyder, James C. "Financial Management and Planning in Local Government," *Atlanta Economic Review* 23 (November-December 1973): 43-47.

Sonenblum, Sidney. *The Environment Facing Local Government Program Budgeting.* UCLA: Institute of Government and Public Affairs, 1973.

Southeastern Wisconsin Regional Planning Commission. *A Land Use Plan Design Model,* III, Final Report. U.S. Department of Housing and Urban Development: April 1973.

State of California, Department of Finance. *Program Evaluation—From Concept to Action.* Sacramento: 1968.

———. *Programming and Budgeting System (PABS).* Sacramento: 1968.

———. *Programming and Budgeting System: The Overall.* Sacramento: 1968.

Steiss, Alan Walter. *Public Budgeting and Management.* Lexington, Mass.: Lexington Books, 1973.

Stone, Daniel E. "The Evolution of Municipal Budgeting in the City of San Diego, California." Master's dissertation, San Diego State College, 1966.

Wall Street Journal. (Editorial.) January 24, 1975.

Wildavsky, Aaron. "Rescuing Policy Analysis from PPBS," *Public Administration Review* 29 (March-April 1969): 189-202.

———. "The Political Economy of Efficiency: Cost-Benefit Analysis, Systems Analysis, and Program Budgeting," *Public Administration Review* 26 (December 1966): 292-310.

———. *The Politics of the Budgetary Process.* Boston: Little, Brown Co., 1964.

INDEX

About the Author

Michael Babunakis has a B.A. and an M.A. in economics from the University of California, Berkeley, and is a legislative analyst for the City of San Diego. He has also served as an analyst for the California state government and for banks in New York and California.